Outclassing the Competition

The Up & Comer's Guide to Social Survival

Outclassing the Competition

The Up & Comer's Guide to Social Survival

the

Competition

Jan Darling

ST. MARTIN'S PRESS/NEW YORK

Design by Mina Greenstein

Library of Congress Cataloging in Publication Data

Darling, J. L. (Jan L.)
    Outclassing the competition.

    1. Social mobility—United States.   2. Social
skills—United States.   I. Title.
HN90.S65D37   1985   395   84-23790
ISBN 0-312-59127-6

First Edition

10 9 8 7 6 5 4 3 2 1

To CWS, with love

*If you take big paces
you leave big spaces.*

—BURMESE PROVERB

*Experience is the worst teacher;
it gives the test before
presenting the lesson.*

—VERNON LAW

Contents

THE V. I. P.'S VOCABULARY GUIDE

Acknowledgments

Though many people contributed substantial time and effort to this book, three were especially instrumental in its completion.

Foremost was Charles Scully. He proofread, brainstormed, and helped in a thousand ways. But most of all, he was my inspiration and support.

My dear friends Andréa Neuss and Jan Harrison provided wonderful suggestions, brilliant critique, and invaluable assistance. I shall always be thankful.

Many people were generous in their responses to my requests for information: New York dermatologist Dr. Pinkas Lebovits; Thomas P. Wolfe, CHA, concierge of San Francisco's Meridian Hotel; André de Beauharnais, former concierge of Manhattan's Pierre Hotel; Don Mikula of Pipino-Buccheri; Philip A. Cooper; plus the staffs of Saks Fifth Avenue, Cunard, Elizabeth Arden, Glorious Foods, Dover Caterers, Cold Spring Harbor Country Club, Brookside Winery, Pebble Beach Country Club, Montauk Charter Service, Manhattan Château Wines & Liquors, Waterfront Liquors, Bergdorf Goodman, and Caviarteria, Inc.

Others who contributed encouragement, ideas, legwork, and/or marketing assistance include Michele Marsh, Margaret Shepherd, David Friend, Irene Maniewski, Avis Pritzker, Sherri Cohen, Kathleen Nykolyn, Katherine Staggers, Tom Alexander, Bob Woolf, and Vincent Cerullo.

For the line drawings in this book, thanks to Mark Mitchell.

For his wonderful suggestions, critique, and friendship, I thank Mark Raclin.

For reasons she knows best, my sincere gratitude to Sallie Gouverneur.

For his brilliance, diplomacy, and endless good humor, many thanks to my editor, Brian DeFiore.

And finally, thanks to my mother, Rosemary Johnson, who supported my decision to write; and to my sister, Sheila Billingsley, who provided valuable criticism and a good example.

Introduction

You weren't born rich? Neither was I. Isn't it dreadful? Billionaire parents could have proved very useful.

You see, long before they send you off to the family alma mater (to which they'll donate a polo field to assure you proper exercise), billionaires have you learn what the up and coming *must* know. And they give you absolute *eons* to polish each technique.

For example, Nanny has you conjugating irregular French verbs a decade before you'll order *Meursault-Charmes*[1] for clients. Ages before your trust fund matures, Mother shows you how to get others to do practically everything for you, from choosing your spring wardrobe to throwing a gourmet dinner for a few (or a few *hundred*) close friends. And Daddy lets you make his *Dubonnet*[2] with-a-splash-and-a-twist, tip the headwaiter, and send your compliments to the chef—all while you're still a junior member at The Club.

Yes, being wealthy is definitely the most pleasant way to acquire the fundamentals—though for an alarming number of us, rich parents aren't an option.

Alas, we are left to struggle through childhood with nary a nanny in sight. And, though we may nevertheless arrive at the right place at the right time, we find ourselves without the right

---

[1]Meursault-Charmes (muhr soh SHARM) is a fine white Burgundy wine. (Note: As a general rule, one does not pronounce a final "s" in a French word.)

[2]Dubonnet (doo buh NÃ) is a sweet aromatized wine.

social skills to feel comfortable with our success. We learn that prosperity can be a ticket to embarassment, that the finer things in life can be the most difficult. Too ambitious to turn back, too proud to seek help, we misuse, mishandle, misconstrue, mispronounce, and, sometimes, miss out!

I've seen it happen too many times. A handsome young man is intimidated by his girlfriend's wealthy parents. An assistant vice-president's career stalls because he lacks the *savoir-faire*[3] required at the highest executive levels. And a top salesperson, because she lets a headwaiter seat her party near the kitchen, and because she accidentally eats her client's salad, loses the deal of a lifetime. Somehow, America—the ultimate classless society—turns out to be the most class conscious of them all!

So, here's the great American riddle: How do you learn what you need to know before you even *know* what you need to know? If you've never heard of a *concierge*,[4] how will you know what to tip one? If you've never been to a polo match, how will you know what to wear? If you've never ridden in a stretch limousine, how will you know if you need one to take clients to the airport?

Why not take advantage of *my* experience? I've already made the transition from Sears to Saks. I've done all the hard work, asked all the questions, made all the mistakes for you. I've learned the French, taken the gourmet cooking lessons, read the required publications, and interviewed the right people.

And, because no hardship was too great, I also spent endless hours drinking the world's finest wines, riding to hounds, dressing for the ballet, and cruising about in assorted yachts and private planes. Courtesy of two grueling years as a Pan Am flight attendant, I traveled to the farthest corners of the globe: from Paris to Buenos Aires, from Hong Kong to Tahiti. Courtesy of my position as a computer-industry executive, I traveled from Manhattan to Palm Beach to Beverly Hills—experiencing the Good Life wherever I went. (Anything for literature!)

So why not make *my* experiences *your* experiences? My

---

[3]Savoir-faire (sah vwarh FEHR), in this case, is social know-how.

[4]A concierge (kahn SYERHZH), in America, is a specially trained social director in an elegant hotel.

mistakes your *triumphs?* By devouring every page of this book, you'll soon feel devastatingly self-assured around impossible clients, your affluent company president, even your wealthy prospective in-laws.

Of course, they'll surely be so dazzled by your worldly wisdom and sophisticated manner that they'll promote you, sign on the dotted line, and/or marry you into the family. But that's the price you pay for having the classiest act in town.

Pronunciation Key

This key will guide your pronunciation of the words and phrases throughout the book. But don't expect to sound like a native. *French* French or *Spanish* Spanish takes years of practice. A slightly Anglicized version sounds better anyway. Heavy foreign accents seem too contrived in the middle of an English sentence.

Pronounce

A	as in m*a*dc*a*p	OH	as in p*o*lo
Ā	as in est*a*te	OO	as in Bl*oo*mingdale's
AH	as in y*a*cht	OO	as in g*oo*d breeding
EE	as in p*ee*rage	OW	as in p*ow*er
EH	as in j*e*t s*e*t	OY	as in r*oy*alty
G	as in *g*entry	TH	as in *th*oroughbred
GH	as in *gh*ostwriter		
I	as in b*i*gwig	UH	as in b*u*tler
Ī	as in h*i*gh soc*i*ety	ZH	as in Lei*s*ure Class

The symbol *n* means that the "n" is not pronounced "en" as in English. It means, instead, that the preceding vowel is nasal, somewhat like the "o" in honk. This French sound is produced by passing some of your breath through your nose.

Capitalization shows stress on a syllable.

Outclassing the Competition

The Up & Comer's Guide to Social Survival

A lovely collection of "tulip" glasses. From left to right: goblets for water, red wine, white wine, champagne, and liqueur. Photograph courtesy of Baccarat Crystal.

1

· WINE WIZARDRY ·

What contemptible scoundrel stole the
cork from my lunch?

—W. C. FIELDS

The first time I served wine, I simply unscrewed a cap and poured. The lively little vino, aged *weeks* in the trunk of a '68 Lincoln, entranced and intoxicated each of my guests. Imagine: no decanters, no corkscrews, no tricky French labels. I had defied convention.

Years passed, as did my *naïveté* (nah eev TĀ). Funny how urbane friends and solvency alter one's perspective. Funny, too, how a great expense account increases one's desire to partake of the finer things in life. In fact, the mere possession of such a perk practically *obligates* one to sample the world's most cherished vintages. After all, when entertaining clients, isn't one almost dutybound to pull out all the stops (or stoppers, as the case may be)?

Finding a Glass With a Touch of Class

Without a doubt, the best way to assemble a wardrobe of wineglasses is to inherit a complete set of Baccarat[1] crystal from an uncle you met only once and didn't like at all. Your next best

---

[1] Baccarat (bah kah RAH) is one of the world's finest glassmakers.

alternative is to call Baccarat or Steuben[2] directly and order four dozen glasses each for white wine, Rhine wine, red wine, and champagne—bearing in mind that custom-made designs are so much more *you* than off-the-shelf varieties.

Of course, there is another alternative: one acceptable to *oenophiles*[3] and social arbiters alike, one that requires very little expertise and only a moderate amount of cash. It entails buying several dozen all-purpose glasses. That's it! You need more specialized styles only if you regularly accompany dinners with both red and white wines, or if your passion for champagne is getting out of hand.

THE ALL-PURPOSE WINEGLASS

Why is this one glass acceptable for so many different wines? Let's take a close look.

Because it is simple, clear, and free of fancy etchings, it reveals the wine's beauty *and* exposes any impurities. In addition, its large eight- to twelve-ounce bowl serves up generous portions and provides ample aeration, while the tapered shape efficiently collects the wine's *bouquet*.[4]

When it comes to quality, let your pocketbook be your guide. Though you need a glass that's beautiful, you *don't* need one that will draw too many tears on the occasion of its demise. Which will usually be much sooner than you think.[5]

---

[2]Steuben (stoo BEHN) is another world-class glassmaker.

[3]Oenophiles (EE nuh FĪLS) are wine lovers. (Note: This word is of Greek origin, not French.)

[4]Bouquet (boo KĀ, *not* boh KĀ) is the wine's fragrance.

[5]Many people buy "open stock" glassware believing that replacements will be available forever. But open stock means only that you can purchase items one at a time, rather than in a set. It has nothing to do with design longevity.

Grand Openings

The Corkscrew and You

I learned to open wine thirty thousand feet above ground, in turbulence, in the dark. But I never lost a cork. Here's the secret.

Find a private place, away from prying eyes. First, remove the price sticker, if any. Then use a small knife to cut away the portion of the metal capsule covering the top; wipe the lip clean.

Next, insert a wing-type corkscrew[6] straight into the cork's center and turn the handle on top till the "wings" rise fully. Push them back down, draw the plug, and carefully blot up any debris. *Voilà!*[7] The job is done; the wine is ready to be tasted, then aerated or consumed. (Note: Champagne, white wines, and *rosés* [roh ZĀ] should always be opened after chilling.)

Uncorking the Bubbly

Movie scenarios notwithstanding, it is considered just the tiniest bit tacky to send champagne stoppers flying, or to let bubbly spew onto rugs or into your mouth. Fortunately, such occurrences are easily avoided by following these steps:

1. Place the champagne in an ice bucket for twenty minutes or in the refrigerator for two hours. Slip glasses[8] into the refrigerator for at least ten minutes.
2. Hold the chilled bottle by the neck and quickly wrap it with a towel.
3. Grasp the bottle's neck firmly with your left hand and tilt it away from you at a 45-degree angle. Remove the foil or metal capsule covering the stopper by cutting just below the swell at the top of the bottle.
4. Holding a cloth tightly over the stopper, untwist and re-

[6]Wooden-top counterscrews are also good; crumbly corks respond well to air-injection models and "Screwpul"; and old bottles with extra-long stoppers fare best with "T-type" screws.

[7]Voilà (vwah LAH) means "There!" or "There you have it!"

[8]Use delicate champagne tulips or flutes if you have them. (See the picture opening this chapter.) Otherwise, use an all-purpose glass.

move the retaining wire, then ease out the plug. (It should hiss, not pop.) A word of caution about plastic plugs: Once you start pulling them, continue; they have a nasty habit of popping out on their own.

5. Keep the bottle tilted for several seconds after opening to prevent an overflow, then wipe away any moisture and discard both cloths.

Note: When opening sparkling Burgundy for a dinner party, remember one thing: Don't. It does nothing for food, *or* your reputation.

Preliminaries

Aerating the Wine

Some wines improve when exposed to air. Others deteriorate. (Don't you adore absolutes?)

For information on a particular bottle, check with your merchant or see the "Which Wine?" chart, beginning on page 11.

If neither is handy, try to remember to:

Serve champagne, *Beaujolais* (boh zhoh LĀ), *rosé,* and white wines immediately after opening.
Air aged red wines up to an hour in a cool room.
Let young red wines, and most Italian reds, aerate two or three hours.

At a restaurant, order red wine as soon as possible and have it uncorked immediately. If it requires further aeration, have the wine steward decant it (pour it into a decanter). If he cannot accommodate you, let the wine aerate in the glass.

At home, leave plenty of time to aerate wines, or decant them as explained in the next section.

Decanting

You may decant any still[9] wine, but don't. Save that exquisite Steuben decanter for unimpressive wines, dessert wines, red wines requiring instant aeration, or old wines heavy with sediment.

Note, though, that handling a sediment-laden wine can be tricky. Why not let the butler do it?

Or, if the butler is off attending to the kitchen staff, do it yourself: Stand the bottle upright for two or more hours till it comes to room temperature and the dregs settle. Then, with the decanter in front of a light (candles are traditional) begin pouring. If sediment threatens to pass, stop immediately. When the sediment has resettled, resume pouring. Never resort to a metal strainer as it will spoil the taste.

Remember, even the most elegant decanter can't replace an impressive label, so don't decant unnecessarily. Also, don't decant a good wine and refill the bottles with a lesser wine. (You are too likely to get caught!)

Pouring Like a Pro

Pouring wine is an art ignored by most, mastered by few, and noticed by everyone. Think: Do friends admire your dexterity with a bottle? Or do they play connect-the-dots with your dribbled drops of Burgundy?

If you suspect that your performance is anything less than brilliant, study the steps that follow:

1. Allow bottles to stand undisturbed as long as possible.
2. Assemble appropriate glassware, allowing one sparkling goblet per guest per wine. Frost glasses for chilled wines by popping them into the freezer for five to ten minutes.
3. Pour yourself a few ounces. Taste it. (See page 36 for rituals.) Is it good?

---

[9] Still means not sparkling, not bubbly. One does not decant champagnes and the like because it destroys the bubbles that cost a fortune to produce. Note, too, that white wines are seldom decanted.

4. Show the bottle to your guests. Let them see what they'll be drinking, but don't make a big fuss about it.

5. Grasp the bottle around its lower middle. (Choking up on the neck is considered *déclassé*.[10]) Fill each goblet one-third full for red wine and one-half full for white wine and champagne. Keep the bottle just above the glass's rim, never allowing them to touch. (Note: You will surely have fewer spills if goblets are on level surfaces rather than in wriggly hands.)

6. As you finish pouring, rotate the bottle slightly to avoid leaving a trail of drops.

7. Occasionally wipe the bottle's lip with a clean cloth napkin, and blot away any moisture. Don't wrap the napkin around the bottle, as it obscures the label.

8. When you change wines, change glasses.

9. During the meal, be attentive to your guests' needs. Quickly refill empty glasses; most people feel uncomfortable helping themselves. If you need assistance, hire someone or ask a trustworthy guest to help.

A few more hints: When serving guests at the dinner table (don't you detest the staff's day off?), begin with guests of honor, standing behind and to their right; move clockwise till glasses are filled. When finished, place the bottle on a coaster or in a cooler. (If you have two bottles, leave one near the host, the other near the hostess.)

Perusing, Choosing, and Using

Servin' Several

When you need two bottles anyway, why not serve two *different* wines? Or even three?

Enjoy a lovely dry white *Graves* (GRAHV) with your fish

---

[10] Déclassé (dā klah SĀ) means "very tacky."

course, a dry red *Bordeaux* (bohr DOH) with the beef, and a sweet *Sauternes* (soh TEHRN) with dessert.

Here are a few rules to help you with selection and service:

Limit wines to one country or region; that is, serve German wines, or Burgundies, but not both.

Serve dry wines before sweet wines, young wines before old, white wines before red, light wines before full-bodied, and average wines before great wines.

Set the table properly. Place the glass for the first wine on the far right, the glass for the second to its left, and the water goblet to the left of that. As you change wines, clear away used glasses and bring extras as needed.

If you're using all-purpose glasses exclusively, set the table for one wine at a time, replacing glasses as you change wines. (Rinsing the glasses is *not* sufficient!)

Wines to Avoid

When appearances are important, avoid:

Wines widely advertised.

Wines you can open without a corkscrew.

Wines with silly or contrived names.

Wines available by the jug.

Wines made from fruits other than grapes.

Chianti (KYAHN tee) in straw-wrapped bottles, *Liebfraumilch* (LEEB frow milkh), pink champagne.

Domestic wines.[11]

The Hostess Gift

Having dinner at a friend's estate? How marvelous! But do remember that choosing the wine to accompany a meal is a task to

---

[11] Like it or not, few domestic wines have achieved the universal snob appeal of imports. For though a good vintage from one of the smaller California wineries can be as delightful as many of Europe's top wines, the average consumer is still more likely to be impressed (and positively won't be disappointed) by a fine wine from France, Germany, or even Italy.

be botched by the host or hostess, not a dinner guest. So if you take wine, offer it as a gift, not an addition to the menu.

Certainly, if you know what is being served (don't ask), you should try to bring something appropriate. Consult "Which Wine?" for ideas, and don't be too extravagant or too stingy. (And don't forget to remove the price!)

Otherwise, take something festive (and neutral) like champagne, or take a wine you especially enjoy. Or take wine coasters, or any small gift.

What's in Store

About Buying

A good wine merchant can be as difficult to find as the proverbial honest man. But it is well worth the try.

First locate a really ugly store with a huge inventory. Everything about it should suggest wine is the *only* business, or at least the most important. If the racks are marked with pronunciations, histories, or service hints, so much the better.

Speak with the manager or owner. Let him or her know you need someone to handle *all* your business, then start asking questions.

Is he, or one of his salespeople, truly knowledgeable about wine? You would be surprised at how many dastardly souls sell wine simply to make money.

Do they deliver? At what cost? How far will they travel? How late are they open?

And what of their selection? A merchant with no '75 *Dom Pérignon* on his racks certainly is not to be trusted![12]

Listen carefully to the merchant's pronunciation. If he can correctly pronounce *Rothschild* (roh SHEELD), or *Montrachet* (mohn rah SHĀ), marry him off to a close relative.

---

[12] Dom Pérignon (DOHn pā ree NYOn) is a lovely, but costly, French champagne.

When you finally find your shop, find another. Compare benefits and prices; they can vary dramatically. When you decide on a winner, make a sizable purchase and turn on the charm. Have them remember you. Fondly.

Shopping Hints

The prudent buyer, one who finds the finest wines, saves the most money, and throws the best parties will:

Buy wines early because they're always better after several days rest. (Aren't we all?)

Tell the merchant whether the wine is for immediate, or future, consumption. Premature uncorking is expensive, monetarily *and* socially.

Buy 50 percent more than necessary. Wine keeps, but thirsty guests—who'll consume at least eight to twelve ounces each—won't. To judge your requirements accurately, know that an average bottle holds 25.4 ounces, a magnum 50.7 ounces, and a split 6.3 ounces.

Purchase champagne and immature wines in magnums. The extra space helps them age.

Make specific requests. When you say "I'm looking for a dry white wine of good vintage, perhaps a *Chablis Grand Cru* (shah blee grahn KROO) or a *Meursault* (muhr SOH)," you set price and type, and peg yourself as a knowledgeable buyer. (See "Which Wine?" on page 11 for suggestions.)

Remember that the term "vintage" implies high quality only for French Champagnes and Portuguese Ports. Otherwise, it simply indicates the year when the grapes were harvested.

About Storage

Wines detest light, heat, extreme cold, temperature swings, vibration, and standing upright. A place that protects them from these evils will make them very happy.

Of course, if you want them to be ecstatic, a wine cellar is just the thing. A climate-controlled cavern several stories beneath the ground would be nice. See what your architect can whip up. And don't be put off by the inconvenience of trekking all that way just to retrieve a bottle of wine. You may send the butler, but do get him an elevator.

Did you have something a bit more simple in mind? Well, I have been known to store a few bottles of red wine in a convenient closet, and some white wine and champagne in the refrigerator (my emergency rations). Naturally, I am careful to keep them on their sides and to drink them within a few months. A climate-controlled wine closet, available in many sizes, can work well too—especially if you plan to lay down (that is, store and age) several cases of good wine. Place it under the stairs or in the basement, or lock it in a closet.

Whatever you do, keep it away from Cook. You know her tendency to sneak a nip or two!

Which Wine?

Wine and food must be complementary in tone and style as well as flavor. Delicate meals require subtle wines; simple meals, ordinary wines; formal meals, spectacular wines. In other words, no champagne with pot roast; no *vin ordinare*[1] with *haute cuisine*.[2]

"Which Wine?" will supply everything you need to know. Augment it with "Wines and Related Terms" ("VIP's Vocabulary #2"), and you're ready for anything!

---

[1] Vin ordinaire (va*n* ohr dee NEHR) is ordinary table wine.
[2] Haute cuisine (OHT kwee ZEEN) is the art of fine French cooking which emphasizes the use of butter, heavy cream, and sauces.

Wine Type	Food Choice	Service Hints	Suggestions
DRY WHITE WINE Many of the best white wines come from Côte de Beaune (koht duh BUHN), Côte de Nuit (koht duh NWEE), and Chablis—all areas in Burgundy, France; good wines are also produced in Mâcon (mah KAHn).	Seafood Poultry Veal Pork —delicately seasoned	*Glass:* all-purpose or smaller of two sizes *Temp:* 45°F *Open:* just before use *Age:* 4-7 years for the best French wines; 2-3 years otherwise. *Decant:* no *Hints:* The best Burgundy whites are labeled Grand Cru (grahn KROO); the next best are Premier Cru (prehm yā KROO).	WILDLY EXTRAVAGANT Le Montrachet (luh mahn rah SHĀ) IMPRESSIVE Any Chablis Grand Cru (shah blee grahn KROO) or Premier Cru (prehm yā KROO), like Les Blanchots (lā blahn SHOH) Meursault (muhr SOH) Pouilly Fuissé (poo yee fwee SĀ) GOOD Mâcon-Villages (mah KAHn vee LAHZH) Mouton-Cadet Blanc (moo TAHn kah DĀ BLAHn)

FRUITY WHITE WINE

The finest fruity wines come from the Rheingau (RĪN gow) and Mosel (moh ZEHL) regions of Germany.

Seafood
Poultry
Veal
—full flavored

Glass: as above
Temp: 45°F
Open: just before use
Age: 4-5 years
Hints: The finest dry wines are labeled Qualitätswein mit Prädikat; the next best, simply Qualitätswein.

They're further labeled in order of ascending rarity and sweetness: Kabinet (kah bee NEHT), Spätlese (SHPÄT lä zuh), and Auslese (OWS lä zuh).

WILDLY EXTRAVAGANT

Bernkasteler Doctor (BEHRN kahs tul luhr DOHK tor)

Schloss Johannisberger (SHLAWS yoh HAN is behrk uhr)

Steinberger (SHTĪN behrk uhr)

IMPRESSIVE

Bernkasteler Graben (BEHRN kahs tul luhr GRAH buhn)

Wehlener Sonnenuhr (VĀ luhn ehr ZOHN uhn ohr)

GOOD

Alsatian Gewürztraminer (ahl SAH shun guh VOORTS trah mee nuhr)

Wine Type	Food Choice	Service Hints	Suggestions
CHAMPAGNE The world's great sparkling wines are from Champagne, France.	Any elegant food that is not too highly seasoned is complemented by *dry* champagne. Any elegant dessert is complemented by *sweet* champagne.	*Glass:* Best in a tulip-shaped, or fluted, glass; an all-purpose, or red-wine, glass will also suffice; what will *not* do is a saucer-type champagne glass. *Temp:* 45°F *Open:* just before use (see instructions in preceding chapter) *Age:* Drink better wines within 10-15 years of bottling; drink lesser wines within several years. *Bottle Size:* Champagne ages more agreeably in magnums. *Decant:* never *Hints:* Brut (BROOT) designates the finest, driest champagne. Other terms, by ascending sweetness, are Extra Sec (SEHK), Sec, Demi-sec	WILDLY EXTRAVAGANT Dom Pérignon (DOHn peh ree NYOn) Taittinger Blanc de Blanc (teh tan ZHĀ BLAHn duh BLAHn) Perrier-Jouët Fleur de Champagne (pehr YĀ zhoo Ā fluhr duh SHAHn PAH nyuh) IMPRESSIVE Moët et Chandon, White Star Extra Dry (moh EH teh shan DOn) Bollinger Brut, Special Cuveé or Vintage (boh lan ZHĀ BROOT SPESH uhl koo VĀ) GOOD Korbel Brut (kohr BEHL BROOT) Kornell Brut (kohr NEHL BROOT)

(deh mee **SEHK**), and Doux (**DOO**).
"Vintage" champagne is from a great year. Vin de Cuvée (*van duh koo VĀ*) is a shipper's best wine.

AVOID
Pink Champagne

SWEET WHITE WINE

Sauternes (soh **TEHRN**), from Sauternes, France, and the quality wines of Germany are among the finest white dessert wines in the world.

Fruit
Dessert
Blue Cheese
Especially good with:
tarts
apples
puddings
ripe pears
honeydew melons

Glass: all-purpose or smaller of two sizes
Temp: 45°F
Open: just before use
Age: 10 or more years
Decant: to store remainder of unfinished bottle
Hints: The best Sauternes carry the Bordeaux classifications of First or Second Growth.
The best German wines are labeled, in order of ascending sweetness and rarity, Beerenauslese and Trockenbeerenauslese. They are made from late-picked grapes with "noble rot."

WILDLY EXTRAVAGANT
Château D'Yquem (shah toh dee **KEHM**)
Any German wine labeled Beerenauslese (BĀ ruhn OWS lā zuh) or Trockenbeerenauslese (TROHK uhn BĀ ruhn OWS lā zuh)

IMPRESSIVE
Château Climens (shah toh klee MAHn)
Château Guiraud (shah toh ghee ROH)

AVOID
Domestic and inexpensive wines

Wine Type	Food Choice	Service Hints	Suggestions
SHERRY The finest Sherries come from Jerez de la Frontera (hā RETH dā lah frohn TĀ rah), Spain.	Appetizers, and soups spiked with sherry, are complemented by *dry* sherries. Chocolate and nuts are complemented by *sweet* sherries.	*Glass:* six-ounce sherry *Temp:* dry sherry—45°F sweet sherry—65-68°F *Open:* just before use *Age:* young *Decant:* if you like *Hints:* Though sweet sherries keep well, dry sherries do not.	IMPRESSIVE Purchase the best Spanish sherry you can afford. The types, ranging from light and dry to full and sweet are: Manzanilla (man zah NEE yah) Fino (FEE noh) Amontillado (ah MOHN tee YAH doh) Oloroso (oh loh ROH soh) Cream
ROSÉ Tavel (tah VEHL), and Anjou (ahn ZHOO), France, produce the finest rosé wines.	Best for lunch or a summer meal with food that is not too heavy or well-spiced.	*Glass:* all-purpose or larger of two sizes *Temp:* 45° *Open:* just before use *Age:* 1-5 years for Tavels; 2-3 years for Anjou rosés	GOOD Tavel Rosé (tah VEHL roh ZĀ) Rosé de Cabernet (roh ZĀ duh kah behr NĀ)

SPARKLING RED WINE	NONE	DON'T	When you crave bubbles, serve champagne.
FRUITY RED WINE The best are produced in Beaujolais (boh zhoh LÃ), France.	Best for lunch or a summer meal with any of the foods listed under LIGHT DRY RED WINE	*Glass:* all-purpose or larger of two sizes *Temp:* 65-68°F *Open:* just before use *Age:* 1-3 years	IMPRESSIVE Any Grand Cru (grahn KROO) Beaujolais (boh zhoh LÃ), like: Moulin-à-Vent (moo lan ah VAHn) Fleurie (fluh REE)
LIGHT DRY RED WINE Bordeaux (bohr DOH), France, produces the finest red wines in the world. The important districts are Médoc (mā DOK), Pomerol (poh meh RAHL), and Saint-Émilion (san tā mee LYOn).	Steaks and chops Veal, pork, or poultry in a red sauce Roast chicken Red meat cold cuts like roast beef and sausage Cheese served prior to dinner	*Glass:* all-purpose or larger of two sizes *Temp:* 65-68°F *Open:* very old wines—just before use; wines 5-15 years old, but mature and ready to drink—one to two hours; young or immature wines—two to 24 hours *Decant:* if you like *Bottle Size:* Wines age best in magnums.	WILDLY EXTRAVAGANT The First Growths (the world's best): Château Lafite-Rothschild (shah toh lah FEET roh SHEELD) Château Mouton-Rothschild (shah toh moo TAHn roh SHEELD) Château Margaux (shah toh mahr GOH) Château LaTour (shah toh lah TOOR)

Wine Type	Food Choice	Service Hints	Suggestions
LIGHT DRY RED WINE (*continued*)		*Hints*: Bordeaux wines are rated, in order of descending quality, First through Fifth Growths, *crus exceptionnelles, crus bourgeois,* and *crus artisan*. The highest-quality wines are château-bottled: Mis en Bouteilles au Château (MEE zah*n* boo TĀ yuh oh shah TOH).	Château Haut-Brion (shah toh oh bree AH*n*) Also extravagant: Château Pétrus (shah toh pā TROOS) Note: The preceding wines are the finest in the world; try less expensive wines first to educate your palate. IMPRESSIVE Château Beycheville (shah toh behsh VEEL) Château Lascombes (shah toh lahs KOHMB) Château Giscours (shah toh zhees KOOR) Any other Second or Third Growth Bordeaux red wine GOOD Château Mouton-Baron-

TAHn bah ROHn fee LEEP)

Château LaTour-de-Mons (shah toh lah TOOR duh MAHnS)

Any other Fourth or Fifth Growth

FULL-BODIED DRY RED WINE

Burgundy, France, produces marvelous, full, assertive red wines.

Similar, slightly less distinguished, wines are produced in the Rhône Valley.

Hearty beef and lamb dishes like: Boeuf Bourguignonme

Other stews

Roasts

Full-flavored foods in a red wine or tomato sauce

Game, like duck or goose (see especially wines marked with an asterisk)

Blue cheeses (see wines marked with an asterisk)

Glass: all-purpose or larger
Temp: 65-68°F
Open: see LIGHT DRY RED WINE
Age: varies widely: 8-10 years is not uncommon
Decant: if you like
Bottle Size: Wine matures better in a magnum.
Hints: The best wines are classified Grand Cru (grahn KROO); the next best are Premier Cru (prehm yā KROO).

WILDLY EXTRAVAGANT

La Romanée-Conti (lah roh mah NÄ kahn TEE)

Chambertin (shahn behr TAn)

Chambertin-Clos-de-Bèze (shahn behr tan kloh duh BEHZ)

Any other Grand Cru Burgundy

IMPRESSIVE

Any Premier Cru Burgundy, like Clos des Mouches (KLOH dä MOOSH)

Pommard (poh MAHR)

Wine Type	Food Choice	Service Hints	Suggestions
FULL-BODIED DRY RED WINE (*continued*)			Châteauneuf-du-Pape* (shah toh NUHF doo PAHP) Vosne-Romanée (VOHN roh mah NÃ) GOOD Hermitage* (ehr mee TAHZH) Mouton-Cadet Rouge (moo TAHn kah DÃ ROOZH) AVOID Wines labeled simply "Burgundy Red" or "Bourgogne Rouge" (boor GOY nyuh ROOZH). They do not rate a vineyard name.
ITALIAN RED WINE The best wines come from the Piedmont region.	With Italian dishes containing a meat or red sauce, try Barolo or Gattinara With Italian dishes con-	*Glass*: all-purpose or larger of two sizes *Temp*: 65-68°F *Open*: 4 or more hours before use	IMPRESSIVE Barolo, Riserva Speciale (bah ROH loh, ree SEHR vah spech YAHL ä)—This wine is called

taining a cream sauce, try Bardolino

With heavily-spiced Italian food, try Barbaresco

Age: generally 10-15 years

Decant: if you're in a hurry

Label: The terms Riserva and Riserva Speciale indicate a superior, well-aged wine. Chianti (kee AHN tee) lovers should avoid the inferior wines in straw-wrapped bottles.

The King of Italy.

Gattinara, Riserva Speciale (gah tee NAH rah, ree SEHR vah spech YAHL ā)

GOOD

Barberesco (bahr beh REHZ koh)

Bardolino (bahr doh LEE noh)

Chianti Classico, Riserva (kee AHN tee klah see koh ree SEHR vah)

Valpolicella (vahl poh lee CHĀ lah)

SWEET RED WINE

Port, from Porto, Portugal, is the King of after-dinner red dessert wines.

Stilton and Cheddar cheeses

Nuts

Fruit, especially apricots and peaches

Glass: all-purpose or larger

Temp: 65-68°F

Open: just before use

Decant: yes

Age: Vintage Port—15 to 20 years or more; LBV—somewhat sooner;

WILDLY EXTRAVAGANT

Vintage Port (Dow's, Sandeman's, Warre)

IMPRESSIVE

Late-bottled Vintage Port (LBV)

Wine Type	Food Choice	Service Hints	Suggestions
SWEET RED WINE (*continued*)		Tawny—generally ready when purchased.	GOOD Tawny Port
			AVOID Ruby Port
NO WINE The foods listed at right are generally incompatible with wine.	Vinegar-dressed salads Dishes containing anchovies Citrus fruits Chocolate (see Sherry for exception) Heavily-spiced or flavored foods loaded with garlic, onions, curry, chili powder, etc. Ice cream (serve liqueurs instead) Bananas Artichokes	These foods destroy the taste of your wines; either forgo these foods when you are serving a fine wine, or serve a wine of only fair quality. Note: In addition, never serve a *dry* wine with *sweet* food or a *sweet* wine with a savory food.	

The LimoScene

Certain oil barons have been known to supply their infants with chauffeur-driven limousines, no doubt to save them the trouble of learning to walk.

Of course, certain members of the Old Guard believe it is a bit pretentious to have one's own car and driver prior to puberty. For these, and other late starters, here are a few inside tips:

Rules of the Road

One calls one's driver a "driver" or "chauffeur."[1]

One addresses one's driver by his first name, as in "Home, James," or by his last name, as in "We've run out of champagne, Peterson."

Your driver opens and closes the limousine door for you. To do it yourself is disgustingly democratic, and therefore not for our sort.

When a woman enters a limousine with a man (my favorite way to travel!), the man enters *first*, and slides over (just as he would in a taxi).

Drivers carry your luggage. You need to preserve your strength for more important matters.

Rules of the Rental

When calling to rent a car and driver, be certain to ask:

[1]Chauffeur may be pronounced "SHOH fuhr," which sounds suspiciously like gopher, but I prefer the more chic French pronunciation of "shoh FUHR."

What size cars are available? Limousines range from sedan to stretch. To determine the best size for your purpose, you must consider the number of passengers and the degree of comfort desired. (Six need a stretch to be really comfortable; in a smaller car, two would have to ride on jumpseats. Talk about roughing it!)

What is the charge for the various sizes? Sometimes a stretch is as much as four times the cost of a sedan, so if you're not going to be cutting a deal en route, perhaps half of your passengers could ride in a second car. Anyway, motorcades are definitely more *you!*

What colors do they have? White is for Hollywood *premières* (prehm YEHR) only. Burgundy is *not* for a person of your obvious breeding. You need black or gray. Maybe dark blue—because it *is* nice when your limousine matches your eyes.

Are blacked-out windows available? How about a bar? Or television? What other goodies do they have to amuse?

Can they supply a driver who hates to talk? Trying to discuss business with a client while solving your chauffeur's marital problems is tricky at best.

Approximately how many miles will your car have on it? Nothing is less classy than a clattering rat trap. Except a broken-down rat trap.

What year and make is the car? A stretch Edsel just won't cut it.

Are there special rates for frequently traveled routes? Luxury at a discount is the world's greatest bargain.

Can you establish an account? It is such a nuisance to take along a bodyguard to carry your cash! Being billed later seems a far better idea, especially if you're trying to pass off the car as your own. (Yes, Virginia, there are people who actually do that!) If you can't establish an account, *can you at least pay by credit card?* If so, which cards? Don't forget to tip in cash (15 to 20 percent of the tab). Your driver will be forever grateful. And you know how you adore gratitude!

The elegant Palm Court restaurant in the lobby of The Plaza in Manhattan.

2

· RESTAURANT RESOURCEFULNESS ·

*When dining out, it matters not whether
you are rich or poor—as long as you
have plenty of money.*

—*JAN DARLING*

Have you ever been baffled by a wine list, shunned by a head-waiter, or stranded in a bar for hours only to be seated later at a table near three screaming children and a dirty clean-up station? Were you with important clients? Were they impressed?

That bad, huh? Well, cheer up! Solutions to these problems are only sentences away.

Finding Your Place

There are many methods for finding a restaurant, the worst of which is a frantic last-minute thumbing through old magazines and the phone book, the best of which is a systematic, logical, and leisurely search.

If you find the latter approach more appealing, consider these generalities:

A small restaurant with a limited menu is preferable to a large restaurant with an extensive menu. The smaller place must compensate for a lack of variety by serving more imaginative meals. In addition, the chef has more time to spend on each dish, and food is less likely to have been frozen or precooked.

French cuisine is the most popular choice for elegant evenings out; Northern Italian is probably second. For a less grand occasion, try Greek, Chinese, Middle Eastern, or Japanese, saving steak and lobster, Mexican, Cantonese, German, and Southern Italian (spaghetti, etc.) for family dinners.

Older establishments are more likely to please than new ones. Restaurants need at least two months to ten years to work out their problems. Why not let them practice on others first?

Restaurants you can easily afford are preferable to those with exorbitant prices. You must encourage your guests to indulge themselves, something you cannot do if money is a problem.

Certainly, the best way to find a place that meets these criteria is through recommendations from knowledgeable friends. But should that approach fail:

Call the Food Editor of your newspaper or city magazine, the host of a local cooking show, or a favorite headwaiter.

Read reviews in local magazines and newspapers, but disregard advertisements and most multiple listings; the restaurants' owners might well have paid for all the glowing praise.

Check with the Chamber of Commerce when you are in a small town. Big-city bureaus are likely to send you to "touristy" establishments.

When all else fails, check a guide book. Where to Eat in America, published by Random House, is good. Abroad, try the *Guide Michelin* (geed meesh LA*n*) or *Guide Kléber* (klā BEHR).

Note: Make sure you keep a list of the places you enjoy so you won't have to start all over again.

Reservations

Making reservations is not as simple as it sounds. At least, it shouldn't be. This is your first contact with the people who can make or break your meal. So, to ensure success:

Make reservations as far in advance as possible. If you cannot, and you arrive to find no tables available, try palming a five- or ten-dollar bill and shaking the headwaiter's hand. But do so discreetly: Some of those fellows will not be bribed.

Think twice before reserving a table between 8:00 and 9:00 on Friday or Saturday night unless you like long waits, precooked food, and inferior service. If possible, try a less popular night, like Monday or Tuesday. Or dine early (6:00-7:00) or late (10:00). Incidentally, some places offer substantial discounts for off-hour dining.

Ask about appropriate (not minimum) dress, licensing (liquor? wine? nothing?), and payment methods (credit cards? cash? checks?).

Make special arrangements for the opening or chilling of favorite wines; for *banquette*[1] or view tables; for dishes requiring advance preparation; for flowers or special-occasion cakes (which are often free); or for unusual payment of the check.

Forget the old ruse of pretending you're a doctor just to get a good table. Headwaiters are wise to that one.

If you're really out to impress, visit the maître d' (meh truh DEE) *prior to dinner—about 5:30.* Make special arrangements, find out his name, make sure he knows yours, and tip him (five or ten dollars should suffice). While you're at it, take a look at the menu and wine list (so you can check pronunciations), and locate the restrooms and the bar (a "regular" would know where they are).

Always reconfirm reservations 24 to 48 hours ahead (or whenever the *maître d'* instructed) or you may lose your table.

---

[1] Banquettes (bahn KEHT) are tables lining the wall; they generally have both bench and chair seats.

Cancel any reservations you cannot keep. Restaurateurs (reh stoh rah TUHR) hate no-shows and have memories an elephant would envy.

If despite all your precautions you get stuck in the bar, tell the bartender you would like to put your drinks on the dinner tab. Bartenders at better establishments should be happy to comply. When your table is ready, leave a cash tip of 15 to 20 percent, then have the headwaiter transport your drinks from the bar to the table. Better to have *him* spill them than you!

Employee Roster

At the more elegant establishments, the cast of players can be mind-boggling. But here goes.

The first person to greet you, the fellow who can squeeze you in on a busy night, is the *maître d'hotel* (meh truh doh TEL)—the maître d'. Call this dashing, tuxedo-clad male by his first name; he will call you Mr., Mrs., or Ms. Whatever. Expect him to be friendly, never haughty. Tip only for special service;[2] five to ten dollars palmed in a handshake, delivered with a "Thank you, Alan," should be sufficient.

The fellow taking your order, supervising the service, boning your fish, and handling your complaints is the Captain. He should be pleasant, knowledgeable, and attentive. Tip him 5 percent, either delivered in a handshake or noted on the check.

That silver cup or key hung on a chain around the neck of that austerely-proper gentleman belongs to the wine steward, the *sommelier* (suh muhl YĀ). He should, but may not, know a great deal about his job. In any case, at the end of the meal he gets 10 percent of the wine tab, but never less than several dollars.

Those fellows serving your food and replenishing your wine are the waiters. Ideally, they will anticipate your every need, but if

---

[2]Someone having a birthday? Alert the *maître d'* before your arrival and he'll deliver your surprised guest a miniature birthday cake or tart, complete with a candle and a charming rendition of "Happy Birthday." Your guest will hate the embarrassment, but adore the attention!

you're forced to signal them, do so unobtrusively. Lift an eyebrow or a finger. If you must, whisper a name or say "waiter," never *"garçon"* or "boy." (A waitress is called by her name or by "waitress," never by "miss" or "ma'am.")

If especially pleased with your waiter, write down his name so you can request a table in his section on your next visit. Treat him with respect, but don't be too friendly, don't thank him too often, and don't apologize for accidents. ("George, I'm afraid we've had a mishap" is all you need say.) Tip 15 percent (plus 5 percent to the headwaiter) for adequate service. For poor service, tip less (or nothing); for great service, add a few percent more.

The busboy, that attentive lad who refills water glasses, empties ashtrays, and clears after each course, is tipped by the waiter, not you (though a smile is certain to be appreciated).

Others who require tips (I know, the list seems endless) are:

The Checkroom Attendant: 50¢ per item or $1 for several items.

Strolling Musicians: $1–$2 per musician, or $5 per band, for several songs directed to your table.

Valet Parking Attendants: $1 or more depending on the establishment and inconvenience involved.

The Doorman: $1 per special service (like hailing a taxi). Otherwise, nothing.

When dinner is superb, send your compliments (but never money) to the chef. If the restaurant is not busy, ask to convey your appreciation in person; the better you know the cook, the more likely you are to receive special attention on your next visit.

The Right Table

What makes a table "in" or "out" may be mere whim or custom. For example, if tourists are normally shuttled upstairs, locals probably consider that area uninhabitable. On the other hand, comfortable and highly visible banquettes, view tables, and those away from the kitchen and passersby are preferred for good reason, as are tables in private rooms.

Though some high-status locations are reserved for long-time patrons (or their friends), a simple request, or advance notice, should get you seated in an acceptable area. If—heaven forbid— you find yourself headed for no man's land, immediately request another table. Important people like you do *not* accept improper seating.

Once you've been shown to a suitable table, who sits where?

Social *equals* (of which you and I have few!) sit boy-girl-boy-girl as much as possible, with close friends, and couples, separated to improve conversation. *Honored guests* (out-of-town visitors, foreigners, celebrities, elderly friends, etc.) sit to the host's and hostess's right at a rectangular table; seats to their left are next favored. In a booth or banquette, wall seats are usually (but not always) the most comfortable and, thus, are generally considered preferable. (Now you know why King Arthur selected his famous *round* table!)

The Menu and You

Ordering: In General

After seating you, the Captain will take drink requests.[3] Try an *apéritif*[4] if you're feeling chic, a cocktail or non-alcoholic beverage otherwise—but do order something so your companions won't feel uncomfortable.

Order wines and desserts as soon as possible so they can be aired, chilled, prepared, or whatever.

If the menu is entirely French, and you have neither lived abroad nor memorized the "French Menu" section in the back of this book, ask for a translation. Don't worry about being a pest; *you* are the one who is being inconvenienced.

---

[3] Now is the time to arrange separate checks, bearing in mind that too many checks spoil the waiter's disposition.

[4] Apéritifs (ah peh ree TEEF) are drinks that stimulate the appetite.

Ladies, if the evening is Dutch treat, and you are given a menu *without* prices, request one *with* prices, if you like. Go ahead and order, however, if someone else is paying. To be too concerned about cost implies that the host may be unable, or unwilling, to pay. Ordering an obviously inexpensive meal does the same thing.

In these liberated times, should a woman place her order through her host *or* directly with the waiter?

Whichever makes her feel most comfortable.

Ordering: The Specifics

Before ordering, you must determine how the meal will be priced. Here's a crash course:

À la carte (ah lah KAHRT), as you know, means that each item is selected, and priced, separately. This is the least, or most, expensive way to order, depending on your appetite.

Prix fixe (pree FEEKS) refers to a meal of a fixed number of courses, with several choices per course. Its "fixed price" means a lower cost than the same items *à la carte* would fetch.

Table d'hôte (tah bluh DOHT), literally "table of the host," refers to an inflexible, multi-course meal offered at a fixed price. For a given quantity of food, it is the least expensive way to order.

Service compris (sehr VEESS kahn PREE) is not a way of ordering a meal, but as it refers to pricing it is included here. It means that the tip is figured for you. (Since the percentage may be less than you would normally tip, be certain to check it out with the waiter.)

Now, assuming you're not ordering *table d'hôte*, you have a few choices to make. Unfortunately, assembling an array of courses into an elegant, flavor-balanced meal requires a certain amount of knowledge. *Fortunately*, the information you need can be found later in this book.

One other source of assistance you may find extremely useful is your headwaiter. He'll know which pastries were just baked and what seafood is freshest. And who better to reveal the house's real *specialités* (speh syah lee TÃ)? So, when he arrives at your table to take your order, say something like, "I adore fish; what do you recommend?" or "If I could eat here only once, what dishes would I not want to miss?" Headwaiters love to be consulted and will generally make wonderful suggestions.

After he gets to know you, he'll be even more helpful. Wouldn't you like to know about the fresh raspberries the chef is saving for a few special customers? And wouldn't you enjoy trying the dessert he just invented? Or the new sauce for the roast duck? The headwaiter's your man.

Has a dish you adored disappeared from the menu? No problem. If the ingredients are on hand, "your friend" will have it prepared for you.

You may also learn that the restaurant prepares Peking Duck if given a few days' notice, or that a simple request brings lobsters from Maine or veal in cream like Great Aunt Hester used to make. Form a friendship with your headwaiter and these pleasures and more will surely be yours.

The Wine List

Ordering

Too many people resort to the Price-and-Point approach to wine lists; that is, they decide by price and order by pointing. This is not an entirely bad method, I suppose, *if* you don't mind appearing unsophisticated, or drinking inferior wines, or paying too much for value received.[5]

Fortunately, there are better ways to avoid the Wine-List Blues. You may:

> *Carry a wine journal*—a small, good-looking notebook
> containing the names and pronunciations of widely available

---

[5] Here's an insider's tip: The *second* most expensive wine in each portion of a wine list is generally the most popular and is often overpriced.

wines. ("Which Wine?"—beginning on page 11—has all the
information you'll need.) By the way, you needn't fret about
appearing unworldly; many ultrasophisticated types keep
journals so that they do not forget favorite vineyards and
vintages.

Drink your own wines. Some restaurants allow special
customers to store as much as a case in their cellars; others
let anyone bring in one or two bottles at a time. Ask before
planning anything, expect to pay a corkage (handling) fee,
then enjoy the dollar savings and avoidance of wine-list
problems.

Order your wines when you make your reservation. This works
when you've reordered the food, when you're planning to
drink champagne, or when you know in advance what
everyone will be eating.

Ask the sommelier (never the waiter) for advice, remembering
that not all wine stewards know what they're doing, and that
more than a few unscrupulous souls will recommend high-
priced bottles to increase tips and revenues. With this in
mind, make your requests as specific as possible. "Could you
suggest an obscure white *Bordeaux* (bohr DOH) in the ten-
to-fifteen-dollar range?" is more likely to bring something
special than "Bring us a wine to go with fish."

Approving Your Selection

When approving the wine you ordered, think Boston, not Hollywood. Remember, this is but a fact-finding mission, not your last
chance to impress the masses.

Here's what to do:

When the steward brings the wine, *check the label carefully.* Is
it exactly what you ordered? The right vineyard? The right
date? The right color?

Let the waiter handle the bottle; don't try to open or pour it
yourself. It may have been left at your table to aerate or
chill.

When the waiter opens the bottle, he will hand you the cork.

Sniff it slightly if it makes you happy, remembering that sniffing the cork *and* tasting the wine is redundant, and that sniffing the cork of a white wine (or the stopper of champagne) reveals nothing.

The waiter will pour you a small amount of wine. *Grasp the glass by the lower part of the stem, check the wine for clarity* (cloudy wine is spoiled), *quickly swirl it around in the glass* (to develop the bouquet), *then take a sip* (gently swishing the wine in the mouth a few moments before swallowing. No theatrics allowed!).

If the wine has spoiled, you'll know immediately; inform the sommelier and ask him to bring another bottle. But never refuse good wine just to appear sophisticated; truly bad wine is most uncommon, and all wine lovers know it.

If the wine is underchilled, have it chilled further.

If the wine is fine, just nod.

If the wine is merely unpleasant, grin and bear it.

Upon receiving your approval, the steward will serve your guests first, returning to fill your glass last. *Let him replenish the wine as needed.*

Complaints

Never hesitate to complain about poor food or service. The management needs feedback to bring about improvement. Besides, you deserve full value for your money.

Address small complaints (cold or undercooked food) to your waiter. Direct larger complaints (poor service, several badly prepared dishes) to the captain. Follow up major problems the following day with a letter to the maître d'. He will thank you for alerting him to the situation, and may even invite you back for a dinner "on the house."

Never tip the full amount if service was inferior. In fact, you needn't tip at all if you were treated very badly. Just be sure you are punishing the right person. Denying the waiter his due because of a poor chef, or the captain *his* because of a stuffy maître d', is both unfair and unproductive.

The Check

An otherwise perfect evening can be ruined by awkwardness in paying the tab. Don't let this happen to you.

If you want separate checks, request them when you order, remembering that two checks per table is the most a waiter should have to handle.

If you'll be splitting the tab, divide it equally. Hassles over a few dollars are unforgivably tacky.

If you want to pay for everything yourself, open a house account and make arrangements to have a bill sent to your home or office. Or, hand your waiter a credit card on a quick trip to the rest-room; this way, he can return your card after the meal with a slip requiring only the tip and your signature.

If you must pay the check in front of your guests, be as nonchalant as possible. If you find a small error, forget it. Handle a significant error as quietly as possible.

Lay the bill face down on the tray; guests must never, ever, know how much you paid. Place your most prestigious credit card (American Express Gold, Carte Blanche, etc.) on top of the bill. (Yes, most people do notice—especially if they're impressed!)

When the card slip is returned, sign it and figure the gratuities. Better yet, leave a *cash* tip; waiters are simply crazy for the green stuff!

Remove your copy from the credit slip, destroy the carbons, pocket your card, and you're ready to head off to the limousine.

Rating the Experience

Anyone can tell a great restaurant from a rotten one, but when making close calls, restaurant critics look for specific things. For example, they know that the classic test of a chef is his skill with an omelet. Unfortunately, few non-critics know enough about omelets to make a meaningful judgment. If you fall into that category, inspect the seafood cocktail instead; it should be cold, colorful, fresh, and delicious, and must be accompanied by a tasty dip, not one of those disgusting straight-from-the-bottle sauces.

While on your "inspection tour," look for signs of uninspired management: cold bread, cellophane-wrapped crackers, "fake" homemade bread on a board, make-your-own salads (rather than elegant, non-filling mixed greens), salads made with ordinary iceberg lettuce, hot food served on cold plates, or cold food served on warm plates.

Ask to have your food served unsalted. If they cannot accommodate you, the dish was probably precooked.

Request that any sauces be served beside or under the food. In addition to saving calories, you will see the food's true appearance, and know that the dish was not precooked.

When judging service, consider these points. Were ashtrays emptied regularly? Were glasses promptly refilled? Did your waiter rush you? Or ignore you? Did he put his thumb on your plate or inside the rim of a glass?

One final test: Did you pay the check gladly? If so, disregard everything else. You've found a great restaurant.

Tips on Tipping

On my first trip to New York City, some fifteen years ago, an angry and very large bellhop noisily chased me out of my hotel.

"You call this a tip, lady?" he yelled, wedging himself between me and a waiting cab.

Classy person that I am, I would have preferred to have called it a gratuity, as in something given gratefully, in gratitude, for good service. But I should have called it a tip. And evidently, I should have made it bigger.

Young and naïve, I had been painfully ignorant about who got what when. And not surprisingly. You may have noticed that finding a book that supplies useful information on tipping is harder than finding a free taxi during a rainstorm. This is partly because practices vary from coast to coast and from large city to township. But it's also because people in a position to be authorities on the subject believe that discussing it is decidedly *déclassé,* so they won't talk—without considerable prompting.

Fortunately, I eventually cajoled and charmed my way into the following information, consulting knowledgeable sources at world-class salons (and saloons), restaurants, clubs, hotels, and other relevant establishments. My search took me from New York to Hilton Head, from Houston to Beverly Hills. (Not exactly a hardship tour!)

If I have missed a category that's important to you, consult the owner or manager of the establishment in question. Also, remember that:

One never tips owners, managers, or professionals (like nurses, doctors, or golf pros).

Tipping 15-20% of a bill, or a minimum of $1 for a small unbilled service, is generally safe.

Rest assured that there are no *hard and fast* rules on how much to tip. The amounts listed below are simply *suggestions* for gratuities when service has been good. For fantastic service, up the ante; for poor service, lower it or eliminate it altogether.

One last thought. You *must* learn to figure amounts gracefully and quickly. No fingers. No calculators. No big to-do. No exceptions.

Airline Personnel: No tip.

Airport Skycap: Up to $1/bag for good service.

Apartment House Staff: At Christmas—2% of annual rent, distributed among employees, is the general rule, but $10-$20 for employees who've been helpful plus the same for the maintenance staff is generally sufficient.

For Special Services—$1-$10 at time of service.

Baby Sitter: No tip; small reward for exceptional service.

Barbershop Staff:

Barber—$2-$5

Manicurist—15% ($2 minimum)

Shampoo Person—$1-$2

Shoeshine Person—50¢ or more, depending on service.

Note: At very elegant establishments, tip as at Beauty Salons.

Beauty Salon Staff:

Hair Stylist—15-20% of tab, delivered inobtrusively.

Manicurist—15-20% of tab ($1 minimum).

Shampoo Person—$1-$3, depending on quality of service.

Other Specialists—15-20% of tab.

Bellman: 50¢-$1/bag; $3-$4 minimum for several bags and good service.

Building Staff (at your place of business):   Top-ranking employee should contact building management to see what is customary for the area.

Cab Driver: 15-20% of fare for courteous service.

Caddy: 20-25% of fee; more if you play a great game.

Casino Personnel:

 Cocktail Waiter/Waitress—Drinks are free for gamblers; estimate their value and tip 15%.

 Dealers/*Croupiers*[1]—Tip with chips or place a bet for employee if you've been playing awhile and you're winning: 10-15% of your winnings, up to $100 or so.

 Maître d' at Show—$10-$20 for a special table, delivered in advance in a handshake.

Catering Staff:

 This can vary widely; best to check with owner of service. Generally, tip 10-15% to head person present, or add it to the bill as a "gratuity, to be distributed to the staff." (Make certain tip was not already included in the bill.) Never tip owners; tip a smaller percentage for extremely expensive service. Guests at a catered party do not tip catering personnel.

Charter Boat Crew:

 10-15% of charter bill for the mate or hard-working, nonowner captain; $10/head for others.

Chauffeur:

 Of a hired car—15-20% of tab.

 Of a private car—as desired for special services.

 Your own staff—at Christmas, one to two weeks' pay.

Checkroom Attendant: 50¢-$1

Chefs: No tip; just lavish praise for excellence.

Cocktail Waiter/Waitress: 15-20% of tab, depending on establishment and service.

Concierge (kahn SYEHRZH) at Fine Hotel:

 For small services (announcing a guest, holding something temporarily)—No tip.

 For dinner reservations—$5; more if you know that a great deal of work was involved.

 For airline reservations—$5-$20, depending on difficulty securing a seat, special arrangements, etc.

---

[1] Croupier (kroo PYĀ) is a person at gaming table who collects and pays out money.

For theater tickets—$10-$20 for good seats at a very popular show. (Theater tickets, once ordered, must usually be purchased; tickets purchased through the hotel agent may be less expensive because tipping isn't necessary.)

For other services—$5 for a simple phone call on your behalf; up to $100 for a full day's work (arranging a party, obtaining loaner furs or jewelry, etc.).

Note: Introduce yourself to the concierge when you arrive and indicate what services may be required. Tip at the end of your stay, or after a particularly difficult task has been performed. Put the gratuity in an envelope and deliver with a healthy "thank you" and a handshake.

Cooks (in a private home where you are a guest):   Several dollars only if cook consistently prepares special meals for you.

Country Club Staff (private club):

Caddy—20-25% above posted fee; more if you have a great game.

Locker room attendant—guests: $1-$2 for service; members: $2-$5 dollars/month.

Restaurant Staff—Tip as you would at any restaurant or as dictated by Club management.

Note: You will no doubt be asked to contribute to a Christmas fund for the employees. Give $10-$100 +, depending on club usage.

Country Club Staff (public golf course):   Tip slightly less than above.

Delivery Person:

Flowers—$1

Groceries—$1-$5, depending on load.

Western Union—$1 is customary, but not strictly required.

Domestic Staff:

In a home where you're a long-term guest—$1-$2/day.

Doorman:

At your apartment—At Christmas, $10-$20.

At a hotel or club—$1-$5 for services ranging from opening

the door of a waiting taxi, to hailing a cab in the rain, to watching your car while you're at dinner.

Entertainers: No tip; send over a drink or flowers if desired.

Garbage Collector: $5 at Christmas in large cities.

Groom (where you stable your horse): $1-$5 for special services; remember with a small gift at Christmas.

Guides:

Government—No tip.

Hunting—10% above posted fee.

Tour—Offer 10-20% trip cost (if against company rules, it will not be accepted). On a long, expensive trip, ask tour sponsors what size tip is appropriate.

Hairdresser: 15-20% of tab; larger tip or small gift at Christmas. Deliver tip in a small envelope or tuck it into stylist's pocket.

Hotel Staff:

For guests in hotel:

Bellboy—50¢-$1/bag; min. $3-$4 for several bags and good service.

Chambermaid—$2/day

Valet[2]—$1-$2

Valet parking—$1 or more for delivery of auto.

Concierge—See CONCIERGE.

Theater ticket service—No tip; small gift for consistent service beyond the call of duty.

Doorman—$1-$5 for service.

Telephone operator—$1-$2 if heavy use of phone service.

Do not tip:

Desk clerk

Elevator operator (unless special services provided)

Manager or assistant manager

Public stenographer

Social director

---

[2]Valet, also called a gentleman's gentleman, is pronounced "vah LĀ" by the French and "VAL it" by the English; take your pick. (When "valet" refers to a parking or cleaning service, use the French pronunciation.)

Travel clerk

Note: If the manager has sent "VIP" flowers or fruit, send a thank-you note.

For permanent residents in a hotel: Tip as for apartment residents, remembering elevator and telephone operators with a small gift at Christmas.

Limousine Driver: 15-20% of car-rental charge.

Masseur (mah SUHR) or Masseuse (mah SUHZ):

At their establishment—$5-$10 (or 20% of bill).

Out call—Tip usually included in fee; otherwise 15-20%.

Messengers: Tipped $1 by receiver of message.

Movers: $10/head (+ $5-$10/head for pickup crew, if different); $20-$30 for driver; offer cold drinks and use of rest-room facilities; allow no smoking in home or truck.

Night Club Staff:

Bartender—15% if sitting at bar.

Busboy—No tip.

Checkroom attendant—50¢ to $1 (do not check your fur).

Doorman—$1-$5 depending on service.

Entertainer—No tip; send over flowers or a drink.

Headwaiter/Maître d'—5% of tab for special service; designate on bill or deliver $5-$10 in a handshake.

Piano bar player—$5 or more ("Have a drink on me") depending on number of requests played.

Waiter—20% (5% of which may be designated for headwaiter).

Washroom attendant—50¢-$1 for service.

Nurses: No tip; a small gift at end of an extended stay is a nice touch.

Page Boy: $1

Parking Lot Valet: $1 or more for auto delivery, depending on elegance of establishment.

Police: No monetary tip; small gift if especially helpful.

Porter:

Airport—50¢-$1/bag; more for service.

Train—Several dollars/night

Postman: $5 at Christmas.

Restaurant Staff:

Bartender—15% if seated at bar; nothing otherwise.

Busboy—No tip.

Captain—5%, designated on bill.

Checkroom attendant—50¢-$1 (do not check your fur).

Doorman—$1-$5 for service.

Maître d'—$5-$10 delivered in advance in a handshake for a special table, or after a meal for special service.

Strolling musician—Just a smile for one tune; several dollars for more ($5 or more for a group).

Waiter—15-20%, depending on service and elegance of establishment (5% of which may be designated for headwaiter).

Washroom attendant—50¢-$1 for service.

Wine steward *(sommelier)*—15-20% of tab, depending on service.

Ship's Crew:

Practices vary widely, but if you call the ship's public relations office, they'll be happy to advise you. Here's what Cunard suggests is customary (though not obligatory) for good service:

On Queen Elizabeth II, you tip according to your dining room assignment. Your waiter and room steward receive the amount below; your busboy gets half that amount:

Tables of the World—$3/person/day

Columbia Restaurant—$4/person/day

Queen's Grill—$5/person/day

Princess Grill—$5/person/day

On the Cunard Princess or the Cunard Countess, all passengers tip $2/person/day.

Your wine steward should receive 15% of wine bill. Tip all others as you would on dry land.

Shoeshine Person: At least 50¢ for a simple shine.

Supermarket Staff:

Delivery to car—50¢ or so (may not be accepted).

Delivery to car—50¢ or so (may not be accepted).

Delivery to home—$1-$5, depending on size of delivery.

Theater Usher: No tip in America.

Train Staff:

Club car attendant—15% of tab.

Porter—$1 or more/day

Pullman porter—Several dollars/day

Waiter—15%

Washroom Attendant: 50¢-$1 for special service.

What the Rich Read

Don't you hate it when your social secretary absconds with *Town & Country* before you've had a chance to read it cover to cover? Why, our sort is virtually paralyzed without it!

There are a few other magazines and periodicals which show up regularly on the best coffee tables and desks. Are they on yours?

Architectural Digest (international architectural and interior design)
Atlantic Monthly (literature and opinion)
Connoisseur (of the arts)
Elle (French fashions)
Foreign Affairs (politics)
GQ—Gentlemen's Quarterly (men's fashions)
Harvard Business Review
Holiday Homes International
International Review of Food & Wine
M: The Civilized Man
The Manchester Guardian Weekly (global events)
The Nation
National Review (for conservative intellectuals; edited by William F. Buckley, Jr.)
The New Republic (for liberal intellectuals)
New York Review of Books
The New Yorker (literature, theater, opinion)
Robb Report (a must for big spenders and connoisseurs)
SPUR (for thoroughbred lovers)

Unique Homes
W (fashion)
WWD–Women's Wear Daily (fashion)
Washington Monthly (politics)

3

· DINING, DECORUM, DELICACIES, AND DILEMMAS ·

The world was my oyster, but I used the wrong fork.

—OSCAR WILDE

"Waiter, we'll have *slugs* for two, please," said George, looking up to see if I was amused by the way he ordered the *escargots*.[1] Mistakenly, he assumed that the smile on my face signified approval, but what the silly boy was seeing was panic, pure and unadulterated.

How had I lost control of the evening? One's first taste of an exotic food should be taken in loving, understanding company. But here I was with George, a nasty young nabob[2] with the soul of an ax murderer. To eat, or refuse to eat, snails in his presence was socially suicidal.

So what was I to do?

What would *you* do?

My solution was to stall, fumble with the snail clamp, criticize the method of preparation, then accidentally let one of the little darlings fly off the plate onto the lap of my previously-white silk dress.

Your solution, should you find yourself in a similar predicament, will be better. You will have read this chapter.

---

[1] Escargots (ess kahr GOH) are snails raised for consumption.
[2] Nabob (NĂ bob) means a powerful, wealthy person.

The ultimate in formal dining—a private banquet at The Plaza.

Besides pronunciation, descriptions, and eating instructions for dozens of wonderful foods (listed under Pâté, Caviar, Lobsters, etc.), this chapter provides complete information on tackling the finer points of etiquette and formal dinner service.

Read each topic carefully to be prepared for emergencies. And nabobs.

Accidents, according to Dickens in *David Copperfield,* "will happen in the best regulated families." And may I add, the most embarrassing places!

If a mishap befalls you in a restaurant, call the waiter. No apology is required, just a quick explanation of the incident. The waiter should then quickly, and cheerfully, remedy the problem.

Accidents in a private home are handled through the hostess (or host). Apologize sincerely, but briefly, if you have caused any damage. Offer to pay for repairs, but don't persist against continued protests.

If one of *your* guests has damaged something, treat it casually. Make the person feel as comfortable as possible, and clean up any mess immediately. Accept payment for damage only if it was deliberate.

Artichokes, delicious hot or cold, are great fun to eat. Just remove a leaf by grasping the tip with the thumb and forefinger of one hand. Dip its base in the accompanying sauce, and gently scrape off the "meat" by pulling it between clenched teeth. Deposit the leaf on your plate or a "discards" dish.

When you have had enough of that, separate the remaining leaves, and the fuzzy choke, from the artichoke bottom using the tip of your knife. Cut off a piece of the bottom with your fork, dip it in sauce, and enjoy.

Asparagus, when cold, may be eaten with your fingers if it isn't covered with dressing, and if the stalks are not too long. Hot asparagus, on the other hand, is best eaten with a knife and fork; using one's fingers can be a very messy proposition.

Bouillabaisse (boo yuh BEHZ) is a famous Mediterranean stew of fresh seafood cooked in a broth flavored with saffron, onions, garlic, oil or butter, and herbs. Traditionally, it is served in two bowls, the fish in one, broth and a piece of bread in the other.

Many people avoid bouillabaisse, and similar dishes, because most of the seafood has not been shelled. What a waste! It's really easy to eat.

Just get what you can with your fork and spoon, then dig in with fingers and knife. (See *Clams, Crabs, Mussels,* etc., for additional tips.) Enjoy the broth with a spoon, tipping the bowl away from you as needed. Soak up final drops with a small piece of bread speared on a fork.

Bread presents no problem if you remember a few general rules. Break rolls, buns, and sliced bread into smaller pieces; spread with butter just before eating. Butter whole slices of toast before cutting into triangles. Split muffins in half and insert a dab of butter. Never take just half of a roll or slice of bread from a serving basket, leaving the ragged remains behind for someone else to discover.

Caviar is sturgeon roe: fish eggs. Never red (like salmon eggs) nor orange (like carp roe), true caviar ranges from grey to black and should be soft, shiny, and translucent.

Beluga (beh LOO gah) caviar, the finest and most costly, is large, dark, and pea-sized. Next largest in size, but with a less than spectacular taste, is *ossetrina* (ah seh TREE nah).[3] Smaller still, and widely available, is *sevruga* (sehv ROO gah). Though not highly prized for its "everyday" eggs, this fish delivers a rare golden roe every two thousand tries or so. Smallest, and least distinguished, are *sterlit* (STUHR lit) and ship sturgeon eggs.

As important as type is the method of handling. Caviar marked "fresh" or "malosol" has little salt added. It tastes better than

---

[3]Ossetrina is yellowish-brown in color and has a tart taste. According to the manager of Caviarteria in New York City, you probably won't like it.

heavily preserved roe, but spoils more quickly and requires constant refrigeration.

Pressed and pasturized caviar (the best choice for *canapés*[4] and for cooking) may not always require refrigeration, but check the label to be sure.

Purists eat high-quality caviar straight out of the tin. Others prefer to have it accompanied by toast and several condiments. To a small bit of caviar on a toast triangle, they might add diced onion and egg, then a squeeze of lemon juice. They may assemble each triangle straight from the serving tray, or take the caviar and condiments onto their plates. (Note: When someone else is paying, go easy on portions; even lesser varieties are very expensive.)

China Cups are held by their handles: *no* hooking your index finger through the loop, *no* crooking your pinkie.

Chopsticks are easy to use—with a little practice. So, to be ready for that inevitable day when you sit down to a table completely *void* of silverware, collect the sticks, some cooked peas or beans, and start practicing as shown on the next page. (Note: When eating anything tricky, like rice, feel free to bring the bowl closer to your mouth; Orientals do. The alternative is starvation.)

Cioppino (choh PEE noh) is California stew made with chunks of fish, clams, and shrimp plus onion, green peppers, white wine, garlic, and tomato. Eat as you would bouillabaisse.

Clams, both hard- and soft-shell varieties, are harvested year round (except during summer in California). On the West Coast, enjoy clams fried. Or try Pismo, razor, or butter clams on the half shell, eating them *whole* using your cocktail fork, adding lemon and pepper to taste.

---

[4]Canapés (kah nah PĀ, *not* kan ah PEEZ) are small appetizers served on bread or crackers.

USING CHOPSTICKS

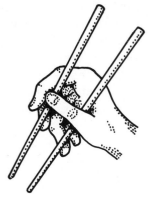

Rest one stick on the base between your thumb and forefinger. Steady with your fourth and fifth fingers.

Hold the second stick parallel to the first with your thumb, forefinger, and middle finger.

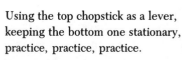

Using the top chopstick as a lever, keeping the bottom one stationary, practice, practice, practice.

On the Eastern seaboard, try hard-shelled *quahogs* (KWOH hahgs)—either littlenecks or cherrystones. They're wonderful on the half shell, with or without sauce.

Steamers (of New England clambake fame) are served in their shells, accompanied by clam broth, lemon wedges, and lots of French bread. To eat, squeeze some lemon into the accompanying melted butter. Then, holding the shell in one hand and grasping the clam's neck with the other, extract the clam, dip it in the broth, and then the butter. Scrape off the meat with your teeth and discard the shell (and the neck if it's tough) onto an empty plate.

Finish the broth with your spoon, avoiding any sand that has settled on the bottom. Soak up the last drops with a bread chunk speared on a fork.

Continental-Style Eating is more worldly, and infinitely more practical, than American-style. Preferred by people who have traveled extensively, it is as proper here as it is abroad.

Here's how to do it. First, assemble a knife, a fork, and some food that requires cutting. (Lamb chops with mint jelly would be nice.) Then, with the fork in your left hand and the knife in your right (lefties reverse), cut off a bite of food; use your knife to push the food more securely onto the fork, if you like. Now, with the fork still in your left hand, carry the food directly to your mouth—tines down. When not cutting, keep the knife low or rest it on your plate; don't wave it about while talking.

When using a spoon and fork (as you would for ice cream and cake), keep the spoon in your right hand, the fork in your left. When using a spoon alone, keep it in your right hand—American-style.

One last note: When dining with unsophisticated clients, switch back to the American method. If they aren't acquainted with the Continental style, they may wonder what you're doing.

Crabs of many species are found in this country. You are probably most familiar with Atlantic and Gulf Coast blues, and the long-legged Alaskan kings. But have you ever tried a blue crab after it has molted? These soft-shelled treasures are consumed whole, body and all, using your knife and fork—that is, when you're lucky enough to find them.

Rock crabs (found in California and New England) and stone crabs (found only in Florida) are highly prized for their delectable claw meats. Rare hermit crabs and tiny oyster crabs are enjoyed sautéed or fried; the latter variety is also consumed raw. Eat crabs in their shells as you would *lobster*.

Crayfish are small lobster-like creatures found from mid to late summer in Lake Michigan, the Pacific Northwest, Europe, and the bayous of the Gulf Coast. To eat, twist off the head of a cooked crayfish, peel the shell off the tail, and eat the meat with your fingers.

Crème Fraîche (krehm FREHSH) is a thick coddled cream used by the French in place of sweet whipped cream. Be advised that you may run across it in a fine French restaurant and be tempted to say something like, "Waiter, this cream is spoiled," in which case the waiter may respond with an embarrassing dissertation on the virtues of *coddled* versus *whipped*. To avoid this, know that coddled cream is heavy and tart; spoiled whipped cream is light and unpleasant. Have your official taster try it and make the final determination.

Egg Cups hold soft-boiled eggs securely for easy consumption. To eat, you must first decapitate the shell by giving it a sharp horizontal whack with your knife, then lift off the top using the knife's tip, add seasoning, and dig in with a spoon. Proceed with care, though, so as not to mix shell fragments with the egg.

Escargots are special snails raised on snail ranches. Most gourmets prefer to have them cooked and served in their shells, though some restaurants save time and money by serving them on dishes or in porcelain shells. (Shame on them!)

To eat snails *not* ensconced in their natural habitats, just spear with the special fork or pick, swish in sauce, and devour. To get at those *in* the shell, grasp the shell firmly with the snail clamp (or your fingers, if they're all that's available). Then, with the fork or pick in your other hand, twist the meat out. Dip it in sauce and eat *whole*. (Don't make a face!)

It is perfectly proper, though horribly messy, to pick up the empty shell and drink its buttery, garlicky juice. A better idea is to soak up the liquid with a bread square impaled on a fork.

Finger Bowls, if mistaken for bowls of soup, can prove most embarrassing. You won't have any problems, though, if you remember that finger bowls are almost always used at the end of a meal (unless you're having lobster, ribs, or some other messy food). Therefore, bowls served early in the meal probably contain broth.

If the finger bowl is accompanied by a liner plate and silverware, use it *after* the next course. Place the utensils on the table at either side of the plate, and move the bowl to where the bread-and-butter plate used to be. Then, after the food, return the bowl to its original position and gently cleanse the fingers of one hand, then the other. (Don't try to wash your whole hand.)

If no silverware accompanies the bowl, the meal is over; rinse your fingertips immediately.

Fish served whole (not my favorite sight) must be decapitated and boned. Start by slicing off the head (ugh!); eat it, using your knife and fork, or put it aside. Next, make a shallow incision end to end, slicing just under the skin; open the fish up flat. Then, cut underneath the backbone with the tip of your knife and lift out the skeleton whole with the aid of your fork. Set it on the plate's edge.

Retrieve any remaining bones with your fork. Or, should you find one in your mouth, use your forefinger and thumb.

Note: At a fine restaurant or formal banquet, you may encounter a fish fork or knife. These utensils are easily identified if they are the only ones on the table—which they often are. Other times, recognize the fork as heavier, longer, and wider than a salad fork; recognize the knife's oddly-curved blade and sharp, curved point. Employ these utensils in the "Continental" fashion. (Hold the knife in your right hand much as you would a pencil, not as you would a regular meat-cutting knife.)

Frog Legs, *Squab,* and *Quail* are eaten with a knife and fork, but feel free to pick up the legs (like fried chicken) to finish them off.

Fruit Pits or *Stones* are taken into the mouth, cleaned off with the teeth, deposited onto a spoon or fork, then lowered to your plate. When unable to eat *around* fruit *seeds,* dispense with them in a similar manner.

Fruits are handled in various ways. Eat grapes, tangerines, and naval oranges with your fingers, and berries, persimmons, melons, papayas, grapefruits, and pineapples with a spoon. Eat most other fruits with a knife and fork.

Hot Food taken into the mouth accidentally is quickly chased with cold liquid. Blowing on food, or creating an air tunnel in your mouth, is punishable by ostracism.

Iced Tea presents but one problem: What do you do with the spoon? When drinking, the spoon should rest on the saucer. If no saucer was provided, keep the spoon in the glass and hold it back with your second and third fingers. Whichever method you choose, keep the spoon off napkins and tablecloths. Tea stains make hostesses very sad—and often vengeful.

Lemon, to be squeezed without incident, should be pierced several times with a fork, then squeezed with one hand, the other hand cupped around it to act as a shield.

Lobsters, contrary to the opinion of many Easterners, come in two varieties: the Northern (Maine) lobster and the spiny rock lobster.

The latter, found in Florida, California, Australia, South Africa, and the Mediterranean, is known for its tail meat. Tender and sweet when fresh and well-cooked, tough and "cardboardy" when frozen or overcooked, rock lobsters are removed from their shells (by your waiter), then eaten with a knife and fork. Cut off a piece, dip it in the accompanying drawn butter, and prepare for ecstasy.

Eating a Maine lobster is a bit more involved. This tricky beauty has meat tucked into every conceivable nook and cranny.

If you're not up to a treasure hunt, order it stuffed, or try Lobster Thermidor, Newberg, or *Fra Diavolo*.[5] Better yet, find a prince like my friend Charles to prepare the lobster for you.

---

[5]Thermidor is cut-up lobster mixed with a creamy mustard–white wine sauce, topped with grated cheese and breadcrumbs, and baked in the shell. Newberg is sautéed chunks of lobster (or shrimp) combined with cream, egg yolks, Sherry, and paprika and cooked in a casserole. Fra Diavolo (frah DYAH voh loh) is sautéed chunks of lobster in a sauce of garlic, onion, white wine, tomato, and spices.

Should you decide to tackle the task yourself, eat Maine lobster as follows:

1. Don a bib, or tuck a napkin under your chin. (In a formal setting, forgo the bib and put the napkin in your lap.)
2. Grasp the shellfish firmly and twist off the legs and claws. Crack the large claws (if necessary) using the lobster cracker or the edge of a heavy knife. Then pick out the meat with the small seafood fork, dip it in butter, and eat. If you are really an enthusiast, you may suck the meat out of the smaller legs.
3. Lift out the tail meat with your fork. Cut off a small piece and dip it in butter before eating.
4. Search through the body cavity. The green stuff is the liver, or *tomalley* (TOM AL lee). Like the scarlet roe of the female, it is considered a delicacy (for some strange reason). Retrieve with your fork, as you would small morsels of meat (also hidden in the cavity); dip in sauce before eating.

Meat, for reasons of health or flavor, should be cooked to appropriate point of doneness. Pork is cooked well-done to destroy dangerous parasites; gourmets prefer lamb medium or medium rare; fine cuts of beef, like *tournedos* (toor nuh DOH), *filets* (fee LĀ), and *châteaubriand* (shah toh bree YAHn), are considered ruined unless served rare or medium rare.

Meats Cooked in Pastry—*en croûte* (ahn KROOT)—are prepared this way primarily to keep them moist. The crusts, therefore, may be crude, even inedible. To avoid a mouthful of inpalatable pastry, taste a small bit before indulging. If it is buttery and delicious, only your waistline need restrain you.

Mushrooms were deemed so precious in ancient Egypt that only Pharaohs were allowed to eat them. Equally enamoured, the ancient Romans called them "food for the gods." In other words, mushrooms are special, though some are more special than others.

Button mushrooms are available fresh almost everywhere. Choose tightly closed buttons with no gills[6] exposed; store them unwashed in an open paper bag or container. Use canned mushrooms only if you cannot find fresh.

Cèpes (SEHP) are yellow-to-brown French mushrooms with small holes instead of gills. They are available canned and sometimes dried, and their strong flavor is a wonderful addition to sauces and meat dishes.

Chanterelles (shahn TREHL) are wild French mushrooms resembling small yellow trumpets. Find them canned at your favorite gourmet shop.

Morels (muh REHLS), or *Morilles* (moh REEL), are cone-shaped, yellow-to-brown, wild mushrooms with honey-combed caps. They are inedible unless cooked, or dried and reconstituted (in water or stock). Find them at better gourmet shops.

Oriental mushrooms come in many shapes and sizes. Buy black mushrooms, or wood ears, dried; reconstitute them as directed. Buy creamy *enokidake* (en noh kee DAH keh) mushrooms canned or in bulk. Their long, skinny stems and tiny caps add brightness, shape, and flavor to your favorite salads. Find any of these mushrooms at an oriental grocery store or a well-stocked gourmet shop.

Mussels, once called the poor man's oysters, are enjoying new popularity thanks to inflation. Enjoy them raw, steamed, or cooked in fish stews.

Mussels in shells are retrieved with a seafood fork, or sucked out (quietly!) when no fork is provided. Eat them whole, after dipping in sauce. Deposit empty shells on a "discards" plate or your bread-and-butter dish.

Mussels in stews are eaten similarly (except the shells remain in the stew). Eat as much soup as possible with your spoon, then spear a small chunk of bread and use it as a sponge.

---

[6]Gills are the dark, feathery growths on the underside of the mushroom cap.

Napkins, believe it or not, are among the most misused items at a table. People forget that when a hostess is present, they should not take napkins to their laps, nor return them to the table, until she has done so first.

They forget, too, that when the meal has no hostess, napkins go to their laps immediately,[7] staying there till meal's end, then returning to an area *beside* the plate—neat, but *not* folded.

Worst of all, they forget that napkins are *never* used to conceal bites of spoiled food. Pity the unsuspecting laundress who would find the remains!

Oysters make up in taste what they lack in beauty. Thank heavens!

Fortunately for them, however, they find each other beautiful: they're *always* spawning in the South, and *elsewhere* except during months containing an "R" (January, February, March, etc.).

Unfortunately for us, spawning does nothing good to their taste, so choose Northern varieties over Southern whenever possible, avoiding oysters altogether during "R" months.

Blue Point oysters were originally just a species from Blue Point, Long Island. Now the name belongs to any oyster two to four inches long. Try this delicious mollusk on the half-shell. Spear each one with the seafood fork, dip in sauce, and eat *whole*. Or try Oysters Rockefeller (baked in their shells with spinach, onion, bread crumbs, bacon, and seasonings) or Oysters Casino (baked in the shell with butter, shallots, celery, green pepper, bacon, and pimento).

When you're feeling wildly extravagant, try tiny Puget Sound Olympias or Virginia *Chincoteagues* (SHIN koh teegs) on the half-shell.

One caution: Oysters eaten raw must be extremely fresh. If you suspect that restaurant personnel might be opening theirs in advance of orders, try this trick: Order yours on the *shallow* shell. Since oysters are normally served on the *deeper* of the two shells, they'll have to open some especially for you!

---

[7] At very elegant restaurants, the captain may unfold your napkin and place it in your lap just before seating you. If he doesn't, you'll have to fend for yourself.

Paella (pah Ā yah) is a classic Spanish dish prepared with chicken parts, sausage, shellfish, garlic, tomatoes, sweet red peppers, onions, and various other vegetables on a bed of saffron[8] rice. To eat, see *Bouillabaisse*.

Pâtés (pah TĀ) are elegant loaves of beef, game, or poultry mixed (usually) with liver, spices, fats, eggs, and, perhaps, brandies and *liqueurs*.[9] Served as appetizers or luncheon entrées, they may be plain and inexpensive, or fancy and costly. To distinguish one from the other, know that pâté:

> *à la Meau* (ah lah MOH) is made with game, and usually liver;
> *à la Périgueux* (ah lah PĀ ree GUH) is elegant pâté made with
>   game, poultry, and *Truffles;*
> *à la Rouennaise* (ah lah roon NEHZ) is made from duckling;
> *de campagne* (duh kahm PAHN yuh) is pâté "of the country,"
>   a coarser variety prepared as a country cook would make it;
> *de foie gras* (duh fwah GRAH) is made from the livers of
>   geese which have been force-fed. Because this practice is
>   illegal in the U.S.A., this marvelously extravagant pâté, if
>   authentic, *must* be imported; look out for domestic
>   imitations!
> *de foie gras truffé* (duh fwah grah troo FĀ) is pâté with truffles
>   added;
> *de foie gras d'oie* (duh fwah grah DWAH) is pâté de foie gras
>   in which 25% of the goose liver is replaced with pork liver;
> *en croûte* (ahn KROOT) means "in pastry crust."
>   Interestingly, pâté was once routinely prepared *en croûte*
>   to keep it moist; its name, in fact, is from the French word
>   for pastry: pâte (PAHT).
> *Note: Terrines* (tehr REEN) are pâtés cooked in earthenware
>   crocks called—surprise!—*terrines*.

Some people adore pâté the moment they try it; others consider it a cultivated taste. In any event, sample it for the first time

---

[8] Saffron (SAF ruhn), the dried stigma of the crocus plant, is used to add flavor and color (yellow-orange) to some foods, especially rice.

[9] Liqueurs (lee KUHR) are after-dinner drinks.

in a quality restaurant. Slice off a square and lift it with your knife onto the accompanying toast triangle. Then pick up the toast and eat it with your hands.

Salads, or rather the eating of salads, present two problems. First: Which one is yours? Answer: The one to your left; only beverages are placed to your right. Second: How do you eat salads containing huge pieces of lettuce? Answer: Use your knife and fork. And try eating Continental-style; it is easier than its U.S. counterpart. (Note: Keep the knife on the liner plate, or propped on the salad bowl, to avoid soiling the tablecloth.)

Salt and Pepper added to a dish you haven't tasted generally means overseasoned food *and* an offended cook. After all, your actions presuppose that the food has been improperly seasoned!

Salt Cellars are tiny, elegant dishes of salt that replace shakers. When they're unaccompanied by little spoons, use your fingers. When the cellar is shared, use the tip of your knife instead.

Scented Towels, hot and cold, are handed to diners between courses, or at meal's end, to allow them to cleanse their hands (not their faces). After use, they are returned *un*folded to the waiter's tray. (Note: They are seldom seen in private homes.)

Schrod or **Scrod** (SKRAWD), according to the National Marine Fisheries, is a size of fish—a filet of 1½–2½ pounds. Though not a particular variety of fish, it is usually haddock or cod.

Scones (SKOHNZ) are delightful English biscuits served at afternoon tea. Eat them with your fingers after spreading the surface with butter and jam.

Servants and Waiters should eliminate problems for diners, not cause them. Still, many diners are unsure of how to deal with them: what to say, when to speak. But remember, waiters, waitresses, and household servants are just people doing a job. They deserve courtesy, an occasional smile, and a "thank you" for extra service.

They also deserve to be left to do their work. Time for conversation is short; time for abuse is nonexistent.

In a private home, the help take orders primarily from the hostess. If you want something—a clean fork, more water—direct your request to her. (If you want more wine, or second helpings, you should wait until it is offered.)

In a restaurant, waiters and waitresses take directions from whomever is paying the check. Although diners may place their own food orders if they like, special requests and problems should be handled through the host. (Note: Dutch-treat occasions often run more smoothly if one person assumes the duties of host.)

Tipping practices vary, depending on the level of service and the type of restaurant. In general, one tips 15 percent in an inexpensive restaurant, and 20 percent in an expensive restaurant, for *adequate* service. See "Tips on Tipping" (page 39) for more details.

Serving Methods at formal meals include:

Plate Service (also called American service). Each guest's plate is prepared in the kitchen, then brought to the table.

Sideboard Service. The waiter fills each plate at the sideboard then passes it to the guest.

English Service. Guests serve themselves from platters and dishes passed by the waiter.

French Service. Waiters serve guests individually from silver platters.

Sherbet or **Sorbet** (sohr BĀ) is eaten with a spoon when served as dessert. When offered between courses to "clear the palate"— that is, refresh the mouth—it is eaten with a fork.

Shrimp with tail shells still attached may be held by their tails or eaten with a fork—as dictated by the formality of the occasion.

An unwieldy shrimp from a seafood cocktail may be bitten in half if cutting would prove too awkward; just don't dip the severed end into a sauce you share with another diner. (Note: At the meal's end, the fork rests on the liner plate, not *in* the shrimp dish.)

Silver Leaf is an edible East Indian garnish that resembles shredded aluminum foil. But don't worry: It's much softer!

Soufflés (soo FLĀ) are puffed-up concoctions of meat, cheese, seafood, poultry, vegetables, sweets, or fruit served as main courses, side dishes, or desserts.

Baked soufflés puff because the beaten egg whites they contain expand during cooking. Cold soufflés, on the other hand, are actually *mousses* (mooss) molded to look like soufflés; gelatin, and freezing, help them maintain their shapes.

Serve portions of a large soufflé on individual plates; spoon any accompanying sauces under—not over—each serving. Eat small soufflés straight from their containers, or unmold if a sauce is provided.

Here's another hint: When eating a world-class soufflé in a great restaurant, ask for both *crème anglaise* (krehm ahn GLEHZ)—a lovely vanilla sauce—and whipped cream. Which one do you like best?

Soup is easy to eat if you remember to spoon *away* from yourself, to sip quietly from the spoon's *side*, and to tilt the bowl *away* from you to get the last drops. One more thing: You may drink from bowls with handles only after eating large pieces of food with your spoon, and only at informal occasions. (Note: *Informal* means a dinner at which you are the only guest, or at least the only guest over the age of two, or one at which most of the guests present are wearing tennis shoes.)

Spaghetti, linguini, and other varieties of long, slippery pasta are eaten by twirling few strands around your fork. Period. Eating with both spoon and fork is amateurish. Cutting strands is downright criminal. And very, very tacky.

Squid and Octopi taste best when they're small; large ones—and those which are poorly cooked—resemble rubber. Consequently, your best chance for success in this particular culinary area lies in a restaurant famous for its fine food. Know, too, that squid is commonly recognized as the more delectable of the two.

Steak Tartare (tahr TAHR): You either love it, or hate it, depending on how you feel about raw, chopped beef. To serve, mix in such condiments as capers,[10] raw egg yolk, diced parsley, and chopped onion. Eat it *on* crackers as an appetizer or *with* toast as a main course.

Table Settings, when properly laid, make dining a breeze. As you no doubt already know, you simply choose utensils and glasses from the outside in. Dishes to the left of center will always be yours as will all glassware to your right.

Chaos reigns, however, when the table is set improperly, when utensils are laid according to size rather than function, or when waiters fail to retrieve unnecessary utensils between courses. When any of these things happen, most of us end up fumbling for this and that, using our dessert spoon to eat the appetizer, using the salad fork to eat the entrée.

Of course, an occasional blunder will not brand you as a complete social clod. Hopefully.

But why risk it when a few minutes spent studying the chart at right will allow you to sail through even the most formal meal?

Truffles are ugly, wrinkled fungi. Sound irresistible? Actually, they are.

These warty little delicacies fetch outrageous prices, primarily because they're so difficult to find. You see, truffles aren't *grown;* they just *grow* here and there among the roots of certain European trees. Once a year, specially trained pigs and dogs dig them up.

Really.

---

[10]Capers (KĀ pers) are tart flower buds from a Mediterranean shrub. They are generally packed in a vinegar solution (which should be washed off) and are used as garnish or seasoning.

1. *Bread-and-butter plate with butter knife*. The knife may also rest on the right edge of the plate. If this plate is missing put butter, and sticky buns or rolls, on the edge of the dinner plate. Nonmessy breads may sit directly on the tablecloth.

2. *Dessert silver*. This may include a dessert spoon (with handle facing right), a spoon and fork (as shown), or a knife and fork (the knife replaces the spoon, its handle facing right).

3. *Water goblet*. If no water is being offered, wineglasses (#4) move to this position.

4. *Wineglasses*. The wine for each course is served in the outermost glass. As wines change, used glasses are removed.

5. *Cup-and-saucer set with teaspoon*.

6. *Seafood fork*. This utensil may also appear to the left of fork #12.

7. *Soup spoon*. If serving iced tea (rare at a formal meal), the long spoon is placed between the knife (#8) and soup spoon.

8. *Dinner knife*. Knives for preceding courses are placed to the right of this one; knives for subsequent courses, to the left. Blades always face the dinner plate.

9. *Napkin*. The napkin moves just to the left of the forks when a soup or appetizer course is present on the center plate.

10. *Main plate position*. Each major course assumes this position until it's replaced by the next course.

11. *Main course fork*. See #12 below.

12. *Salad fork*. When serving salad after the main course, reverse positions of forks #11 and #12.

13. *Salad plate*. When serving salad after the main course, this plate is not preset; it is brought to the table at the proper time.

Northern Italy produces wonderful white (and beige) truffles, but the real prizes are the black *Périgord* (peh ree GOHR) truffles found in Southern France.

The finest are labeled *Truffes du Périgord, Peeled Extra*. Next best are *Brushed Extra*, then *Peeled, First Choice*, and *Brushed First Choice*. Pieces are also sold and are a great deal less expensive than whole truffles or slices.

Add truffles to scrambled eggs, pâté, canapés, salads, sauces—practically anything this side of dessert.

Order truffles in restaurants, too. The terms *Périgourdine* (peh ree goor DEEN) and *Piémontaise* (pyā mohn TEHZ) refer to any dishes containing these delicacies.

Unwanted Food, when passed on a platter, should be taken in small amounts, pushed around on your plate, and hidden as much as possible. This way, the hostess (or host) will not be offended by your passing up the boiled eel she (or he) spent days preparing.

Should unwanted food actually reach your mouth, you must make a quick decision. If it just *tastes* bad, grin and swallow. If it actually *is* bad—that is, spoiled—quietly remove it with your spoon or fork; stick it under some other food on your plate (never in your napkin), and tell your host (at a restaurant) or your hostess (in a private home). He or she will warn others. By the way, your failure to say something may result in the social gathering being moved to the hospital. (Not a proper place for our sort.) So speak up!

Utensils are not touched at a formal meal until the hostess (or host, if no hostess is present) begins eating. At a banquet or large party, however, you may start after the six people nearest you are served—whether or not hosts have begun.

Between bites, utensils are placed where they will neither cause accidents nor signal servants to clear. Soup spoons remain in low soup plates, while spoons and forks used in bowls or glasses are returned to their service plates; knives and forks used on flat plates are placed in one of several ways: When eating American-style, they are placed as shown below left; when eating Continental-style, they are crossed in the center of the plate, the knife blade toward you, the fork tines down over the knife blade.

After use, utensils are positioned in such a manner as to signal waiters or butlers that you've completed the course, and to provide for safe and easy removal. Spoons and forks used in bowls are placed as previously described. Knives and forks on plates are laid as shown below right when eating American-style. Diners eating Continental-style should lay utensils similarly, but with the fork tines down.

Between Bites

After Use

CLASS NOTES

Schools for Socialites

Not everyone who's anyone went to a New England prep school, but almost everyone who's anyone knows which schools count. Do you?

Just in case the name of your alma mater has slipped your mind, here's a list of some of the preppiest:

Insider's Name	Proper Name	Location	Gossip
ANDOVER	Phillips Academy	Andover, MA	Two great rivals that are the
EXETER	Phillips Exeter Academy	Exeter, NH	Harvard and Yale of prep schools.
CHOATE	Choate Rosemary Hall	Wallingford, CT	Very preppy; very famous; sometimes infamous.
MILTON	Milton Academy	Milton, MA	Covers kindergarten and middle school as well as prep school.
DEERFIELD	Deerfield Academy	Deerfield, MA	No women allowed!
HOTCHKISS	Hotchkiss School	Lakeville, CT	Home of New York preppies
ST. PAUL'S	St. Paul's School	Concord, NH	Very liberal academically.

Insider's Name	*Proper Name*	*Location*	*Gossip*
GROTON	Groton School	Groton, MA	Home of the Boston WASP.
MIDDLESEX	Middlesex School	Concord, MA	Strong Boston ties.
FARMINGTON	Miss Porter's School	Farmington, CT	All girls; Jackie O's alma mater.
ETHEL WALKER	The Ethel Walker School	Farmington, CT	All girls; very horsey.
KENT	Kent School	Kent, CT	Coed; very horsey.

Q. What do heads of state give one another?

A. Gifts like the eagle decanter above. Design by Lloyd Atkins.
Photograph courtesy of Steuben Glass.

4

· GIVING TO THE RICH ·

*I explained to him I had simple tastes and
didn't want anything ostentatious, no
matter what it cost me.*

—ART BUCHWALD

Want to infuriate a millionaire? Buy him (or her) a present.

Oh, he'll pretend to adore what you bought. But when he says,
"*Dahling,* you shouldn't have," he'll probably mean it.

You see, he decided what he wanted, indeed, what he
deserved, long before you'd ever thought of giving him a thing. He
even dropped hints. But you, insensitive upstart that you are,
caught not a one. Instead, you selfishly gave him that sculpture it
took you a mere year to complete.

If you think I'm exaggerating, if you think "It's the thought, not
the gift, that counts," if you think others truly believe that giving
is better than receiving, think again. Few of us are saintly enough
to believe that gifts are anything less than measurements of how
others rate us and of how generous, well-bred, and tasteful the
givers are.

So the next time you contemplate a purchase, approach the
task as you would an important business decision: with great caution. A friendship may be at stake, and a reputation—yours!

Here's some help.

Rules for Realists

1. *Never ask the recipient what he wants.* Don't let anyone think you're too lazy or unimaginative to come up with your own ideas. Anyway, asking probably wouldn't do much good. People are generally either too greedy or too embarrassed to provide useful information.

2. *If the recipient lets you know what he wants, and it's something you can afford, get it!* A surprise gift is more trouble, and less likely to please, so why bother?

3. *When you have no clues, choose a present that makes you look good.* Ideally, a gift should both please the recipient and make the giver look good. In reality, few do.

   So select something *your friend* might like, but invest most of your energy in showing what a clever, interesting, and caring person *you* are.

   For example, show your *savoir-vivre*[1] by purchasing a share of topnotch stock for a newborn, instead of the usual blanket or clothes. For newlyweds, try tickets to the hottest new play in town or to the playoffs of a celebrity tennis match; forgo the ubiquitous serving platter.

4. *Buy gifts of indeterminate value for your snobbiest friends.* If people can easily find out what something costs, they probably will. And you don't want them to feel embarrassed that you spent too much, or insulted that you spent too little, do you? So why not circumvent the problem by purchasing gifts with no well-defined market value?

   Try a leatherbound first edition of an old book, or a lovely antique chafing dish. Or have a local artist paint a unique game set. A friend of mine once commissioned a Monopoly set for his love, renaming the streets for those in their town, and making up a revised set of cards and playing pieces. (Now, I'm not saying that this was the perfect gift, but they *were* married later that week!)

   Here's one last thought for any haughty friend. Send a

---

[1] Savoir-vivre (sah vwahr VEE vruh) is the knowledge of how to live well.

check to his favorite charity, museum, or school. The institution will send your friend a note saying that you made a generous donation in his name and—you'll love this!—they will never disclose the amount.

5. *Quality beats quantity every time.* One bottle of vintage *Dom Pérignon* is far better than a case of domestic champagne. One lesson with a master chef beats two weeks with a no-name cook. One date with Robert Redford—oops! I got carried away.

6. *Encourage a passion.* Everyone has an unfulfilled dream. Help her realize it. Give that first flying lesson to a would-be pilot, or lend your cabin in the mountains to that downhill skier or naturalist.

7. *Do not add to a collection.* Collectors fall into two categories: those who are addicted to their hobby and welcome only the unusual and authentic, and those who are sick to death of their hobby and dread *any* addition to it. Neither type seems likely to be thrilled and grateful forever.

8. *Rethink your ideas about homemade gifts.* When a child, or a disadvantaged friend, makes something with his own hands, we cherish it. If we're expecting no gift at all, homemade seems delightful. If James Beard whips up one of his masterpieces, we will be more than happy to accept. Otherwise, homemade gifts will likely go out in the trash with their wrappings. (Sad, but true.)

9. *Give each present at least the illusion of exclusiveness.* If you have purchased thirty identical gifts, don't let on—even if they're perfectly grand. To do so would seem insulting.

10. *Do not ever give unrequested pets, anything from a joke shop, any gift that implies ineptitude* (a sex manual to your lover), *an overly extravagant gift to a non–family member, an intimate present to a nonintimate, anything that is a necessity* (except to the poor), *or money to another adult* (Mother, please disregard!).

Presentation

When presenting a gift, the *how* is almost as important as the *what*. For example, a man who gives a woman a mink coat is generous (and incredibly hard to find!). But a man who flies his true love to Paris for a private showing—now *there's* a man with style (even harder to find!).

Fortunately, style can be exhibited in much less grandiose ways. A gift wrapped in beautiful paper, tied with a perfect bow, and delivered with a personal note (not just your name) is stylish.

Wine packaged in a wine brick, pâté nestled in an exquisite crock, or a monogrammed pen with a box of personalized stationery are also stylish gifts.

If a gift is too large to wrap, have it delivered. (Telling the person to expect "a little something" in the afternoon will drive him crazy all morning!) If the message is delivered in a singing telegram, so much the better.

Once you've presented a gift in person, smile and keep quiet. Nothing spoils a gift, or your image, quicker than a dissertation on how you "wanted to buy something better but ran out of time (money, patience, or checks)." You might as well just tell him he wasn't worth the trouble.

Who Wants What When

Few of us realize how many new gift-giving occasions come with increased social or economic status. But we usually find out—the hard way—after several embarrassing omissions!

To make things easier, here is a list of occasions on which offerings of some sort are required.

Social Events

Dinner at a Private Home:
> *To take or send later:* wine; liqueur; a crock of homemade pâté; caviar and melba toast; silver wine pourer; a wine

cooler or coasters. (Note: If you wish to send flowers, do so the day *after* the dinner; flowers sent *before* may not be compatible with arrangements planned by the hostess.)

Weekend Visit to a Private Home:

To take or send: basket of gourmet food; a Virginia ham; bar glasses; rafts for the pool; basket of guest soaps; steaks or lobsters; *canapé* knives or cutters; linen cocktail napkins; champagne-stopper puller.

To send later: photo display of the weekend beautifully mounted in an album; anything the host or hostess mentioned during your stay; flowers.

Housewarming:

An unusual but hardy plant; a coffee-table book; stationery printed with the new address; baskets; coffee mugs; placecards with holders; book to record party menus and guest lists; attractive bulletin board for kitchen.

Bon Voyage[1] to a Friend:

Monogrammed leather passport case; plant watering service; loan of your electric-current converter; emergency sewing kit; shoe covers for packing shoes; champagne delivered en route to ship, plane, train (arrange with carrier).

Rites of Passage

Anniversaries:

See the preceding "Rules for Realists," keeping the traditional guidelines in mind if you so desire.

Year	Traditional Gift		
1	Clocks	9	Leather
2	China	10	Diamond jewelry
3	Crystal	11	Fashion jewelry
4	Electrical appliances	12	Pearls, Gems
5	Silverware	13	Textiles, Furs
6	Wood	14	Gold jewelry
7	Desk sets	15	Watches
8	Linen, Lace	16	Silver hollowware

[1] Bon voyage (bohn vwah YAHZH, *not* bohn vī ahzh), as you probably suspect, means "have a great trip."

Year	Traditional Gift		
17	Furniture	35	Jade
18	Porcelain	40	Ruby
19	Bronze	45	Sapphire
20	Platinum	50	Golden Jubilee
25	Sterling Silver Jubilee	55	Emerald
30	Diamonds	60	Diamond Jubilee

Births:

A charitable contribution; a silver rattle; gold initials; a leatherbound edition of children's classic; silver picture frame; tickets to a new play and/or a baby-sitting offer for the newly house-bound parents (also see Shower Gifts).

Birthdays: See "Rules for Realists," page 74.

College Graduation:

Wineglasses; a subscription to *The Wall Street Journal*; a briefcase (if appropriate); stock; cash; a gift certificate at a computer store (for computer buffs).

Debut:

Only the family gives the debutante gifts, and their choice is often jewelry.

High-School Graduation:

Cash; electric blanket; portable typewriter; gift certificate for records or cassettes; popcorn popper; cordless telephone.

Showers:

Baby: A subscription to a popular magazine for the new parents; "designer" bibs; hardcover baby books; deluxe photo album; Polaroid-type camera; diary for mother to record thoughts and experiences.

Bridal:

Bed and bath—towels, sheets, etc. (check color preference first); a silver toothbrush holder; monogrammed gold razor; lovely hand mirror; sexy (returnable) nightgown.

Kitchen—practically anything unusual from a gourmet cookware store (no blenders, please); cooking lessons; a subscription to a great cooking magazine (like Cuisinart's *Pleasure of Cooking*); copper pans and bowls; copper measuring set; an accurate scale.

Weddings:

> *First (for younger couples)*—stocks or bonds; Krugerrands; a cordless telephone; glassware, china, and flatware (ask where their patterns are registered); a card table or game sets; a vacuum cleaner; weekly maid service for a month.
>
> *First (for older couples)*—a copper chafing dish; a coffee table book; a lovely frame for wedding picture; a house-plant; crystal wine or bar glasses; a decorative warmer for food service; fine cutlery; breakfast in bed (from a specialty caterer); a standing wine cooler.
>
> *Second, third, etc.*—gift optional (see gifts "for older couples," above).

Illness

In a Hospital:

> Small baskets of scented soaps; a bedjacket for a woman; TV rental; cheery books (like this one!); preparing the home for his return (buying food, putting fresh linens on the bed, etc.); caring for pets or children. (Note: Nothing beats a daily visit or an offer to run errands.)

At Home:

> Any of the above; maid service—even if just for one day; meals served in bed; the rental of a small refrigerator for bedside use; a list of places that deliver food, medication, meals, etc.; records or video cassettes.

Christmas Tips

The people who have been working for you, or serving you, throughout the year are (if you know what's good for you!) customarily remembered just before Christmas, or whenever extraordinary service is given.

Here are some ways to show your appreciation:

Exercise Instructors, Children's Teachers, Clergy, and Other Helpmates:

> A small gift ($10-$20), perhaps a plant, just to show you care.

Shopkeepers Who Have Performed Special Services:

Liquor, wine, or a Christmas plant to dry cleaners, florists, butchers, bakers, etc.

Service Personnel Who Have Performed Their Jobs Well:

A token gift (or $5) to your mail carrier, milk carrier, regular delivery people, answering service employees (try sweets to be divided among them), babysitters, special switchboard or elevator operators.

Apartment House Employees:

$10-$15 or liquor to doormen, security guards, maintenance personnel, building superintendent.

Your Barber, Hairdresser, Favorite Restaurant Employees, Caddy, Etc.:

A larger than normal tip.

Household Staff (Including Part-Time Help):

1-2 weeks' extra pay.

Office Staff:

If you're *head of the company,* give a cash bonus, a gift certificate to a fine store, or a good wine to your *immediate staff.*

If you're *an executive,* give a basket of toiletries, a visit to an elegant salon (like a "Miracle Morning" at Elizabeth Arden), a pen and pencil set, or personalized stationery to your *secretary or clerical assistant.*

Gifts That Spell C-L-A-S-S

To receive is divine. But to receive unexpectedly is *diviner.*

So, if you want to impress someone, or just make someone smile, consider a "just for fun" gift like any of the following:

During the busy holiday season, or when a friend is hard at work, send over dinner. Barbara, a lovely Texas hostess, has her children deliver pots of chili and freshly baked corn bread to close friends. She encloses a note saying, "Have dinner on me."

Arm your vacationing friends with letters of introduction to other friends along their route. Include names and addresses of some favorite restaurants and night clubs, too. Roll the papers like a scroll; secure with ribbon.

When you find a bargain, share the loot. Surely everyone you know would love ripe avocados, freshly caught crabs, just-cut mistletoe, or a half-pint of the season's first raspberries.

Call or write the concierge at the hotel where a traveling friend will be staying and arrange to have flowers or champagne waiting for him. I generally have a note enclosed saying something like "I'm so jealous I could scream!" People love it when you're thoughtful *and* envious. (If he isn't staying at a luxury hotel, call your favorite florist, or try "Wines by Wire," page 216.)

Think of how thrilled your friends will be if on their first visit to your favorite restaurant they are seated at the best table in the house, and if after dinner the captain says, "The Wither-spoons have arranged a lovely dessert for you. May I serve it?" You can arrange it all with a simple phone call to the manager or maître d'.

Have your travel agent arrange a limousine to pick up friends at an out-of-the-way airport and drive them to their hotel. Before they leave on their trip, give your friends a note, not to be opened until they land, describing the details.

Want to see friends across the country? Send *them* tickets. Real high rollers, send your plane.

The Art of Receiving

The way you accept a gift can be a gift in itself. Everyone knows to be gracious, to act happy, to say thanks. But if you really want to please someone, do what my friend Jill did.

I gave her a small pot of glitter powder (sparklers you dust on over holiday makeup). Certainly not an extravagant gift, it was just a small Christmas remembrance for a new-found friend. But by watching you would have thought she'd just received the one gift in the world she had always wanted. She complimented me on the

wrapping, on my thoughtfulness. She gushed, "I adore presents."
With the eagerness of a child on Christmas morning, she tore open
the package and pulled out the powder pot, quickly dusting it over
her face and hands. She "loved it" and had "always wanted some."
She thought it was "the perfect choice—fun, but elegant." Somehow, she wasn't just appreciating my gift, she was appreciating
me.

Of course, Jill didn't stop there. Two days later I received a
lovely note, on exquisite personalized stationery, telling me again
how much she enjoyed the gift and having a friend like me.

Now, I have a sneaking suspicion that the powder was not the
most wonderful gift she had ever received. But Jill, I suspect, *is*
the most wonderful recipient.

In fact, she was actually the one who gave *me* a gift. And she
will benefit immensely. I can't wait for another occasion to buy her
something else.

If you want to generate such a response in others, give *them* a
gift of your enthusiasm, your thanks, and a wonderful note[2] (sent
within twenty-four hours!). And not just when you receive a present. Dinner at someone's house, a favor done, a surprise kindness,
are all excuses for your return generosity.

---

[2] Fold-over notes—called "informals"—are absolute necessities. Have your
monogram engraved on the front. (Begin writing on the lower half of the inside
portion, continuing, if necessary, on the lower half of the reverse side.) Do not
skimp on quality of engraving or paper. Because you'll use these notes for most of
your personal correspondence, they must reflect your elegance and good taste.

Crazy About Catalogs

Ho-hum. Time to do my Christmas shopping. Time for inclement weather, pushy bargain hunters, and cranky sales clerks. Right?

Au contraire.[1] I'll spend most of my shopping days fighting nothing stronger than the bubbles in my bath. You see, I shop by catalog. It's the only way to buy!

Why don't you join me? To begin, you need only ring up Neiman-Marcus and ask them to send each of your favorite couples their annual HIS & HER gift. Over the past decades, this could have meant such non-boring items as HIS & HER oil wells, HIS & HER Chinese junks, or HIS & HER submarines.

Have something a bit more subtle in mind? Why not look through their entire catalog? In fact, why not get catalogs from Saks, Sakowitz, Bonwits—all the big-name stores. Just call each store and open an account. Most offer free catalogs year round to charge customers. And, of course, credit facilitates ordering by phone.[2]

If you prefer not to open an account, or if you want to deal with a merchandise house, simply call or write and ask for their latest catalog. The addresses and phone numbers you'll need follow:

---

[1] Au contraire (oh kahn TREHR) means "quite the contrary!"

[2] Note: When you order gifts by phone, have them sent to you so you can enclose a personalized card. When shopping by mail, you can send a gift card along with orders, giving instructions for its enclosure with the merchandise.

Superstore Catalogs

Bergdorf Goodman
P.O. Box 9598
Church Street Station
New York, NY 10249
(212) 753-7300
Catalogs at Christmas and
throughout the year: $5

Bloomingdale's
P.O. Box 2052 FDR Station
New York, NY 10022
Christmas catalog:
(212) 355-5900, $3
At your service:
(212) 705-3136
1-800-368-3438

Bonwit Teller
1120 Avenue of the Americas
New York, NY 10036
(212) 593-3333
Catalogs at Christmas and
throughout the year: $5

Gump's
250 Post St.
San Francisco, CA 94108
(415) 982-1616 or
1-800-227-3062
Catalogs at Christmas and
throughout the year: $3

Henri Bendel
10 W. 57th St.
New York, NY 10019
(212) 247-1100

I. Magnin
135 Stockton St.
San Francisco, CA
(415) 362-2100

Lord & Taylor
424 Fifth Ave.
New York, NY 10016
(212) 391-3344
Multilingual personal
shopping staff
Catalogs at Christmas and
throughout the year: $3

Marshall Field & Company
P.O. Box 1165
Chicago, IL 60690
(312) 781-1050
Catalogs at Christmas and
throughout the year: $5

Neiman-Marcus
P.O. Box 2968
Dallas, TX 75221
(214) 821-4000
Catalogs at Christmas and
throughout the year: $5

Sakowitz
1111 Main St.
Houston, TX 77002
(713) 759-1111
Personal Shopping:
(713) 877-8888

Saks Fifth Avenue
611 Fifth Ave.
New York, NY 10022
(212) 753-4000
  *International Shopping
    Service; Fifth Avenue
    Club*

Merchandise Offers

Arts and Artifacts

Collectors' Guild, Ltd.
601 W. 26th St.
New York, NY 10001
(212) 741-0400

Metropolitan Museum of Art
P.O. Box 225
Gracie Station
New York, NY 10028
(212) 326-7050

Museum of Modern Art
11 W. 53rd St.
New York, NY 10019
Art Lending Service Booklet:
(212) 708-9400

Smithsonian Institution
P.O. Box 2456
Washington, DC 20013
(202) 357-1826
(202) 357-1826

Auction News

Sotheby Parke Bernet
171 E. 84th St.
New York, NY 10028
(212) 606-7000
  *Newsletters throughout the
    year*

Books

Books on Tape
P.O. Box 71405
Los Angeles, CA 90071
1-800-626-3333 (outside
  California)
1-800-432-7646 (in California)
  (Free catalogs)

Children's Goods

The Dollhouse Factory
157 Main St.
Lebanon, NJ 08833
(201) 236-6404

FAO Schwartz
P.O. Box 218
Parsippany, NJ 07054
(201) 334-7715
1-800-228-2028 Ext. 50
Free catalogs

Clothes[3]

Brooks Brothers
346 Madison Ave.
New York, NY 10017
(212) 682-8800
Free catalogs

FBS
659 Main St.
New Rochelle, NY 10801
(914) 632-5777
1-800-228-5200

Spiegel
1061 W. 35th St.
Chicago, IL 60609
(312) 986-1088
1-800-345-4500
Catalogs: $3

Sportpages
3373 Towerwood Dr.
Dallas, TX 75234
(214) 247-3101
Free catalogs

Crystal

Baccarat
55 E. 57th St.
New York, NY 10022
(212) 826-4100

Steuben Glass
Fifth Avenue at 56th Street
New York, NY 10022
(212) 752-1441
Catalogs: $4

Equestrian Needs

H. Kauffman & Sons Saddlery
Co.
139-141 E. 24th St.
New York, NY 10010
(212) 684-6060

Miller's
123 E. 24th St.
New York, NY 10010
(212) 673-1400

Furniture

Conran's
145 Huguenot St.
New Rochelle, NY 10801
(914) 632-0515
Catalogs: $1

---

[3]Some of your best clothing values are available through the Superstore Catalogs.

Roche Bobois
200 Madison Ave.
New York, NY 10016
(212) 725-5513
Catalogs: $5

Gift Ideas

Trifles
P.O. Box 44432
Dallas, TX 75234
1-800-527-0277
Catalogs: $2

Gift Ideas for the Super Rich

Tova International
Tova Corporation
8920 Wilshire Blvd.
Penthouse
Beverly Hills, CA 90211
1-800-852-9999
*Ask for the Winter Wish
Book: about $3*

Hardware and Gadgetry

Hammacher Schlemmer
147 E. 57th St.
New York, NY 10022
(212) 421-9000 or
1-800-368-3584

Hennikers
3825 W. Green Tree Rd.
Milwaukee, WI 53201
(414) 352-0425

The Sharper Image
755 Davis St.
San Francisco, CA 94111
1-800-344-4444
Free catalogs

Jewelry

Cartier
Fifth Avenue at 52nd Street
New York, NY 10022
(212) 753-0111
Catalogs: $5

Tiffany & Co.
727 Fifth Ave.
New York, NY 10022
(212) 755-8000
1-800-526-0649
Catalogs: $3

Leather

Gucci
685 Fifth Ave.
New York, NY 10022
(212) 826-2600
Color catalogs: $9.50

Mark Cross
645 Fifth Ave.
New York, NY 10017
(212) 421-3000

Sporting Goods

Hunting World
16 E. 53rd St.
New York, NY 10011
(212) 755-3400

L.L. Bean
Freeport, ME 04033
(207) 865-3111

Northwestern Golf
4701 N. Ravenswood Ave.
Chicago, IL 60640
(312) 275-0500

5

· WING TIPS TO WHITE TIE ·

With an evening coat and a white tie,
anybody, even a stockbroker, can gain a
reputation for being civilized.

—OSCAR WILDE, *1891*

Hey, handsome! Take a long look at yourself. Have you been so busy *becoming* a success that you haven't taken the time to start *looking* like one?

In years past, you could have hired a valet to help you appear as commanding and sophisticated as you and I know you are. He would have made short work of *monsieur's*[1] caviar-stained tie and the dangling button on his navy vest. Even more importantly, he would have delivered the *coup de grâce*[2] to those madras trousers and that spiffy green belt strewn with minuscule yellow golfers.

Today, thanks to inflation and Yankee ingenuity, there is a bargain alternative: the full-length mirror. Buy yourself one, take firm hold of your ego, and prepare to get gorgeous!

---

[1] Monsieur (muh SYUH, *not* muh SHOOR) is, of course, "mister."

[2] Coup de grâce (koo duh GRAHSS, *not* koo duh GRAH) is a fine, merciful death blow. This word is commonly mispronounced because people think that one does not pronounce the final consonant of a French word. Although this rule holds true some of the time, it does not hold true when the consonant is followed by an "e" (and some other times as well).

A classic fall suit in a subtle Glen plaid. From Saks Fifth Avenue:
Collections Privé.

A Few Specific Generalities

A Colorful Start

According to Hemingway, "The very rich are different from you and me." And one of the ways they show it is by their choice of colors. Why, a debonair man about town would sooner trade his Lamborghini for a Corvair than be caught wearing lavender, purple, fuchsia, turquoise, lime green, mint green, chartreuse, mustard, peach, or hot pink. Such colors are simply too unflattering to his aristocratic complexion, not to mention a touch too enthusiastic for his refined, patrician tastes.

Are *you* willing to risk being branded *"bourgeois"*[3]? Or worse? Then you had best rid yourself of all ignoble colors. Of course, this may mean tossing out half the contents of your closet, but it's for a good cause: your sterling reputation. Anyway, you can still wear all your favorites—so long as they are white, cream, beige, tan, camel, khaki, blue, navy, gray, black, taupe, cocoa, or (if you have brown hair or brown eyes) brown.

If you crave some more color, you can always add red or yellow anywhere *above* the waist. For business, you can also add pink shirts; for play, you can throw in teal, olive drab, or Kelly green—in moderation. But you must use color with the utmost subtlety. Too many shades, too little class.

Don't Print It!

As long as I'm on an honesty binge, we might as well get another touchy subject out of the way. It's time to talk about prints.

Let me start off by saying that in this area, less is more—always. And cute isn't—ever. In fact, most prints are too boring, banal, or blatant for most tastes. In addition, they are entirely too memorable to wear well, and aren't nearly sleek enough for a dashing man like you.

Why not purge your closet now, before you find your sweet

[3] Bourgeois (boor ZHWAH) is an adjective meaning "middle class"; the group called "the middle class" is the *bourgeoisie* (boor zhwah ZEE).

self purged from some important social or business occasions? Just ring up your favorite charity (other than yourself!) and have them pick up:

> Anything with writing on it. (If the world wants to hear from your T-shirt, they'll call.)
> Anything suggestive of beer or other commercial products.
> Anything plaid (unless it's so subtle that squinting erases it).
> Anything littered with landscapes, flowers, people, hearts, or animals (except possibly the odd gator-encumbered polo shirt).
> Anything with horizontal stripes (unless you're a beanpole).
> Anything with patches or made of patchwork (which is acceptable only after bankruptcy).
> Anything with polka dots (except a tie with very civilized dots).

Did I condemn some of your favorite things?

Sorry; someone had to do it. Better me than your boss. Or your in-laws. Or a client. Or . . .

A Few Fabrications

There are rumors wafting from boardrooms across the land that clothing made from fabrics other than silk, cotton, wool, and linen will soon be made illegal. To get the jump on the competition, a chief-executive friend of mine even developed an allergy to everything else.

Smart move. These fabrics are exceptional in comfort and ease of wear. And, though they must occasionally be blended with another fiber to prevent wrinkling (Linen, I'm talking to you!), they are unparalleled in appearance. But man-made fabrics, well, I've always felt that man was vastly overrated as a producer of fine fabrics. Mummy Nature is much handier; she's been at it longer and has far better taste.

Quality, Not Quantity

You may—you must!—purchase the best clothes you can possibly afford. Look for brand names reflecting quality: Brooks Brothers, Polo, Burberry, Paul Stuart. And insist on classic styles and expert workmanship. If that means you are able to afford four suits rather than five, or two blazers rather than three, so be it. You can always add variety with interesting (but not *too* interesting) shirts, pocket squares, and ties.

It's Only Fitting

Every bit as important as quality and style is the fit. Shoulder seams must match shoulders, sleeves must be of correct length, and waistbands must never bind. Trousers must ease over buttocks and hang straight at the crotch, falling three-quarters of an inch longer in back than in front. Otherwise, you've wasted your money.

Fortunately, any store worth its price tags has one or more tailors on the premises. Use them. And find a good tailor to work on the clothes you already own, bearing in mind that there is no law against having casual clothes fit, and that looking fantastic can be as rewarding socially as it is professionally.

Heads of State

Seldom does a man achieve success without a good head on his shoulders. Here's a top-to-bottom look at how to get yours.

High Hat

Hats keep the rain off and the cold out, which is about as much as you can say for most of them. Wear sparingly: perhaps a spiffy Panama to fend off the summer sun, a chic and warm felt safari hat or fedora to ward off the cold.

On Top

Hair, on the other hand, should be worn as often as possible. Have it cut by an expensive stylist, remembering that the end product should be neat, flattering, and *au courant*[4]—but not heavily lacquered or styled. Remember, too, that too short hair is too boring and too long is, too.

One more thing. Don't let anyone talk you into something radical. If you were truly meant to have jet black hair, blond streaks, frizzy curls, or a full head of hair where none is currently growing, you would probably already have it. For free.

If you are nonetheless compelled to make a major change, do take an aristocrat with you. An objective opinion can be invaluable. And, should you both be wrong, you will have someone great to blame!

Eyes Only

I once met a man with purple eyes. You doubt it? So should he have when he ordered purple contact lenses.

Purple (or green or red) lenses on sunglasses are not sensational either. And mirrored lenses, well, if I wanted to chat with a mirror I would undoubtedly have chosen one capable of far deeper reflections.

Highbrows

About brows. If yours resemble pregnant caterpillars, or if you have one long brow stretching from eye to eye, then get thee to a pluckery. Any good salon will soon root out the problem.

Snooty Snouts

If your nose is large and you hate it, consider a chat with a board-certified plastic surgeon.

If it's red and veined, or pimply, or always shiny, call a good dermatologist.

---

[4]Au courant (oh koo RAHn) means current, up-to-date.

If it's constantly in the air or in other people's business, cut it out.

A Close Shave

For the most part, executives of large corporations frown on long sideburns, mustaches, and beards, believing that such things are best left on barbershop floors. I personally prefer a clean-shaven look anyway, unless the gent in question has terrible acne, a weak chin, or worse yet, a tendency toward trendiness.

After shaving, attain the sweet smell of success with a splash of cologne or *eau de toilette* (oh duh twah LEHT), but not so much that passersby drop to their knees gasping for air.

Smile Pretty

If your teeth are not white, straight, and scrupulously clean, then beg, borrow, or brush until the situation is rectified.

Incidentally, the new "invisible" braces are wonderful for adults. And bonding is a fast, inexpensive alternative to capping. Find a pro and consider the facts; then, if it makes sense, ACT!

Oh, there's one more thing. Do you smoke?

Don't. Especially domestic cigars. The ability to pollute the air and/or nauseate[5] others is a social skill not currently in high demand.

Getting Down to Business

Lest you be accused of being just another pretty face, we had better spend some time on the rest of you—starting with your business attire.

Shirt Tales

Believe it or not, shirts worn with business suits need not fit like duffle bags, and may even be moderately tapered. Under no cir-

[5]A little reminder. Popular usage notwithstanding, if one feels sick to one's stomach, one is *nauseated*, not *nauseous*. If one is, in fact, nauseous, then one is probably making other people sick—and should cease and desist at once!

cumstances, however, may they be short sleeved. Cuffs must extend below the jacket sleeve. There is a law requiring this, written somewhere in stone.

When it comes to colors, you have a wide latitude—as long as your shirts are a pale shade of light blue, taupe, gray, pink, or yellow. Or a striped mixture of any of these colors and white. Or a tattersall. Only once in a great while will you want all white; save it for your pinstriped suit (when white is the best choice) and for summertime (when the white won't drain the color from your face).

For important occasions—a board meeting, dinner at *Ma Maison* (mah meh ZAHn)—select something special. I must admit a personal preference for a light blue shirt with white collar and cuffs, especially when the cuffs are French and are held together by exquisite gold links. Talk about a million-dollar look!

More about those collars: My hands-down favorite is the pin collar, worn with a simple gold (or gold-filled) pin or bar. Incidentally, if you have your shirts tailor-made for you (at someplace like the Custom Shop), not only will they fit better and wear longer, but they will also be more flattering. The collar can be designed to hide jowls and wrinkles, to shorten a long neck, or to lengthen a short one.

So get yourself to a fitter. (No, the butler can't go for you.) Then fortify yourself for all the compliments ahead.

Fit to Be Tied

Men doing business wear ties. That's written in stone next to the law about shirts. So be it.

The most elegant ties are a classic 3¼-inch wide, and all silk. They are generally wine-red, navy, pale blue, pale yellow, or gray and may be plain or subtly dotted, patterned, or striped. They are never purple, green, or white, nor do they serve as backgrounds for little animals, stirrups, fish, or mustard stains.

Bow ties are for geniuses, eccentric millionaires, and, in some minds, con men. Normal folk fare far better with the traditional, never-offensive Windsor-knotted tie.

A silk foulard square *barely* peeking out of your jacket pocket finishes the look. Nonmatching, but coordinated, patterns or colors are generally best. Too much of a good thing is seldom effective.

Suit Yourself

It is truly a jungle out there. But you know that. You also know, don't you, that the King of the Jungle hasn't changed his style in years? And neither have his subjects.

All the King's men wear suits of navy worsted or gray flannel, sometimes plain, sometimes in a subtle Glen plaid, occasionally with narrow pinstripes (though they are careful not to resemble Al Capone in any way). The more conservative among them buy their suits at Brooks Brothers (that venerable home of the Ivy League suit); others shop at Lord & Taylor's or Saks, or chic designer boutiques. Their suits usually have natural shoulders and, quite often, a vest (the bottom button of which they are careful to leave undone). Rarely, if ever, do they wear sweater vests, for though a preppy man may look nice in Daddy's clothes, the converse is so seldom true.

Whether their trousers are cuffed or not is strictly a matter of personal taste and prevailing style. But let me say this: Whereas cuffed pants may hang somewhat better, cuffs tend to cut the long line of the leg. And lord, how I love the look of long legs!

Now, about color. For the most part, the King's men avoid black, saving it for funerals and formal occasions. They avoid brown suits at all times, not wishing to be mistaken for low-level managers or unambitious computer programmers.

In summer or California (whichever comes first), they wear lightweight suits in beige or tan, or beautifully tailored blue seersucker. For more casual occasions, they don the obligatory navy blazer with chinos, eggshell linen, tan gabardines, or lightweight gray flannel. Incidentally, they almost never wear all white; you might say that the rich and powerful have no sense of good humor, man. (Sorry, I couldn't resist!)

Getting It All Together

Putting together the elements of a great look isn't too difficult once you get the hang of it. Some people think that the only truly tough part is coordinating several stripes or patterns, but they're wrong. That's easy. Just don't do it!

True sophisticates realize that each piece of an ensemble must shine on its own, *sans*[6] competition from the others. Thus, if the suit is plain (which it should be if you want it to last for years), then select a striped shirt or a tattersall with a solid tie. If the suit is a pinstripe or Glen plaid, or the jacket is tweed, then everything else must be plain (though by *plain* I do not mean boring!).

Want a little more help? On the next page, some classy combinations.

Accessories to a Climb

Before pronouncing yourself impeccably dressed, you are going to have to take care of a few important details: namely, your accessories.

A Timely Suggestion

You need a good timepiece; one that's reliable, stylish, and reasonably expensive. A Rolex is the classic choice. Slick florentine-gold bracelet watches, though quite beautiful, are a bit ostentatious and should probably be avoided until after your hundredth million.

Watches that double as calculators, computers, or hot plates are not altogether dreadful, but you must try not to get so carried away by the gadgetry that you forget that style is the important thing. Anyway, if auxiliary functions must be performed, it is so much more chic to call the butler than to punch away at a gadget on your wrist.

And if your granddad left you his gold pocket watch, what then?

---

[6]Sans (sah*n*z) means "without." Note that in this instance, the more correct French pronunciation of "sah*n*" is inappropriate because it sounds artificial.

Suit	Shirt	Tie	Pocket Square	Appropriate Wear
Navy	Light blue	Wine/navy pattern	Wine	Business
	Yellow	Yellow/navy/ red stripes	Red	Business
Gray	Light gray	Gray/yellow pattern	Yellow	Business
	Pink with white collar and cuffs	Dark pink	Pink/white pattern	Special occasion
Navy Pinstripe	White	Wine red	White	Business
Taupe	Taupe/white stripes	Brown	White	Business
Navy blazer, gray flannel trousers	Pale blue with white collar and cuffs	Yellow	White	Special occasion
	Blue/white stripes	Wine	White	Casual business, special occasion

A handsome double-breasted suit by Giorgio Armani. Perfect for the tall, lean man. Photographed by Saks Fifth Avenue.

Do all your suit trousers have belt loops? Is the watch really an heirloom (yours or somebody else's)? Then wear it. Antiquity is always timely.

Rings and Things

Signet rings are nice, as are wedding rings (if you're married and plan to behave accordingly).

Other rings, however, are tricky. Even in these enlightened times, there are still diehards who believe that pinky rings are a sure sign of homosexuality or Manhattan residency—though which they consider more decadent I've been unable to discover.

About rings encrusted with diamonds, rubies, class insignias, and the like: Leave them home. Perhaps, if luck is with you, an undemanding jewel thief will make off with them and you can use the insurance money to get something less ostentatious (a new yacht? another Rolls?).

Nailed Again

You do know to keep nails clean, short, and unbitten, and cuticles smooth and pushed back, don't you? I thought so.

Don't Be Brief

Gentlemen of taste carry a sleek *attaché* (ah tah SHĀ) of fine leather or reptile. *Briefcases* are too large and awkward, and generally look as though they had been thrown off stagecoaches and ransacked by bandits (as do most wallets). Certainly, big-city life can be challenging, but a sophisticate never allows wear and tear to show on his personal belongings, especially those which are constantly shoved under very important noses.

Middle Ground

If I see another white belt, or a yellow one, or one with little fishes or other junk on it, I may become violent. I can take only so much;

I am not made of steel. Sure, I'm a strong woman, but some things are just too horrendous to bear.

What do I think of beltless pants? For other than very casual wear, not much. Classic suspenders, or a fine belt (leather or lizard) in black, brown, or cognac, add a nice finishing touch to *monsieur's* ensemble and are, therefore, far preferable.

Sock It to Yourself

Though I hate to appear too picky, I wonder if I could ask you just one tiny favor. Will you please (pretty please!) wear calf-length socks under your trousers? Few things ruin an otherwise well-dressed man's appearance faster than a patch of hairy leg.

Well-Heeled

Leave shoes outside your European hotel room (a practice that could prove interesting in New York City), and you will find them returned polished early the next morning. Europeans realize how important well-tended shoes and boots can be to a gentleman. So do all executives; and most prospective in-laws.

Custom-made shoes are especially appreciated. A certain New England patriarch is known to have worn the shoes his father gave him all the way from graduation exercises at Harvard to his first corporate presidency. Naturally, the valet kept them in good repair, resoling them two or three times. Those wonderful shoes lasted twenty years. Maybe more. Yet another case of quality being a bargain.

Big names in shoe biz include Church, Ferragamo, Peal, Gucci, and Bally (among others). And, of course, some of the very best people have their shoes and boots custom-made. Why not send your footman[7] to handle all the little details?

A few more things. You do know, don't you, how dreadful your Gucci loafers look with a three-piece suit? And your Church's wing

[7]The footman, an endangered species, is a male servant who runs errands, waits tables, and such. He has nothing to do with feet, except that the best ones generally have two.

tips look with your chinos? And brown shoes look with navy or gray suits? And white shoes look with anything and everything? Thank heaven. Tell your friends.

Playing Around

You're not one of those silly men who look like a million at the office, but like small change on the weekends, are you? Do you realize how damaging such behavior can be to your image as a sophisticate?

Above the Belt

Contrary to popular belief, polos are not the only casual shirts in existence. Not that I haven't been fond of them for years. In fact, I'll happily go on record as saying that no polo player should ever be without one.

Men who do not play polo (a rather large group, I suspect) should occasionally consider wearing something else: a navy shirt with white pinstripes, a rugby shirt, a short-sleeved tattersall—something that fits well (but not so well that it has to be *poured* on), and something that isn't made of fishnet fabric or covered with grommets, macho metal studs, or a dozen unnecessary zippers.

Now, about bodies. If you have a generous belly, wear a sports jacket whenever you can. It's a great camouflage.

If you have a great chest, keep it to yourself. Don't unbutton your shirt more than two notches and, for heaven's sake, forget the gold chains! Even if you are King of the Discos, *especially* if you are King of the Discos, make it your secret. The rest of the world will be forever in your debt.

Below the Belt

When it comes to selecting walking shorts or slacks, a gentleman need only keep four things in mind. One: Color counts, so restrain yourself. Two: Ill-fitting slacks and too-tight jeans are not particularly attractive. Three: Heiresses, employers, and in-laws tend not to be enthusiastic about tears, holes, and paint stains. And four: As no world-wide flood has been forecast, there seems to be no *raison d'être*[8] for pants which fail to fall to a proper length. Need I say more?

In the Swim

Whereas I am sure your entire anatomy is the stuff of poetry, I prefer not to know all the gruesome details upon meeting you casually at the beach. My sisters throughout the world, I suspect, are in concurrence.

Therefore, would you please wear boxer-type swim trunks rather than body-hugging briefs? Laguna makes some attractive ones, as do Polo, Ocean Pacific, and Calvin Klein. Perhaps you can save your briefs for the beach at St. Tropez (san troh PĀ). Since the women there are topless, they'll be in no position to criticize.

Formalities

Now it's time to talk formal wear, so listen and listen well!

Dinner jackets are black. Always black. Only black.

Dress shirts are white. Never ruffled. Never blue.

Cummerbunds are black. Not red. Not ever.

Bow ties are tied, not clipped on. Bow ties are also black, which is why semiformal dress is called *black tie*. (No one of *your* stature ever uses words like "tuxedo" or "tux." You say "dinner jacket" or "black tie." Or you say, "We are dressing for dinner.")

I know that your father told you nothing was black and white, but he was wrong. Not only is *black tie* black and white, but so is the more formal *white tie*, worn only when "full dress" is specified. Which is almost never!

A rental shop located in a high-rent area will have details on the many "musts" surrounding white tie and tails. Lord, I do hope

---

[8] Raison d'être (reh zahn DEH truh) means "reason for being."

they remember to tell you that no one ever wears a dinner jacket or tailcoat before 6 P.M., and that when a gentleman needs formal wear early in the day he dons the gray cutaway and striped tie of traditional morning dress. But then you already knew that, didn't you? I can't tell you a thing!

An Epilogue, More or Less

Well, now you're gorgeous (as promised). Or you will be soon. But I know you'll want to take a look at the Class Notes on Personal Shoppers so you won't have to spend your entire life updating—and upscaling—your wardrobe. After all, you've got places to go. And people to meet.

Garb for Gadabouts

You just won't sit still, will you? Today, the opera. Tomorrow, polo. The next day, only heaven knows what. Now, I don't wish to be a spoilsport, *dahling*, but what on earth are you going to wear? Here are a few suggestions.

Where You Are Going	*What to Wear*
BALLET	Business clothes are always appropriate; "black tie" is optional for benefits and opening nights.
BOARD MEETING	Your finest conservative business attire is required.
COCKTAIL PARTIES	Chic business attire is appropriate unless "black tie" is specified.
CROQUET MATCH	*Players:* The Croquet Association of America specifies all-white attire, including slacks or walking shorts, a casual pullover or shirt, and flat shoes. *Spectators:* Wear casual clothes.
CRUISE (*ocean voyage*)	In general, those who wish to wear "black tie" while dining do so all nights but the first and last, and when putting into or leaving port; others dine in chic business attire. For lunch in the dining room, men wear coats and ties; women wear sundresses. Other times, casual sportswear is suitable.

DINNER AT TOP
RESTAURANT

Don chic business clothes or "black tie," depending on where you've been before dinner or where you're going afterwards.

GALLERY, OPENING
OF AN EXHIBIT

Weekdays: Chic business attire is suitable.
Weekend: Wear chic casual clothes (sports jackets for men) unless "black tie" is specified.

GOLFING

In general, men wear slacks and a polo or other casual shirt. Women wear casual shirts or polos, and slacks, walking shorts, or skirts—depending on the rules of the course in question. Cleated shoes (which may be rented) are always required, and a glove and a visor or cap is strongly suggested.

HORSEBACK
RIDING

Casual hack[1] in the country: Wear boots appropriate to the style of riding (Western or English)—no tennis shoes or loafers—and jeans or riding pants with a casual top.
City-park hack: Wear appropriate boots with jeans for Western riding or riding pants for English riding. Hunt caps are sometimes required.
Hack on a large estate/cub hunting[2]: Don English riding boots and pants, hacking jacket, and hunt cap. A turtleneck, or shirt and tie, is suitable for gentlemen; a "ratcatcher," or shirt and tie, is appropriate for women.
Fox hunting[3]: Formal hunt attire is designated by the Master of each hunt. "Pink" coats (which are really red), and boots with brown tops, are solely for hunt members who have been awarded "color." Jewelry, other than a watch and tie pin, perfume, and cologne are prohibited. Cognac or Sherry in a flask is strictly encouraged.

HORSE SHOWS

Dress casually for *outdoor* events, remembering what you might have to walk through. And don't bring your dog! For *indoor* events with names like "*Grand Prix*"[4] or "International Cup," more

Where You Are Going	*What to Wear*

formal attire is required. In general, the better your seats, the better your dress—ranging from jeans in the upper balcony to chic business wear in the box seats; hunt members and officials' friends sometimes wear "black tie."

IRS AUDIT — Wear inexpensive, conservative attire. No jewelry. No furs.

OPERA — See Ballet.

PHOTO SESSION — Wear clothes with classic lines so photos are not immediately dated; select fabrics with interesting textures (raw silk, beautiful knits), but avoid fussy prints. For color photography, don something in a flattering hue—but nothing too garish. For black-and-white, wear medium tones, like pastels and grays.

Men: You will need some light powder to combat shine. Apply concealer to any blemishes and/or under-eye circles unless photos will be carefully retouched. For color photos, you may need a *touch* of blusher and lipstick to avoid looking washed out. (If other superstars can stand makeup, so can you!)

Women: Select a foundation *exactly* the same color as your face and neck, and powder face liberally. (Shiseido's stick make-up combined with their Powdery Foundation provides a wonderfully matte, long-lasting finish and is favored by many makeup artists.) Concealers should be used liberally on imperfections and under-eye circles. Apply several coats of mascara and a *medium*-toned lipstick; clear lip gloss should be dabbed on the lower lip only. For black-and-white photos, makeup should be used more heavily than normal. Shadows and blushers are used for contour only. (Dark areas recede; light areas come forward.) For color shots, stay with subtle hues. No bright blue shadows. No true red blushers.

RADIO TALK SHOW

Wear something suitable to your subject. Though you won't be seen by the audience, you will need to build credibility with your interviewer and with the station management.

SAILING

Dress comfortably and casually in layers which include a waterproof jacket or windbreaker; it is always cooler on water than on land. You *must* wear rubber-soled shoes with treads. A cap or visor, coupled with the vigorous use of a sunscreen, is a good idea, as is a swimswuit and cover-up. Bright colors will help others find you if you fall overboard. Take a seasickness preventative unless you're an "old salt."

SKIING

Downhill (Alpine): Your clothes must keep you dry and warm, allow for freedom of movement, and look great—all of which spells *expensive*. For your first trip, borrow as much as you can.[5] If you must buy, get a pair of warm-ups or stretch pants, a warm and colorful parka, a sweater, a cotton turtleneck, a kerchief, ski glasses, ski gloves, a cap, long underwear, and wool socks. For *après ski* (ah prā SKEE) you will need boots which will fit over heavy socks, a swimsuit, and warm casual attire (appropriate to your particular resort).

Cross-Country (Nordic): Clothing is lighter than for downhill; dress in layers which include long underwear, wool or corduroy knickers, long colorful socks, a sweater, wool gloves, and a hat. Bring *après ski* wear as designated above.

Where You Are Going	*What to Wear*

SPEAKING ENGAGEMENTS

Don attire befitting your topic. Don't wear anything that requires constant adjusting. If you tend to perspire noticeably, wear a jacket and bring a linen handkerchief. Wear roomy, comfortable shoes if you'll be standing. If you'll be sitting, remember to wear over-the-calf-length socks (if you're a man), and a fullish, longish skirt—not a straight skirt, not pants (if you're a woman).

SYMPHONY

See Ballet.

TELEVISION INTERVIEW

Clothing: Wear simple, classic lines, making certain to heed the suggestions under "Speaking Engagements" regarding appropriate attire for standing or sitting. Red, gray, and blue are generally the most flattering colors; white, black, yellow, green, and brown are usually *not* flattering. (If you'll be interviewed on a news program, ask what color they'll use for *chromakey* during your segment, then *avoid* that color. Failure to do so may bring about cancellation of your interview since the camera would blot out your clothing, making your head appear disembodied.) Take care, too, to avoid checks and narrow stripes (which tend to strobe). Ditto shiny fabrics and light-catching jewelry.

Makeup: Apply cosmetics as for color photography. Take special care to avoid dark lipsticks, colorful eye shadows (brown, mauve, and gray are better), and red blushers (brown, used *sparingly,* is best). Do your own basic makeup even if you are offered the services of a makeup pro at the station; you know your face better than anyone else. Let the pro finish your face, though, just to be on the safe side.

THEATER   See Ballet.

YACHTING   *Small boat with no crew:* See Sailing.

Large yacht with crew: For an extended cruise, men will need chic resort attire plus a blazer-and-tie and a dinner jacket. Pretty sundresses and several cocktail dresses and evening gowns are suitable for women.

---

[1] Hacking is riding "on the flat" as opposed to "over fences."

[2] Cub hunting, also called cubbing, is fox hunting before the formal season opens. Designed to train young hounds (which are never called dogs), it also serves to accustom new horses and riders to the sport.

[3] Unless you are an excellent rider, do not accept an invitation to hunt. It can be very dangerous. If you are a good rider and really wish to learn the sport, ask if you can join the "hill-topping" group which follows the hunt at a safer speed and jumps fewer fences.

[4] Grand Prix is pronounced "grahn PREE," not "GRAND PREE."

[5] Ski resorts of almost every description rent skis, boots, and poles. Some of the larger, more exclusive areas even rent clothes, though for a hefty fee.

Playing Around With Polo

So you've misplaced your polo ponies again! What are we going to do with you?

I'll bet you've forgotten all sorts of other things about the game as well. Perhaps a quick refresher course will help jog your memory.

About the Game

A person unafraid of mixing metaphors might describe polo as hockey played by horsemen on a gigantic football field (about 300 yards by 160 yards).[1]

The aim of the game is to score goals by hitting a ball through the opponent's goal posts. Goals are located at either end of field; posts are placed eight yards apart. Teams change sides after each goal is scored.

The ball is hit with the *side* of a mallet head mounted on a long flexible cane. This stick (or mallet) is held only in the right hand.

The game is *usually* divided into six "chukkers" of seven and one-half minutes each. There is a three-minute rest period between each chukker; at half time, there's a fifteen-minute break.

At major games, there are two mounted umpires and one off-

[1]Arena polo is a variation played indoors or out in a ring about one-third the size of a standard polo field. As each team consists of only three players, one *forward* is eliminated. Games are timed somewhat differently.

field referee. Less important games may have only an umpire.

Polo ponies are no longer required to be pony-sized (under 14.2 hands high),[2] but the term "pony" nevertheless remains. Today's mounts are more apt to be 15 to 15.2 hands high. Many are Thoroughbreds who weren't fast enough to race successfully. Others are highly prized animals imported from Argentina.

There are four players on each team: two offensive riders called *forwards*, one defensive rider called a *back*, and one rider who may play either offense or defense called a *half-back*. The players wear shirts numbered, respectively, from one to four.

Players are permitted, even *encouraged*, to "bump" other players and to "ride off" (push against each other) to spoil an opponent's shot. No one is allowed, however, to purposely endanger a pony or rider.

Riders are ranked according to their abilities. A beginner starts with a handicap of −2 goals; an expert may be rated as high as +10 goals, though 10-goal players are few and far between. The *team* handicap is determined by adding the handicaps of all the players. For all practical purposes, the higher-ranked team has a goal penalty roughly equal to the difference between the teams' handicaps. This penalty is deducted from goals scored to determine the winner of the match.

Tied games end in a "sudden death" chukker. The first team to score a goal wins.

About Watching Polo

Some matches are free. At others, you will have to pay an admission fee per person or per Mercedes.

---

[2]A "hand" is four inches, so named because it is roughly the width of a man's hand. Horses are measured from the ground to the top of the shoulder (or "withers"); thus, a pony standing 14 hands high (abbreviated 14 hh) is 64 inches tall at the withers. A pony 14.2 hh is 66 inches tall.

Spectators are advised to remember that galloping horses and flying balls can be hazardous to one's health. Thus, you must be certain to sit beyond the safety zone (which extends ten yards on either side of the field and thirty yards at each end). And be prepared to move quickly.

Though bleachers are usually available, you can often pull your car right up to the edge of the safety zone. Thus, you can sit *on* your car or *in front* of it.

Picnicking and tailgating are very popular pastimes at matches. But remember, polo isn't just any ol' game, and its spectators don't eat just any ol' food. Especially at the more prestigious matches, you'll find crystal flutes of champagne alongside silver trophy bowls and platters mounded with smoked salmon, pâté, cold roast capon, marinated mushrooms, cheese, and the like. (Needless to say, Cook will require plenty of notice to whip up something suitable.)

Clothing for spectators is generally very casual, but chic. Men usually wear slacks and polo shirts (talk about imagination); women wear shirts with slacks, walking shorts, or casual skirts. Panama hats are absolutely everywhere! (In Palm Beach, one should not be surprised to see *some* men in summer suits and, for reasons one can only surmise, shoes *without* socks. Their ladies will often wear pretty sundresses and broad-brimmed hats. A few will carry ruffled parasols.)

During intermission, spectators are asked to "step on divots," that is, stomp down clumps of dirt and grass on the playing field that have been kicked up by the horses. Queen Elizabeth often helps; perhaps you should, too.

A last hint: Barking dogs and polo ponies (like hecklers and *prima donnas*[3]) mix rather poorly, so leave Rover back at the compound.

---

[3] Prima donnas (pree muh DAH nahs), strictly speaking, are female opera stars; the term also refers to anyone who demands superstar treatment while lacking superstar credentials.

6

· THE SILK STOCKING SET ·

Where's the man could ease the heart
Like a satin gown?

—DOROTHY PARKER

You've come a long way, baby. But does it show?

Alas, few women achieve a look of sophistication and elegance without exasperating years of trial and disaster. Instead, most of us tend to tumble, at least to some degree, into one of four ruts; let's call them Too Sweet, Too Safe, Too Sensational, and Too Sexy. (I am nothing if not a master of the all-encompassing snappy label.)

You'll probably recognize some of your friends in the descriptions which follow. They might also recognize you. But don't fret; updating your image to reflect your new position in life takes only painful self-appraisal and incredible courage, easy virtues for someone like you.

Type-Casting

Too Sweet: You know her well—strictly Easter-egg colors, itsy prints, ruffles, and Peter Pan collars. Once the perfect ingenue, she may now be closing on thirty and is a homemaker, a secretary, or maybe a pediatrician. Too Sweet is a true romantic, lovely and

An enchanting suit for the international woman by Vicomtesse Jacqueline de Ribes. Photograph courtesy of Saks Fifth Avenue.

soft, cute as a bug. Wonder why she didn't update her wardrobe after leaving twenty-two?

Too Safe, on the other hand, is grown-up and deadly serious. Probably climbing the corporate ladder or making her way in a male-dominated profession, she long ago decided that *joining* them was easier than *beating* them. A slave to navy and khaki, Too Safe adores suits, striped shirts, and neat little bow ties. In fact, her clothes would be indistinguishable from her husband's if it weren't for the skirts. (Real corporate women don't wear pants.) You will recognize Too Safe immediately when she dons her Adidas to walk to the water cooler.

Next we meet *Too Sensational*, the merchandiser's dream. This lover of trendiness was born for "hot" colors, bizarre prints, *ne plus ultra*,[1] *le dernier cri*.[2] Often seen in "sweats," leg warmers, and high heels with ankle socks, Too Sensational is known for her terrific fashion sense of humor. What a shame that business clothes weren't meant to be amusing.

Finally we have *Too Sexy*. So bountiful are this lady's assets that everything she slips into appears tight and too revealing. Not really meaning to appear overly seductive, she just accentuates too much of her positive, resulting, alas, in a negative. Think Dolly Parton in *Nine to Five* and you have a classic portrait of Too Sexy.

Be honest now. Are you just a little bit Too Sweet, Too Safe, Too Sensational, or Too Sexy?

Most women are. Fortunately, you can maintain your natural love for romance or conservatism or drama or excitement and still look as polished as any socialite. Listen, even aristocrats must learn to dress with style and grace. Let's just say *you* are starting fashionably late!

Socialite Style

If you want to look as though you had been born rich (and who but an IRS auditee would ever wish otherwise?), then you must first determine your Socialite Style.

[1] Ne plus ultra (nuh ploo ZOOL truh) is "the ultimate."
[2] Le dernier cri (luh dehr nyā KREE) is the latest fashion.

Start by studying the following profiles and adopting the one which seems the most *you*. But please be honest with yourself. All the wishing in the world won't change your Lauren Bacall into a Jaclyn Smith, or vice versa. Nor should it. By being absolutely true to their own styles, Bacall and Smith have risen to the top of their professions. By being true to yours, I suspect you will do the same.

The Grande Dame[3] (A class image for adults who were previously Too Safe or Too Sweet)

Image: aristocratic
Taste: ultraconservative
Profession: executive, politician, professional (or wife of same)
Figure: thin to slightly overweight; mature
Hair: requires frequent visits to a salon; very neat; generally chin length or shorter
Makeup: conservative
Nails: perfectly groomed; practical length
Pants: seldom if ever
Favorite Outfit: suit, blouse with tie neck
Favorite Fur: mink
Favorite Shoes: plain pumps, sensible height
Favorite Purse: structured traditional alligator bag
Favorite Jewelry: pearls, wedding ring, gem earrings
Designers: Chanel, Valentino, Adolfo, Castleberry
Possible Pitfall: coming off as too prim and proper
Famous Grandes Dames: Dina Merrill, Nancy Reagan, Audrey Hepburn

The Belle (A beautiful look for Too Sweet or Too Sexy)

Image: contemporary Scarlett O'Hara
Taste: feminine
Profession: Miss America, secretary, jet setter, flirt
Figure: round, feminine

---

[3] A Grande Dame (grahnd DAHM) is a great lady.

Hair: soft, wavy, often long
Makeup: pretty, emphasis on eyes and mouth
Nails: long and polished
Pants: soft, pleated, or dressy
Favorite Outfit: ruffled, full-shirted ball gown
Favorite Fur: fox
Favorite Shoes: high heels
Favorite Purse: medium-sized envelope or basket
Favorite Jewelry: family heirlooms, cameos, diamond studs
Designers: David and Elizabeth Emanuel, Kasper, Betty Hanson
Possible Pitfall: falling back into Too Sexy or Too Sweet
Famous Belles: Jaclyn Smith, Jane Seymour, Marisa Berenson, Ann-Margret, Connie Stevens

The Sportswoman *(A wonderful new look for Too Safe)*

Image: all-American
Taste: California casual
Profession: businesswoman, busy mother, gymnast, actress
Figure: well-toned, athletic
Hair: wash and wear
Makeup: natural
Nails: fairly short; sometimes buffed rather than polished
Pants: all kinds
Favorite Outfit: jumpsuit or pants with a top
Favorite Fur: coyote
Favorite Shoes: sandals, low-heeled pumps or boots, sneakers
Favorite Purse: casual and roomy shoulder bag
Favorite Jewelry: sports watch
Designers: Calvin Klein, Anne Klein, Perry Ellis, Ralph Lauren
Possible Pitfall: losing sight of one's femininity
Famous Sportswomen: Cheryl Tiegs, Dinah Shore, Susan St. James, Farrah Fawcett

The Sophisticate (A great image for Too Sensational or Too Safe)

Image: trend-setter

Taste: haute couture,[4] dramatically tailored to theatrical

Profession: entertainer, sales representative, advertising executive, model

Figure: lean, small-busted, often tall

Hair: distinctive color, striking style

Makeup: dramatic

Nails: long; bold polish

Pants: all kinds

Favorite Outfit: three-quarter-length jacket with padded shoulders, straight skirt with a slit, broadbrimmed hat

Favorite Fur: lynx or sable

Favorite Shoes: high heels, fashion boots

Favorite Purse: large envelope

Favorite Jewelry: diamonds, emeralds, bold costume jewelry

Designers: Bill Blass, Norma Kamali, Karl Lagerfeld, Claude Montana

Possible Pitfall: going to extremes

Famous Sophisticates: Diahann Carroll, Jill St. John, Joan Collins, Lauren Bacall, Diane Von Fürstenberg

Million-Dollar Style

After finding the right style, your real work begins. (Sorry, but domestics can't do everything for you!) Anyway, you need only revise some of your anachronistic purchasing habits.

This may mean forsaking quantity in favor of quality, passing up fads for more enduring styles, and paying more attention to color and fit. (And just when you thought it was safe to go back into your jeans.)

Silk and the Ilk

There are but a few truly elegant materials: silk, cotton, wool, linen (if it's blended with another fabric so it won't wrinkle),

[4] Haute couture (oht koo TOOR) is high fashion.

Jacqueline de Ribes's knock-out dinner dress with white satin lapels and cuffs, jeweled buttons, and a black satin hip bow. Photographed by Saks Fifth Avenue.

suede, Ultrasuede Facile,[5] and fur. Polyester and other such man-made fabrics do not exist, but are merely figments of your accountant's imagination.

Fad Versus Fashion

It's a cinch to tell a passing fad from an enduring fashion. Fads are impractical, rarely flattering, ultimately expensive, and generally *déclassé*. In addition, fads are most always composed of cheap materials, no doubt in anticipation of their impending demise.

Fashion is the opposite.

Need more clues? Check out the following lists.

PASSING FADS (AT LEAST WE CAN HOPE!)

Army fatigues (too exhausting!)
Army boots
Fishnet fabric
Fun furs (which seldom are)
Green nail polish
Green, orange, or magenta hair
Leg warmers (for nonathletic endeavors)
Metallic fabrics for daytime

Miniskirts
Over-the-knee boots
Plastic shoes, clothes, etc.
Shoes in iridescent colors
Socks with high heels
Sweats (charming though the name may be)
Tattoos
Too-tight pants
Torn or patched clothing
Wild color combinations

ENDURING FASHIONS

Blazers with mid-width lapels
Boots reaching nearly to the knee
Capes
Envelope handbags
Flat shoes and sandals
Fur coats and jackets from unendangered species, in natural colors

Pumps with medium or high heels
Red, pink, or coral nail polish
Shoulder pads (which may be removed if they temporarily fall from grace)
Silk blouses with high necks, stock ties, and/or pleated fronts

---

[5] Ultrasuede Facile (fah SEEL) is a new butter-soft washable suede-like material; it is wonderful and very expensive.

Kid gloves in neutral colors	Three-quarter-length coats
Mid-calf-length coats	Trenchcoat-style raincoats
Pleated skirts	Wrap jackets and coats

Am I completely against trendy clothes and accessories?
Well, yes. And no.

At an event where even one business associate or "important other" is present, the nix is on. Otherwise, strictly for play, an occasional fad can be fun. Just don't blow your silk-and-suede budget to keep up with the latest rage.

Color You Beautiful

Five years ago, I cleared my closet of everything I had not worn for two years or more. To my complete surprise (and let me say here that I do not surprise easily), virtually all remaining garments were red, black, or white.

Everything I loved, everything that had consistently brought me compliments, was one of three colors. Half-instinctively, half-consciously, I had selected colors that best complemented my own coloring and fashion image.

Don't you owe it to yourself to find your own special colors? Once you see how lovely you look in the right shade of blue, the perfect red, the best gray, you will wonder how you endured the "wrong" colors for so long.

Which, I'm afraid, brings up an important point. After discovering the importance of color, you may become extremely depressed at the prospect of suddenly having nothing to wear. But take heart. Garments in uncomplimentary colors will eventually wear out (especially if the butler stomps on them a bit). And, of course, there are hoards of charitable organizations without your exquisite taste that are simply clamoring for donations. So don't empty your clothing vaults tonight. But *do* vow to never again buy anything in a color that is not wildly flattering. Within no time at all you'll have the basics of a wardrobe you can build on forever.

COLOR SEARCH

I used to wear nothing but "earth" colors (brown, orange, mustard, olive), thinking they looked good on me. They didn't. Now I realize that I liked these colors because I lived in California, where *everything* is earth colored. When I moved to a big eastern city (where almost *nothing* was earth colored), I realized the error of my ways and switched to the reds, blacks, and whites I should have been wearing all along.

To find *your* most flattering colors, I suggest you do one of two things. If you like to get your information from books (in which case my publisher and I would like your name and address), then buy one that describes your special "seasonal" colors. Or, if you prefer a more do-it-yourself approach, get thee to a fabric store. Select scarf-size remnant squares of the shades you (and others) have always liked on you, plus those you've admired on friends or actresses who have coloring similar to yours. Choose at least thirty swatches to start, being careful to select varying hues of each basic color. (I wouldn't be caught dead in Chevrolet red, but somehow—I don't know why—Ferrari red is definitely me!)

Now, back at the family estate, remove your makeup, wrap yourself in white (a sheet will do, but ermine is more *you*), and stand in front of a mirror well bathed in natural light. Drape each fabric around your neck and study its effect on your hair, eyes, and complexion. (A debutante friend with your coloring could prove very useful here.) What you're looking for is any shade which makes your face glow and causes it to appear more important than the fabric. When you find such a hue, have the maid guard it with her life. You will have found one of your colors.

One caution. Just because lime green flatters you doesn't mean you actually have to wear it. Though no color is inherently good or bad, some (for reasons sexual, ethnic, racial, or nonsensical) provoke quite pleasant—or adverse—effects in a great many people.

To determine which colors create or destroy that coveted "Daddy has money" look, I informally polled several thousand of my most intimate (and rich) friends. Scoff at the results if you wish. Ignore them at your peril.

Classy Colors for Major Wardrobe Pieces

Neutrals: white, ivory, cream, beige, taupe, tan, camel, khaki,
cocoa, chocolate brown, olive drab, navy, gray, black

Blues: powder blue, heather, royal, gray-blue, pale aqua, teal,
Chinese blue

Greens: emerald, forest, jade, moss

Reds: true red, scarlet, wine, rust, cinnamon, cranberry

Pinks: powder pink, rose, dusty rose, pale peach, pale apricot

Yellows: lemon, icy yellow, mustard

Fun Colors (great for accents, evenings, and play)

Blues: turquoise, bright aqua

Greens: Kelly, bright green

Pinks: hot pink, bright pink, coral, salmon

Purples: lavender, plum, grape, orchid, magenta, lilac, mauve,
periwinkle

Nighttime Only

Metallics: gold, silver, bronze

Colors to Recommend to Your Enemies (they are almost impossible
to wear well)

Greens: lime, olive, iridescent green

Purples: fuchsia, violet, puce

Yellows: hot yellow, chartreuse, gray-mustard

Oranges: true orange, bright red-orange

MIXING THINGS UP

To my mind, the current tendency toward mixing the unmix-
able is one to be nipped in the bud, prior to real damage being
done. Whereas a crimson dress with a purple belt and yellow accessories may warm (make that *scorch*) the hearts of some, for
other than strictly casual wear I just can't see it. (Though everyone
else within miles surely will!)

For more interesting occasions (donating another Rembrandt to the museum, receiving an honorary doctorate from Harvard), a bit more subtlety seems in order. This is not to say that you should stick with tired old color combinations like red, white, and blue; or navy, white, and green; or that awful scourge of the preppy, bright pink with Kelly green. Quite the contrary. I expect you to come up with something more innovative, more exciting.

One of the more stunning combinations of the current fall line is Bill Blass's powder pink and camel; who would have ever thought that these two colors would be wildly compatible? Pink, in fact, has become a surprise neutral, looking splendid with red, dark brown, black and white, and navy and white.

Other color combinations that may strike your fancy include:

royal blue and black	red and black
cream and olive drab	camel and gray
gray with yellow and white	Chinese blue and ice blue
taupe and black	cream and silver-gray
red with turquoise and white	blue-gray and rose-beige

You can, of course, attain striking results with a simple mix of gray and white, navy and white, or my all-time favorite, black and white. And, for a truly elegant look, I've always loved a combination of complementary intensities of the same basic color: For example, a charcoal skirt with a medium-gray jacket and a pearl-gray blouse. Try this with blues, yellows, pinks, creams, and beiges, as well.

To pull your colors together, use smashing accessories. Particularly important are earrings and belts. But don't overdo it. If everything looks too matched, too Wednesday-afternoon-at-the-bridge-club, you'll never get a mention in the "Eye" column of *WWD* (*Women's Wear Daily*). Then, how will your old school chums know you've returned from Cannes (kahn)?

MAKING LESS MORE

Well, are you completely exhausted from the limitless permutations of colors and shades? Dazed by all the accessories you'll need and the many servants required to color-coordinate your closets and vaults?

Good. Why not simplify your life?

I did. Subconsciously at first, then quite deliberately, I selected red, white, and black as my "signature" colors. Here's why.

- I can mix and match my colors at will: red with white, white with black, or black with both red and white.
- I can afford exquisite accessories because I have fewer colors to accessorize.
- Shopping is greatly simplified because anything that isn't one of my colors is automatically eliminated.
- New purchases go with things I already own; no more suits hanging in the closet for want of the right blouse.
- I can travel for days with just one pair of shoes and one handbag.
- One coat goes with everything.
- One shade of nail polish goes with everything.
- Most importantly, my wardrobe has become special—my colors remind others of me.

Have I convinced you of the advantages of "signature" colors? Then why not start assembling *yours* today? Select one light neutral, one dark neutral, and one or two bold colors.

If you're a fair-skinned brunette like me, you might try my colors, maybe adding pink or royal blue as a fourth shade. An auburn-haired beauty might prefer cream with chocolate and rust. Or maybe *you* would like beige with honey and navy, or buff with cocoa and gray-blue. Just remember to select colors you really love, that flatter you *and* each other.

The Solid Facts

Because I spend a fortune on beautiful fabrics and exquisite tailoring, I want my clothes to last forever (at the very least). And the plain fact of the matter is that prints don't wear all that well; they're simply too memorable.

Solids, on the other hand, will serve you for many years. They are far easier to mix and match and there are no problems with competing patterns. Also, garments of one color can be changed radically by the mere switching of accessories; a new belt, new earrings, and you have a new outfit. Try that with a zebra-print dress!

Having a Fit

You may think me unduly demanding, but I insist on being able to do several fun things while wearing clothes: namely, eat, move, sit, and breathe. To guarantee this, I sit, bend, inhale and exhale deeply, and walk around in any garment I consider buying. While I'm at it, I also check for fabric tears and stains, proper sleeve and pant length, shoulder fit, and well-sewn seams. (Better to discover problems in private than in front of important clients!)

If a garment flunks my tests, I have it altered. If it cannot be altered, it is discarded. I never make exceptions.

There is one more test a garment must pass prior to becoming a debit to my charge. Because I think a companion valet adds a bit too much to the cost of a garment, I insist that the fabric in question be resistant to wrinkling, soiling, and self-destruction. Call me picky. (But also call me impeccably dressed.)

From the Bottom Up

Now that you've got the basics down pat, let's take a toe-to-tresses trip through the Socialite Look, starting just this once where none of us ever want to be: at the bottom.

News on Shoes

There are damsels, I understand, who would happily blow their champagne-and-caviar budget on shoes and boots alone. *Chacqu'un à son goût,*[6] I suppose.

---

[6]Chacqu'un à son goût (shah KUHN ah sohn GOO) means "each to his own taste."

Personally, I think most of us (save those rare lean beauties with size six tootsies) are better off calling as little attention as possible to our feet. It is far better to elongate the body and shorten the foot by drawing attention upward. So keep bright colors near the face, and wear shoes no lighter or brighter than the color of your garment's hem. You'll be delighted by the difference this simple technique makes.

COLORS

Choosing the best shoe color to accompany any ensemble is a breeze if you've adopted my signature-color wardrobe scheme. Simply match the light and dark neutral colors you've selected.

If you're not yet a convert, you can still fare quite nicely with just two basic colors, though deciding *which* two may be a bit tricky. To choose the first, I recommend that you do what private color consultants often suggest: Look to your hair. Black hair? Buy black shoes. Gray hair? Try gray shoes. Blond hair? Well, you get the idea. And it's a pretty good one. If you've selected apparel to complement your skin, eyes, and hair, then shoes the color of your hair should, in turn, complement your clothes.

To choose your other neutral, match a prominent color in your wardrobe. For a dark shoe select among wine, navy, charcoal, black, or dark brown. For a light shoe try oyster, bone, cream, beige, taupe, or pale gray.

You might notice that I've omitted white. And for good reason. *White shoes are awful!* They make your feet look like gunboats and, worse yet, capture the eye so effectively that no one notices your pretty face. So, for spring or summer, why not instead try "spectators," those classic pumps with white tops and black, navy, or brown bottoms? For boots, try an off-white suede or switch to a darker or skin-colored neutral.

For summer playtime, go ahead and buy flats and sandals in any color you like: red, green, blue, even the *verboten*[7] white. Fortunately, flat shoes do not pull the eye down nearly as badly as heels and boots do.

---

[7] Verboten (vehr BOHT n) means "forbidden."

ABOUT STYLE

Only marginally less important than the right color is the style. Though your mirror is your best guide to proportion and appropriateness, the chart on page 132 may also help when it is particularly important to put your best foot forward.

Up the Lower Extremities

Not long ago, there was but one proper length for a skirt and one correct length for pants. But no longer. Today, almost anything goes, though a few rules of decorum and fit will probably never change.

For business, you must take the conservative route. More than a few chief executives are still less than thrilled about the idea of women in business, let alone businesswomen in jeans or harem pants. So my advice is never, *ever,* wear casual trousers in a corporate or professional environment, even if others in your firm wear them. Even if *most* of the women in your firm wear them. If the men in power wear conservative suits, women in power (and elsewhere) must wear suits or well-tailored dresses. Whether your suits have skirts or slacks is up to you and to the practice in your particular firm.

Sound unfair? Sound silly?

Sound advice: Do it anyway!

Trousers and skirts must fit properly. They must ease over the body: no cupping under the buttocks, no pulling at the zipper, no "smiling" across the crotch. The front hem of pantsuit trousers should just brush the front of your shoe; the back should fall just a touch longer. Skirt hems must be even and "blind" stitched, and should fall no shorter than mid-knee in conservative business environments and not significantly shorter whenever a "class" appearance is important (which is always!). So get yourself a tailor (or dressmaker) and visit him or her often.

A Good Belt

Belts go from single to multiple, from narrow to wide, from macho to feminine. The mere fact of their constantly changing makes them invaluable accessories. So have fun with whatever is new, but do remember that:

A rich-looking belt can make an inexpensive outfit look expensive; conversely, a cheapo belt can make even a designer original look dreadful.

A soft belt should never be pulled so tight that it crinkles like the wrinkles in your faithful family retainer's chin.

A light, or brightly colored, belt should be worn only by a woman who disappears when turned sideways.

A belt has too much hardware on it if you suddenly start noticing junk dealers hanging around your estate.

Bosom Buddies

To bra or not to bra, that is the question.

The business answer?

Wear one.

The casual answer?

It depends. Who is present? How obvious is your bralessness? One point worth remembering is that you can never go wrong looking tasteful, but boy, can you get into trouble looking otherwise!

High-Rent Blousing

Blouses are the excitement of your wardrobe. They make the boring, fun; the dull, fantastic. Or they ruin the whole look. *Which* is up to you. To my mind, the perfect suit blouse is always a lovely color and invariably has beautiful detail: pleats, French cuffs, lovely buttons,[8] something to make it special. Most likely, it is silk.

---

[8] Inexpensive blouses can be greatly enhanced by replacing their buttons with mother-of-pearl, brass, or fabric-covered buttons.

Clothing	Occasion	Shoes	Hosiery	Special Concerns
1. *Conservative-length* dress or skirt	Business	Dress pumps with little or no trim	Ultrasheer, in a color matching shoes; in spring or summer, off-white stockings with black pumps	"Spectators" are for spring and summer only, as are open toes, sling-backs, and patent leather; suede is solely for fall and winter; socks with heels are for trendy teens only!
2. *Calf-length* skirt or wide-leg pants	Business, casual	Flat or mid-heel boots or shoes	Semi-opaque or sheer in a color-matching shoes or boots	Hem of garment must cover top of boot. Shoes must not be too delicate.
3. *Short* skirt, dress, pants, or shorts	Casual	Flats or sandals	Nude; off-white or pale pink sheers with black or red flats; in winter, opaques or knits	Avoid ankle socks, opaque white hose, and chunky shoes.
4. Long trousers	Business, casual	Mid- to high-heel boots; sandals; flats; sporty pumps	Semi-opaque, knit or sheer, in a color matching shoes	Avoid dress pumps and chunky high-heel sandals.

5. Narrow-leg pants	Casual	Boots (to tuck pants in); flats	See # 3 above	Our sort does not tuck skin-tight pants into boots because our sort does not wear skin-tight pants.
6. Evening wear	Semi-formal, formal	Dressy silk pumps; delicate high-heel sandals	Ultrasheer, in a color matching shoes; perhaps with sparkles or rhinestones	Avoid patent leather, grosgrain bows, and rhinestone clip-ons.

The perfect blouse does not gape at the bust, nor does it expose brassiere straps. More often than not, it has a high neck with a special collar, a stock tie, or a beautiful large bow. Incidentally, bows at the throat are all right, but if your eyes droop a bit at the corners, as do mine (yet another burden of excessive brains!), you might look better with a bow tied to the side. Or if you want a fun new look, turn the bow into a rose instead:

Wrap tie ends once around the neck and make a half-knot. Twist the ties together to form a cord, coil the cord at your throat, then tuck the ends under and up through the center. *Voilà!* A rose.

Trail Blazers

Men of taste buy beautiful suit jackets and blazers and have them tailored to a perfect fit. Smart women do the same.

Smart women also look for high-quality buttons and conservative lapel width. Most importantly, they know that a too-long jacket on a too-short figure, or a too-short jacket with too-long legs, makes the body seem out of proportion. They would rather look perfect. As should you.

A Scarf, A Shawl, and Y'all

Scarves and shawls are among the trickiest items in any wardrobe. Not one woman in a thousand knows how to wear them. As a result, they are thrown or tied on in a manner which is inevitably too sloppy or too prissy—not exactly the adjectives one yearns to hear. Therefore, I suggest you wear only those scarves and shawls that are sold as part of an ensemble (so you can blame mistakes on the designer), and that you purchase such ensembles only with the help of a chic salesperson (so you can blame her, too).

If you feel compelled to disregard this advice—and there is a bit of the rebel in the best of us—then at least:

Drape shawls so that Boy Scouts are more compelled to whistle at you than to help you across the street.
Refrain from borrowing scarf-tying techniques from Italian

counts, sore-throat victims, refugees, headache sufferers, downstairs maids, and Roy Rogers. Instead, toss a giant scarf over one shoulder, secure with a pretty pin, and tuck the ends under your belt. Or fold a large square diagonally, tie it loosely around your neck, and drape it so that the point falls over a shoulder. Or wrap a scarf sash around your waist and coil the ends into a "rose." Or tuck a small silk square into your jacket pocket.

Check the latest issues of your favorite fashion magazines for more ideas.

Carry On

One of the many advantages of a signature-color wardrobe (I *have* convinced you by now, haven't I?) is that you need but four hand-bags for the entire year: one for evening, two for day and casual evenings out (one light neutral, one dark), and one for playtime. Thus, you can afford really beautiful bags, a point of no small importance given the visibility of this item.

For evening, I personally prefer a black silk envelope clutch with a pretty rhinestone clasp, something just large enough to accommodate a lipstick and some madcap money. You, on the other hand, might prefer a small bag in gold or silver mesh, or perhaps a lovely beaded clutch.

For everyday use, I like a large, simple leather envelope, especially one with an attachable shoulder strap for those glorious occasions when my hands are full of little blue boxes (from Tiffany's, of course). To find the perfect bag for *you,* check your profile in the section on Socialite Style, remembering that crocodile, kid, and lizard are much less costly than the insults you'll receive for carrying plastic or crude leather.

Whichever bag you chose, have your personal maid clean it regularly, and for heaven's sake don't overstuff it. To accommodate all those bothersome little items required in business, get yourself a beautiful *attaché* (ah tah SHĀ) case—not a clunky old beaten-up briefcase like those carried by mansion-to-mansion salespeople. To accommodate your gym clothes—if you're one of those diehards who actually *like* to perspire—you need a chic, clean, zippered bag. Dirty socks toppling out of an open canvas tote will do nothing for your hard-won image as a socialite. Nothing *good,* that is.

Fur Sure

A classy lady like you needs a fur jacket or coat to help ward off those frigid nights in Zermatt (tsehr MAHT). I know what you're thinking: *Elles sont trop chères!*[9] But they're not as expensive as you might think. You won't have any trouble affording one (two? three?) if you just stay out of Bijan (bee ZHAHN) for a few weeks and if you consider that:

> *One of the more durable furs will last ten to fifteen years.* Raccoon, mink, nutria, seal, lamb, and sable are all long-lasting. (But watch out for luxuriously soft furs like lynx and fox; they can evaporate before you can say charge-it-and-send-it.)
>
> *In many professions* (sales, performing, advertising, investment consulting), *looking successful is every bit as important as being successful.* The right image, in fact, actually contributes to success. And nothing but nothing makes you look more prosperous than fur!
>
> *The best way to meet people of wealth* (you know, our sort!) *is to look like a person of wealth yourself.* Rich people wear furs. And so should you.

Can you afford *not* to have a fur? I thought not. But before buying, you must educate yourself. Here's how.

SHARP SHOPPING

To fully appreciate the various furs, you must see them up close. Have your driver drop you at the finest salon in town, easily recognized by its location in a high-rent district. Tell the shop's sales staff that you'll be buying a coat or two in the very near

[9] Elles sont trop chères (ehl sahn troh SHEHR) means "they are too expensive."

future. They'll probably sweep you off to a private room, spend ages discussing each pelt's pros (they won't remember any cons), maybe even ply you with champagne. (Lord, I hope they select a decent vintage!)

One caution, though. With such treatment you may be tempted to reach for your Gold Card. But *don't*. Visit *several* salons first. Try on dozens of coats and jackets. Drink champagne. Have fun. And learn. Don't worry about bothering the merchants. They have their mark-ups to sustain them.

When you're ready to buy, go back to your favorite among the salons. You see, unless your social secretary is prepared to become an expert on fur, you must stay away from discount furriers. Discounters too often sell several-year-old remainders that may well have been improperly stored (which can cause their pelts to dry up like *your* skin does when you can't summer at Bar Harbor).

If you want a bargain, you'll fare better at the August and post-Christmas sales at the better furriers. (Saks Fifth Avenue has such a good one you may have to wing off to Monaco each December to avoid buying their entire caravan!) Fifty percent off is not uncommon at such sales (which, of course, gives you an excuse to buy one for your favorite author as well).

CARE AND FEEDING OF YOUR FURS

To be mistaken for a post-deb, you must behave in public as though you have been wrapped in sable since childhood and have actually become quite bored with it. Not that you shouldn't be careful with your fur. You wouldn't want to check it in just any old restaurant cloakroom and, naturally, you'll never leave it in a shared office closet or in an unguarded area at any but the most exclusive *soirée*.[10] You'll just keep a very low profile about your concern.

Private care is an entirely different matter. To keep your fur full and lustrous, you must resist the almost irresistible urge to stroke it; hands are too oily. To avoid bare spots, never brush it. And never carry a bag with an over-the-shoulder strap; it will surely carve the path to your fur's ruination!

[10] Soirée (swah RĀ) is an evening engagement or party.

Between wearings, keep your fur on a broad hanger, enclosed in a silk case (never a plastic one, which would suffocate the poor darling), and hang it in a cool closet where it won't be crushed or overheated.

Before running off to your summer residence, have your furrier clean, glaze, and store your coats and jackets; this is a must if you want them to last. Then, around Halloween, have the butler fetch them. Should they become drenched because the silly fellow forgot his umbrella (good help is *so* hard to find!), remember that a *damp* fur can be hung to dry in a well-ventilated area, but a *wet* fur must be returned to the furrier right away.

Not Fur

I suppose you'll need something to wear during those few boring months before the family lake freezes. And then there's the period after the spring thaw. (Wearing furs too early or too late looks a bit *nouveau*,[11] don't you think?)

Why not splurge on something really beautiful: a true classic in fine wool gabardine, in a color that will take you through both autumn *and* spring? Perhaps a muted pink, or taupe—one of your neutral colors.

Oh dear, I guess you'll also need a warmer coat for those unbearable occasions when the furs are at the furrier or on loan to a needy friend. Something glorious will do: perhaps double-breasted. Maybe with padded shoulders. (Calvin Klein and Bill Blass both have little numbers any sensible woman would kill to possess.)

Whatever you choose, make certain that it fits correctly, is roomy enough to cover your bulkiest jacket, and is long enough to cover the hem of *all* your winter skirts. (Mid-calf should be about right.)

Then pray for snow in the East, or a première in the West, so you'll have an excuse to get your furs back!

---

[11] Nouveau (noo VOH) means new; in this case, it is short for nouveau riche (noo voh REESH): newly rich.

It's Raining

A classic London Fog or Burberry trenchcoat is always a safe choice, but if you prefer something a bit more dramatic, try a waterproof hooded cape in one of your neutral colors. A matching umbrella is also a nice touch, and is ever so handy for thrashing through throngs of persistent *paparazzi!* [12]

Playtime

Long have I marvelled at the folly of the woman who looks like a top-flight executive in the boardroom, but like a trollop at the company picnic. So silly. The tastefulness (or tastelessness) of a color, fabric, or fit are not altered by the mere locking of an office door. Fuchsia is still fuchsia, polyester is still polyester, and too tight (too short, too low) is still tacky.

Not that I'm one of those fanatics who dress to the teeth simply to run to the corner store. That would be too exhausting. On the other hand, if you always look terrific, you will increase your chances of meeting some pretty terrific people. But then, maybe you don't care about that sort of thing. (What are you, crazy?)

Things Are Going Swimmingly

When selecting swimwear, the wise woman heeds certain rules that have been passed along through the ages:

1. Bikinis are for perfect, young bodies; maillots (mah YOH)—one-piece suits—are for everyone else.
2. If a woman needs a bodyguard to make it from the snack bar to the diving board, she should suspect that her suit is cut either too high in the leg or too low in the front or back.
3. If a woman would be *embarrassed* to have her dear old sainted mother see her suit, it is probably too daring. If she would be *delighted* to have her see it, it is probably too tame.

[12] Paparazzi (pah pah RAHTZ ee) are street photographers who snap the rich and famous.

Partytime

Le smoking.[13] The very phrase conjures up visions of David Niven in his finest dinner jacket. The woman on his arm: Isn't that Audrey Hepburn? Don't you simply adore her flowing white gown, the white fox boa, the Cartier diamonds? Ah, elegance. Ah, Hollywood.

For a real-life black-tie affair, m'lady is more likely to be turned out in a beaded cocktail dress, sexy evening pajamas, or her favorite little black dress. Only for white-tie or "full dress" occasions would she insist on a floor-length ball gown and long white kid, or doeskin, gloves.[14] And you know by now, don't you, that white-tie invitations are harder to come by than *nouvelle cuisine*[15] at McDonald's (mak DAH nuhldz)?

Now, about your choice of dress. Here are a few hints.

Think simple, so you can accessorize it differently and wear it again.

Think elegant and tasteful, so you'll be the classiest woman there.

Finally, *think correct fit,* so you can sit in it, lean over in it, dance in it, conceal your undergarments under it, and get at least one well-born friend to pass on it. Otherwise, don't wear it.

Consider this the gospel according to good taste.

Bewitched, Bothered, and Bejeweled

Ear Bobbles

Earrings add dash, a special polish. With the click of a clip, the ordinary becomes extraordinary; the mundane, world-class. But not just *any* old bobbles will do.

---

[13] Le smoking (luh SMOH keeng) means "dinner jacket" or "black tie."

[14] Long formal gloves, in white only, are an optional accessory for short-sleeved or sleeveless ball gowns.

[15] Nouvelle cuisine (noo vehl kwee ZEEN) is a lighter style of French cooking relying less on heavy sauces than did haute cuisine (oht kwee ZEEN).

An elegant black velvet evening gown, perfect for a "belle's" next "black-tie" occasion. By Jacqueline de Ribes. Photographed by Saks.

To begin your search for the most flattering styles, stand in front of a full-length mirror (something antique and beveled would be nice) and have the maid hand you various sizes and shapes. Do you look wonderful in large discs or tiny studs? In triangles or squares? In short dangles or long? In buttons or loops? In silver or gold?

Now, consider your style. Are you a Sophisticate? Today's *faux*[16] jewels and high-fashion earrings were designed just for you. Are you a Belle? You simply *must* have antique gems for those beautiful lobes of yours. Sportswomen, choose something simple and fun. And Grandes Dames, we know you'll want something medium-sized, conservative, and, of course, outrageously expensive.

One thing all you lovely ladies might want to remember: One hole in each ear will nicely accommodate the diamonds you so richly deserve. Two holes in each ear are, at best, redundant.

Ring Around the Collar

Whereas your basic diamond necklace has a certain *je ne sais quoi*,[17] alas, most necklaces don't. In fact, many are quite boring. Or worse. (I hope you're not in the habit of shooting the bearer of bad tidings.)

Topping the "boring" list is the ubiquitous single-strand pearl choker. Tell me, where is the artistry? The creativity? The imagination? To make magic, why not try a neck hugging multi-strand choker with a nice jewel in the center? Or how about several strands of salt-water pearls? Or miles of pearl rope to loop several times around your neck (some loops long; others short). Or a 36-inch-long pearl necklace coupled with one of crystals or semi-precious jewels?

Moving on to the "worse" list, let me just say that if you cannot, in good conscience, describe your costume necklaces as *true works of art*, toss 'em. A strand of red plastic beads does not a masterpiece make. Ditto fake gold. Ditto yesteryear's gold chains.

[16] Faux (foh) means false; or, in this case, obviously fake.
[17] Je ne sais quoi (zhuhn sā KWAH) means "I don't know what" or "that special something."

The truly trendy must follow *current* trends. If you have any doubts about the appropriateness of a necklace, leave it off. Understatement and elegance are virtually synonymous.

Ring Around the Finger

I have a marvelous garnet ring. It's large, oval, and antique, left to me by my maternal grandmother. Because of its deep red color, it goes with everything I own. Because it is unusual and dramatic, it never fails to draw compliments. Yet, surprisingly, it is the least expensive piece of jewelry I own. Just goes to show you: Style is really everything.

Incidentally, I seldom wear more than one ring on each hand. If a ring is beautiful, it shouldn't have to fight competition. And if it isn't beautiful, why wear it?

Grooming for the Great

One of my least favorite television advertisements tells the tale of a strikingly beautiful young woman who has lost Mr. Right because (brace yourself) she scratched her head. Much to his horror, the lady had D-A-N-D-R-U-F-F!

Well, I for one know who's the *real* flake in this commercial, and shampoo couldn't help him. Still, this poignant little slice of life *does* point out the importance of good grooming. And though one scratch will probably not ostracize you from polite society forever, chipped polish and purple eye shadow aren't likely to win you any well-placed friends either.

So, the moral to this charming little tale is this: Pay attention to your grooming or no one good will pay attention to you. (Or something like that.)

Hands-On Experience

Few things betray a woman's status faster than her hands. Those of a working woman too often expose (if you'll pardon the expression) signs of labor, while a socialite's hands reveal absolutely nothing.

The lady of wealth treats her hands like prized possessions. Do you? Do you slather them with oodles of cream and lotion, and have weekly manicures? Do you keep them under cashmere-lined kid gloves while wintering in St. Moritz (san moh RITZ)? And do you don special gloves when riding to hounds or racing your Maserati?

And what about your fingernails? Are they brittle, always breaking? Do they curl down at the tips like claws, or turn up like miniature ski jumps? Then my advice is: Keep them short, and use only a subtle, nonfrosted polish; better yet, shine them with a buffing compound. Drawing attention to our imperfections is not one of our major goals.

What should you do if you really *must* have long nails? Well, if your compulsion is teamed with plenty of time and money, then you might consider having porcelain nails applied. Go to a world-class salon and investigate the process thoroughly. You may discover that the possible damage to your own nails makes this investment pretty risky.

What's that? You were born with fantastic nails? Lucky you. Make the best of this asset by keeping them long (though not Manchurian) and colorfully laquered. As you may have guessed, I prefer a clear, true red polish (today's favorite is Elizabeth Arden's Restless Red), though you might like coral, wine, pink, tan, cinnamon, rose beige—anything that isn't glaring, too bright, too pale, or frosted (which I think causes nails to peel). Incidentally, I believe that *no* polish is the worst thing for fingernails. Polish strengthens nails and makes them more resistant to peeling and breaking. And, because it's a royal pain to keep reapplying, it makes you think twice before using your nails for crowbars.

Of course, even if you pamper your nails, the polish will eventually chip. The very second yours does, smudge the area using a cotton swab soaked in polish remover, rinse and dry hands, then apply a small "patch" of lacquer. When polish has set, give the whole nail a new coat. *Et voilà!*[18] Perfection.

---

[18] Et voilà (eh vwah LAH) means "And there you have it!"

If the chip is the result of a tear or break—perish the thought!—repair the nail before proceeding. For little breaks I use instant glue. For real trouble I use instant glue and Revlon's "Nail Mender" papers. Together, these form a bond which could have kept even Sonny and Cher together.

The Sweet Smell of Success

Which fragrance you choose is up to you and your true love, but please remember:

> *Parfum* (pahr FUHM) is finer than *eau de toilette* (oh duh twah LEHT), which in turn is finer than *eau de cologne* (oh duh koh LOH nyuh), which in turn is finer than anything called a "scent" or a "splash."
>
> If you're going to wear an inexpensive scent, choose a brand that the whole world won't immediately recognize.
>
> Apply scent long before entering boardrooms, elevators, automobiles, and my immediate vicinity. Please. Fragrance should be obvious only to someone close enough to kiss.

The Aristocratic Face

Though you will never create the illusion of wealth with mere makeup alone, inept application can destroy all your other efforts.

What makes a face look priviledged? What makes it look *middle class?* As luck would have it, this section has the answers.

Upper-Class Complexions

Wealthy young matrons have beautiful skin. Their dermatologists and facialists wouldn't have it any other way. Here are some of their pesky former problems, along with their very classy solutions. (I'm a real sucker for happy endings.)

Pesky Problems	Instant Relief	Long-Term Solutions
ACNE	Sparingly dot on a medicated cover-up cream under your foundation. (Stop picking!)	New acne treatments are absolutely astonishing. Ask your dermatologist about Retin-A creams, about an over-the-counter cleanser called Hibiclens, and about a cream called Clear by Design. People with really severe acne which has not previously responded to treatment should ask about Accutane.
AGING SKIN	Retard the aging process and ease dryness with moisturizers (applied to slightly damp skin); select one with a sun block to protect against sun damage; use it year round. Dab eye cream at corners of each eye.	Ask your dermatologist about various techniques designed to soften wrinkles, fine lines, and small scars: peeling, dermabrasion, and the new process of collagen injection. Make sure to investigate side effects and contraindications, and consult several doctors before proceeding.
BROKEN CAPILLARIES AND RED BIRTHMARKS	Conceal redness with green-tinted cover-up cream (like Shiseido's "Green Veil" stick foundation) under your makeup base.	Dermatologists can remove many of them, though some may return.

Pesky Problems	Instant Relief	Long-Term Solutions
BROWN BIRTH-MARKS AND FRECKLES	Use a good foundation, but go easy on attempts at concealment; your efforts may simply appear chalky and artificial.	Discuss possible removal with your dermatologist; ask if you might expect a tiny scar. Also, be certain to show your doctor any brown mole that itches, bleeds, or changes color; it could be dangerous.
DARK CIRCLES UNDER EYES	Apply a good concealer (like Germaine Monteil's Super Moist Hides Anything) *only* to dark parts of the area. Finish with a foundation with top coverage, like Shiseido's Stick Foundation.	Ask your dermatologist if anything can be done to improve the appearance of the area. Always treat eyes with utmost care; dab on make-up and creams—do not rub.
DRY SKIN	Moisturize! Moisturize! Moisturize! (Even people with oily skin should use a light moisturizer after age 35.)	Have your dermatologist prescribe a special cleanser or use a mild soap like Neutragena.
LIVER SPOTS	Proceed as for "Brown Birthmarks."	Speak to your dermatologist about removal.
SCARS	Try a good cover-up under your foundation.	If the scar is recessed, proceed as for solutions listed under "Aging Skin." If it's elevated, ask your doctor what could be done to improve the appearance.
SHINY NOSE/OILY "T" ZONE	Try a water- or glycerine-based founda-	Dermatologist and skin-care salons have special

Pesky Problems	Instant Relief	Long-Term Solutions
SHINY NOSE/OILY "T" ZONE	tion and a light dusting with translucent pressed powder; use linen blotting tissues.	cleansing lotions to help control oil flow. Also, ask your doctor about wearing Clear by Design under your makeup.
UNEVEN PIGMENTATION	Apply cover-up creams under your foundation: green cover-up for reddish areas; skin-colored creams elsewhere.	Dermatologists may be able to help. Also, try discontinuing your brand of perfume; some cause hypersensitivity to the sun which may result in mottling. Birth control pills may also cause uneven pigmentation, so speak with your gynecologist if you suspect they could be causing the problem.

Prominent's Cheekbones

For reasons only a few geneticists truly understand, trust funds cause high cheekbones. Shocking, yes. But true.

Fortunately, though we upwardly mobile types have a hard time conjuring up trust funds, we can easily create the illusion of great bones. Here's how:

STEP ONE: Apply under-eye concealer, as necessary, to obliterate traces of your champagne hangover. Then, using short upward strokes, blend a thin coat of foundation over the face. (Make certain that foundation color matches jawline and neck color *exactly*.)

STEP TWO: If you have dry skin, mix a small amount of cream blush with a few drops of moisturizer in the palm of your hand. If you have oily or blemished skin, whisk powdered blush onto a large sable brush (not the brush that comes with the blush). *Blow off the excess.* (Note: Blush color should complement lip color.)

STEP THREE: Suck in your cheeks like a well-bred fish and apply blush from a point directly beneath the center of your eye, along the underpart of the bone, all the way to your hairline.

STEP FOUR: Blend very, very well.

STEP FIVE: Repeat Step Two and apply a hint of color to your temples, forehead, chin, and the bridge of your nose.

STEP SIX: Dip a clean sable brush into translucent powder, blow off the excess, and dust your entire face.

STEP SEVEN: Blot face with a slightly damp silk sponge to remove excess powder and create a soft look.

STEP EIGHT: Pucker up again. You're bound to be kissed!

Patrician Proboscises

Chiseled noses are *de rigueur*[19] for women of wealth, though I would venture a guess that seven out of ten have been, shall we say, surgically assisted. As such help is far less expensive than it used to be, you might consider giving Mummy Nature a little help yourself—if you're not thrilled with her original handiwork. If you *do* opt for surgery, be certain to consult a board-certified plastic surgeon, and insist on chatting with several of his patients. Better for *him* to get his nose bent out of shape than you! *N'est-ce pas?*[20]

Of course, you can always improve on what nature gave you without such drastic measures. Just pull out your contour pencils and powders and either draw a light strip down the center of your nose or subtly shade down both sides. Blend the contouring well, so no one can tell.

Elite Eyes

You could read thirty books on eye makeup techniques and still make mistakes. Some encouragement, eh?

[19] De rigueur (duh ree GUHR) means "fashionable" or "required."
[20] N'est-ce pas? (ness PAH) means "Is it not so?"

Because each eye is a special combination of brow, bone, lid, and color, you really need the individual attention of a pro. Better yet, *two* pros. So why not sign up for lessons with *several* makeup artists (found at hairstyling and facial salons—not department stores). Of course, each lesson may cost thirty or forty dollars, but if you're like me, that's but a fraction of what you've already wasted on unflattering cosmetics.

One caution. Though your artists will no doubt be absolute whizzes at contouring and highlighting, they may be unaware that you travel in such rarefied circles. So after learning a few tricks of the trade, you might want to make certain that you also:

Use a soft brow powder to lightly feather in brow hairs and add color (after having your brows shaped by a professional). Strive to avoid a harsh, artificial look. Keep brows in place all day with a sealer. My favorite is from Vidal Sassoon.

To help keep shadows beautiful all day, try Elizabeth Arden's Eye-Fix Primer (or a similar product). Apply foundation and translucent powder, then shadows.

Select lid colors to match your eyes, not your clothes. This means gray shadow for gray eyes, brown for brown, etc. If you have blue eyes, proceed carefully. Teal or gray-blue will be far more flattering than a color that is bluer than your eyes.

If you like, add soft color just under your lower lashes with an eye pencil that matches your shadow color.

For dark contouring, raven-haired beauties should use gray; brunettes and redheads should use brown; blonds should use taupe.

For light contouring, use cream, peach, or pink. White too often looks artificial and harsh.

Under the brow use only the most subtle neutral tones. Reddish shadows make you look like you just plucked your brows. And yellowish shadows, well, one shouldn't have to pay to look jaundiced.

About mascara: Charcoal and brown-black are for brunettes; brown or gray is for everyone else (except carhops, who look sensational in blue and green). Apply several coats to upper

and lower lashes, remembering that you are looking for a
pretty fringe, not a gooey curtain.

Throw out your false lashes unless you have no lashes at all.
They look hopelessly dated.

Remember that less is always more, especially for daytime.
Your goal is merely to enhance your eyes, not advertise for
Estée Lauder.

For evening, intensify daytime colors. Add gold or silver
"sparkle" if you like.

Millionaire Mouths

A sexy mouth consists of perfect teeth and beautiful lips. More
specifically:

THE TEETH

The first thing a new celebrity does upon achieving notoriety is
have her teeth straightened and/or capped. She knows the value of
a beautiful smile. Do you?

If you want to look rich and famous, but your teeth are less
than straight, visit an orthodontist. Modern techniques are less
costly, and more invisible, than you would ever believe.

If you would like whiter teeth, have a chat with your dentist.
He, too, has new techniques—like bonding, an inexpensive alternative to capping. Listen to what he says, and if it makes sense,
proceed.

THE LIPS

Sumptuous, kissable lips are as easy as counting to five:

1. Select a lipstick that matches, or complements, the color of
   the neckline of your garment. If the outfit you're planning
   to wear would necessitate your choosing an unflattering lip
   color, find another outfit. *You* deserve to look sensational!
2. Carefully outline lips using a pencil that *exactly* matches
   your lipstick. Trace just inside the lip line to lessen fullness,
   just *outside* to increase it.
3. Using a lip brush, apply lip color. Add a *slightly* lighter

shade to the center of your lower lip, if you like, to produce a sexy "pout."

4. Blot lips. Reapply color and blot again for more intensity.

5. Apply a light coat of clear gloss.

Hairdos and Don'ts

Real Style

If there is anything I regret, it is having waited so long to take my hair to Vidal Sassoon. They are so particular there! My regular stylist spends an hour just trimming my hair (shampoo and blow dry add another thirty minutes). And if you can believe it, on a recent visit to New York my sister had to have her cut approved before they would even consent to set it! You see, when you walk out of Sassoon's, they expect you to look perfect. And you generally do.

Don't *you* wait another day to invest in the very best cut your money can buy. Call the top salon in the nearest "big-time" city. (Find them advertised in magazines like *Mademoiselle* [mahd mwah ZEHL] and *Glamour*.)

If the owner still takes private clients (Vidal doesn't), try to get an appointment—even if you have to wait six weeks, even if he charges more than the other stylists.[21] If the owner isn't available, say something like "I have short curly hair and work for a conservative law firm (sing in a rock group, never leave home); can you suggest a stylist for me?"

Expect to spend at least two hours in the salon, more if you're having a manicure, brow arching, waxing, or makeup lesson—all of which I highly recommend. (You and I are so good at being pampered!)

One caution. While you're there, resist the urge to tell your stylist how to do his or her job; you would be surprised at how often he has to dissuade someone from trying Farrah's or Joan Col-

---

[21] Never inquire about price prior to making an appointment. And don't gasp when they respond. It's considered bad form.

lins's newest cut. You've come to the best; trust him. Tell him only what he needs to know: information on your lifestyle, your basic image (sophisticated, sporty, etc.), how much time you're willing to spend maintaining your hair, how tall you are, and any coloring or permanent solution currently affecting your hair. Then, if your *coiffeur*[22] suggests that the time has come to cut your hip-long tresses, or grow out your Mohawk, or loose the magenta streaks, listen! Ask his reasoning, and if it appears sound, forge ahead. If, however, it sounds as though he is merely pushing the look-of-the-month, keep on questioning. You need a style that's right for you.

Now, let's say that it's a week or so after the styling, you've adapted the cut to your life, and you love it. Unfortunately, your new hairdresser is too far away. Or too expensive. What should you do?

Quick! Take a half-dozen photographs of your new do—from various angles. Then, you can have your regular stylist copy it. (If you have no regular stylist, or hate the one you have, stop several well-coiffed women and ask them who does their hair. They'll be so flattered they'll certainly tell all.)

What if you don't like your big-time cut? Well, you did check out the other hairdressers while you were there, didn't you? Then go back, and keep going back, until you look great. I assure you, the investment in time and money will be well worth it.

Mouse-Brown to Marvelous

Few things alter your appearance as radically as a change in hair color. This is good *if* you are making a choice which looks both natural and more flattering (which, in reality, few do), and *if* you are willing to be scrupulous in its maintenance (which, in reality, few are). Given these constraints, those who are determined to proceed should consider these points:

Hair color is but one aspect of overall coloring. Thus, to
improve your appearance, you must also consider your

---

[22] Coiffeur (kwah FUHR) refers to a male hairdresser; a female is called a coiffeuse (kwah FUHZ).

complexion and eyes. Desire must never be primary!

Young women with dark brown or black hair are invariably better off with their natural colors. Frosting and streaking always look artificial. If you *must* make a change, go only a shade or two darker—but never all the way to jet black.

After age forty, women with very dark hair may want to go a shade or two lighter to soften their appearance. If so, those women who look best in earth tones should select "warm" browns or auburns. Those who look best in true red, Chinese blue, or black should choose ash browns; for them, reddish tones could be disastrous.

Women with light brown hair who want to go blond should take similar care. Those who look best in soft earth tones (honey, peach, cream) should move towards the golden blond shades; those flattered by pastels (powder blue, powder pink, lavender) must select ash tones. A last hint: Frosting can look very rich and chic on both younger and older women, may be entered into gradually, and requires less maintenance than a complete "dye job." Why not give it a try before resorting to dye?

Whatever you do, don't go so light or so dark that your hair color looks unnatural. If you suspect that you've crossed the fine line between exquisite and artificial, why not ask a few trusted friends (telling them, just this once, to be absolutely honest)? If they nix the color, do it over again. What is money, after all, when your reputation is at stake?

Madcap Hatter

You're not going to squash that beautiful new *coiffure*[23] of yours under a hat, are you?

Well, maybe.

The right hat at the right time on the right woman can look

---

[23] Coiffure (kwah FOOR) is a hairdo.

positively smashing. But the wrong hat, the wrong time, the wrong woman: What a mess!

If you look great in hats, you probably already know it. Envious friends (and your mirror) will have told you so many times. Still, it is important to remember to:

Select a hat appropriate to the season. Straw is for spring and summer only; felt and wool are for winter and fall only.

Check the size, shape, and proportion of the hat in relation to your body as well as your face and head.

Feel free to wear your hat while drinking or dining, but remove it if you'll be indoors for an extended stay.

Never wear a hat to a Broadway play; at today's prices, obstructing someone's view could be hazardous to your health.

Fashion Passes, Style Remains

—Coco Chanel

Knowing *what* to wear is but half your battle. *How* you wear it still remains.

A woman of style is more than well-dressed and well-groomed. And she is much more than beautiful.

She is elegant. Charming. She is polite to other people.

She walks head high and tall, as aware of others as she is of herself.

So, as fashion passes and fads are laid to rest, she still has what it takes. In short, she is a lady.

Shopping for Socialites

Well, lady, don't just sit there! It's time to go shopping. But don't worry, it won't tire you, nor will it muss a single hair on that exquisite head of yours. You need only turn the page.

Personal Shoppers

Personal shopping services, designed for those of us who would rather make deals than purchases, come in as many varieties as Tiffany has diamonds.

If money is no object (Lord, I love how that sounds!), you can employ an *independent* personal shopper. He or she, who may also be a wardrobe or color consultant, can handle any number of tasks for you. (Some buy wholesale and can even save you money.)

Locate shoppers in your Yellow Pages. (In Manhattan, they're under "Shopping Services—Personal.") Talk to several before making a choice, and ask for references. Expect to pay by the hour, day, or job.

If you don't mind making all your purchases at one establishment, you'll adore the free, or almost free, services available at many of the larger stores. Manhattan's Saks Fifth Avenue, for example, has five such services. To acquaint you with all the wonderful things they (and others) will do, and to suggest ways to enjoy them to the fullest, I have outlined them below.

THE INTERNATIONAL SHOPPING SERVICE boasts multilingual operators, fluent in 29 languages, to assist patrons who prefer shopping in a language other than English. *Français* (frahn SĀ), anyone?

THE PERSONAL SHOPPING SERVICE does for all of us what secretaries used to do for their bosses. (No, not that!) I mean they shop for us when we're too busy, and they're absolute wizards at finding the perfect gift. Just ring up your shopper when you need a navy blazer, and she'll assemble the finest in your size and hold them for your approval.

When you can't decide what your mother-in-law deserves for her birthday (be nice now), your personal shopper will find something divine for you; then she'll wrap it, charge it, and have it delivered to the lady's door. You'll never have to set foot in the store (or your mother-in-law's house). Now that's a bargain!

Here's a trick of a rich matron who adores trying on lovely frocks, but detests the waiting, charging, and totting aspects of shopping. After selecting what she wants, she records all the pertinent information (style numbers, designers' names, sizes, colors, etc.), then leaves the store.

Later, after a massage and facial at Arden's, she calls her personal shopper. The purchases are sent over before the effects of the massage have worn off.

THE EXECUTIVE SERVICE, for women only, is the *crème de la crème*[1] of personal shopping services. An annual membership fee of fifty dollars (at this writing) gets you your own personal shopping consultant—someone who knows you, keeps records of your sizes and preferences, and reminds you to buy a gift for your parents' anniversary.

She will arrange for priority alterations and same-day delivery. And should you grow ravenous while browsing through the Anne Klein boutique, she will arrange light sustenance; should you collapse from the excitement of finding that perfect gown, she'll arrange a private car to whisk you home, and bill the fare to your account.

Naturally, you'll get advance notice of "happenings" in the store: fashion shows, designer visits, and such. And did I mention that when your agent needs to find you in a hurry, your shopper will speed the message to you?

Saks has two other special services that may be of interest:

---

[1] Crème de la crème (krehm duh lah krehm, *not* kreem duh lah kreem) means "best of the best."

THE CONVENTION AND VISITORS SERVICE exists to pamper visitors to New York, offering them deluxe personalized shopping. Call in advance or make arrangements through the Saks store in your home town.

THE STUDIO SERVICE will help you with your wardrobe when you're ready to star on Broadway or be a guest on the "Tonight Show." They wouldn't hear of your making your debut without their expert advice!

Another Way

If you've sunken into despair because you neither live in Manhattan nor have plans to visit soon, relax. Other Saks branches offer personalized shopping, as do Bloomingdale's, Filene's, Marshall Field, Lord & Taylor, Sakowitz, Neiman-Marcus—the list is as long as that of first-class department stores. Call one in your area, or consult "Crazy About Catalogs," page 83.

If you live so far from the madding crowd that you shop exclusively in *boutiques*,[2] you can acquire personal shopping attention with minimal effort.

Start by cultivating good working relationships with experienced sales clerks in your favorite shops. Good manners, charm, and continued patronage will bring wonderful results.

Next, establish charge accounts with several of this country's best stores—say, Saks, Bergdorf Goodman, Neiman-Marcus, and Bloomingdale's. Between their shopping services and catalogs, you'll have access to the world's most exquisite merchandise.

Professional Advice

A last word about the care and feeding of personal shoppers and sales clerks. Remember that these people are professionals, de-

---

[2] Boutiques is pronounced "boo TEEKS," not "boh TEEKS."

serving of your consideration. So don't tip them when they perform difficult or time-consuming tasks for you. Send flowers instead, or at least a lovely note. Letters of praise to their superiors are a nice idea, too. Besides, after they went to all the trouble of having that elegant stationery personalized for you, the very least you can do is use it.

Designer Dictionary

You may never have seen a dictionary quite like this one before. And for good reason!

Even members of a single family are often at odds on how to pronounce the family name. They may even disagree on how to spell it! Thus, arriving at a consensus can prove to be a bit challenging.

But then, challenge is my middle name, especially if it means hours wandering through Saks, Bergdorf's, Bonwit's, Bloomies. . . .

Anyway, here's what I found:

Adolfo (ah DAHL foh)
Armani, Giorgio (JOHR gee oh   ar MAH nee)
Balenciaga (bah lehn CYAH gah)
Balmain, Pierre (PYEHR   bahl MA*n*)
Borghese, Marcella (mahr CHĀ lah   bohr GHĀ zeh)
Cacharel (kash ar REHL)
Capraro, Albert (kah PREHR oh)
Cardin, Pierre (PYEHR   kahr DA*n*)
Cerruti, Nino (NEE noh   chehr ROO tee)
Chanel (shah NEHL)
Chereskin, Ron (sheh RESH kin)
Chloé (KLOH ee)
Courrèges (koor REHZH)
De la Renta, Oscar (dā lah REHN tah)
De Ribes, Jacqueline (zhah kleen   duh REEB)
Ferragamo, Salvadore (sahl vah DOH rā   fehr rah GAH moh)

Ferre, Gianfranco (gyan FRAHN koh   fehr RĀ)
Dior, Christian (krees TYEHn   DYOHR)
Fabergé (fah behr ZHĀ)
Gernreich, Rudi (ROO dee   GEHRN rīk)
Givenchy (ZHEE vahn SHEE)
Grès, Madame (mah DAHM   GRĀ)
Grethel, Henry (GREH thul)
Gucci (GOO chee)
Guerlain (guhr LEHn)
Hechter, Daniel (dahn YEHL   hesh TEHR)
Hermès (ehr MĀ)
Herrera, Carolina (kehr oh LEE nah   heh RĀR rah)
Houbigant (oo bee GAHn)
Jaeger (YEH guhr)
Kamali, Norma (kah MAH lee)
Krizia (KRIT zyuh)
Lanvin (lahn VAn)
Lancôme (lahn KOHM)
Lagerfeld, Karl (LAH guhr feld)
Lauder, Estée (ess tā   LAH duhr)
Lauren, Ralph (LOHR rehn)
L'Oréal (loh rā YAHL)
Matsuda (maht SOO tah)
Monteil, Germaine (zhehr MEHN   mohn TEH)
Missoni (mih SOH nee)
Nipon, Albert (NIP ahn)
Pablo (PAH bloh)
Patou, Jean (ZHAHn   pah TOO)
Pietrovanni (pyeh troh VAH nee)
Pucci (POO chee)
Rabanne, Paco (PAH koh   rah BAHN)
Ricci, Nina (NEE nah   REE chee)
Rykiel, Sonia (SOHN yah   ree KYEHL)
Rochas, Madame (mah DAHM   roh SHAH)
Ruffini (ruh FEE nee)
St. Laurent, Yves (EEV   san loh RAHn)
Shiseido (shuh SĀ doh)

Trigère, Pauline (tree ZHEHR)
Ungaro (OON gah roh)
Valentino (vah lehn TEE noh)
Versace, Gianni (GYAH nee vehr SAH chā)
Vittadini, Adrienne (Ā dree ehn vih tah DEE nee)
Vollbracht, Michaele (MĪ kuhl vohl BRAKT)
Von Fürstenberg, Diane (vahn FUHR stehn berg)
Yamamoto, Kansai (KAHN sī yah mah MOH toh)
Yamamoto, Yohji (YOH gee yah mah MOH toh)

7

· THE BEAUTIFUL PERSON'S BAR GUIDE ·

*I always keep a supply of stimulant handy
in case I see a snake—which I also keep
handy.*

—W . C . FIELDS

Clients and employers can drive you to drink. But that's the *good* news. The *bad* news is that they are likely to join you.

So how's your martini? Your Manhattan? Your *Pousse-café* (POOSS kah FĀ)? Can you make an *Americano* (ah meh ree KAH noh)? And turn it into a *Negroni* (neh GROH nee)? Can you pronounce *Curaçao* (KOOR uh SOH)? And *Byrrh* (BEER)? And *crème de menthe* (krehm duh MAHNT)?

If your bartending prowess leaves something to be desired, you are going to love this chapter. It's filled with enough information about *apéritif* (ah peh ree TEEF), cocktail, and *liqueur* (lee KUHR) service to turn you into the best bartender in town (though I remind you that your mother expects more from you than that).

The Bar

Whether you drink or not, you need a bar in or near your entertaining area. Nothing too extravagant: an antique brass cart, a

Exquisite crystal "Rotary" flacon and bar glasses from Steuben Glass.

small corner table, a well-appointed wet bar—all will do nicely. What will *not* do is six feet of studded black leather, matching macho stools, and a sign reading "Joe's Place." A miniscule area beneath the kitchen sink isn't any better.

The bar should reflect your good taste, your knowledge of fine liquors, and your desire to please your guests. It should be well-stocked with an assortment of popular beverages, mixers, condiments. But don't overdo; guests might suspect you have a drinking problem.

The expense of setting up a bar might seem staggering—especially if you're starting from scratch—but you may relax in the knowledge that the equipment lasts for years; some of the liquor, almost as long. Besides, alcohol is so much a part of your business and social life, can you really afford to skimp?

Here's what you'll need.

Equipment

blender
bottle and can openers
cocktail napkins
cocktail picks
cocktail strainer
cocktail straws
corkscrew
cutting board
ice bucket and tongs
ice pick
jiggers: 1½ ounce and 2 ounce
juice extractor
mallet or ice cracker

martini pitcher and stirrer
measuring cup
paring knife
shaker
slotted spoon
swizzle sticks
towels
water pitcher

Optional
ice crusher
lemon zester
refrigerator

Staples

Mixers
bitter lemon
bottled spring water

Flavorings
Angostura (an gos TOOR ah)
  bitters

Mixers (continued)

club soda/Perrier (pehr YĀ)
cola
diet soda
ginger ale/7 Up
juices (tomato, orange, etc.)
mineral water
tonic water

Garnishes
cocktail olives
cocktail onions
lemons and limes
maraschino (MEH ruh SHEE
 noh) cherries

Flavorings (continued)

Grenadine (GREHN nuh
 DEEN)
salt and pepper
sugar: superfine and con-
 fectioners'
Tabasco sauce
Worcestershire (WUHS tuh
 sheer) sauce

Optional
cinnamon
mint
nutmeg
Orange Flower Water
oranges

The Class Glass

Glassware needs vary dramatically from one household to another depending on family size, dining and entertaining preferences, and drinking habits.[1] Most households, however, will need at least a dozen each of the following glasses:

All-purpose wine   Highball   Old-fashioned

At least eight of these glasses are also needed:[2]

Cocktail   Brandy Snifter   Liqueur/Cordial

Choose among the more specialized glasses pictured on page 168 according to your needs.

Cocktail Napkins

Drinks served without napkins or coasters invite the clothing stains and table-top rings that make your maids so cranky! Beautiful coasters and monogrammed linen napkins are nicest, though plain or monogrammed paper napkins—without cutesy jokes or pictures—are always acceptable.

To display paper napkins for a party, try placing a stack of napkins (at least one inch high) on a flat, non-skid surface and cover with a small saucer. Press down on the saucer with the palm of your hand, and slowly rotate it clockwise. Stop when the napkins are fanned into a crescent, or continue until they form a full circle.

---

[1] For anything other than poolside use, plastic glasses are tacky. Your guests deserve fine, handblown glassware of the best quality you can afford. If you need large quantities for a party, rent them from a caterer or party supply house.

[2] Note: Hold goblets by their stems to avoid warming cold drinks. Cradle brandy snifters in the hand to heat the liquid, thereby improving the flavor and bouquet.

Saucer-type "Champagne"
or Sherbet Glass
(not recommended for champagne)

Champagne

Pilsner Beer Glass

Sherry

Tending Bar

More important than the finest ingredients, more necessary than
the latest equipment, is technique. Make yours perfect by following these suggestions.

    Always chill glasses for cold drinks. Place them in the freezer
      for a few minutes, or the refrigerator for a few hours.

    Go easy on the liquor. When Mark Twain said, "Too much of
      anything is bad, but too much whiskey is just enough," he
      failed to consider the effect of too much alcohol on the taste

of a mixed drink or the nervous system of an unsuspecting guest.

Use only the freshest, finest ingredients. Carbonated drinks must bubble briskly; lemon and lime juices must be fresh; liquors must be of fine quality (unless they will be mixed with sweet or sour ingredients); and instant mixes and bottled mixed drinks must be avoided.

Use bottled water for mixing drinks and making ice unless your community has wonderful tap water. Make ice early and keep in bags to avoid freezer odors. Better yet, buy ice the day of your party.

Stir clear drinks gently. Shake cloudy drinks vigorously (or add the liquor last and stir well).

Handle ice with tongs, condiments with picks. You wouldn't stick your fingers into a guest's martini, so keep them off his ice and olive!

Measure all ingredients accurately and use the proper terminology and techniques:

MEASURES

dash   6-8 drops; ⅙ teaspoon
jigger   1½ ounces
large jigger   2 ounces
pony   1 ounce

TERMS

frosted   glass placed in the freezer until it looks frosty
frosted rim   glass rim first dipped in citrus juice, then in salt or sugar
neat   drink containing no mix or ice
muddle   mash together ingredients using a pestle-like muddler
squeeze   small wedge of lemon or lime squeezed over a drink, then dropped in
standing   drink with no ice (usually refers to martinis)
stir   mix gently

straight   drink with no mixer added

twist   1½-by-¼-inch sliver of lemon rind twisted over, then
   dropped into, a drink

up   drink containing no ice

Garnish drinks properly. A martini isn't a martini without an
   olive. In fact, the mere swap of the olive for an onion turns it
   into a Gibson. Garnishes do count!

Handle the drinks carefully. Avoid mishaps by filling glasses no
   more than two-thirds full and by wiping away excess moisture. When passing several drinks, use a tray. And keep your
   fingers away from the glasses' rims.

Save decanters for sediment-laden wines, Vintage Ports, and
   "no-name" brandies and liqueurs. Fine liquors are more impressive when displayed in their bottles (so others can see the
   labels).

Match the drink to the occasion: apéritifs before meals, cocktails
   at parties and during the afternoon, and brandies and liqueurs
   after dinner and late in the evening. Complete details ahead.

Apéritifs

Sweet cocktails, or multiple servings of any liquor, destroy the
appetite. So save "hard" drinking for cocktail parties and evenings
at the disco. Before meals, be kind to your palate; drink apéritifs.

When entertaining, offer apéritifs casually: "I'm having sherry.
Will you join me?" And don't forget to consider the character of
the meal ahead.

Try *Pernod* (pehr NOH), *Kir* (KEER), or *Dubonnet* (doo buh
NÃ) before a French meal; before Italian food, *Campari* (kahm
PAH ree); before any delicately-flavored meal, dry champagne,
dry sherry, white wine, or vermouth *Cassis* (kah SEESS).

But first, a word of warning. Just as Scotch is seldom appreciated the first time it is tasted, neither are many apéritifs. So don't
give up too soon.

Here are some drinks to try.

Americano (ah mehr ree KAH noh)
   Into an old-fashioned glass pour:
      2 ounces Bitter Campari
      2 ounces Italian vermouth (sweet)

   Add ice, stir well, and finish with a twist of lemon.

Bitter Campari (kahm PAH ree) is an Italian bitters flavored
   with orange peel and herbs.
   Into a highball glass pour:
      1 ounce Bitter Campari
   Fill glass with:
      Club soda

   Note: You may want to add a dash of Grenadine until you
      become accustomed to the bitter taste.

Byrrh (beer) is a French wine-based apéritif flavored with
   quinine. Serve it over ice in an old-fashioned glass.

Champagne is served in a tulip- or flute-shaped glass, or an all-
   purpose wine glass—never the shallow, saucer-shaped glass
   usually associated with champagne; that glass allows all those
   expensive bubbles to escape too quickly. Choose a well-
   chilled extra dry *(brut)* champagne to serve before meals. A
   domestic wine will do nicely; save magnificent imported
   wines for formal dinners and special occasions. (See "Which
   Wine?" on page 11 for more details.)

Champagne Cocktail
   Into a champagne, or all-purpose, glass put:
      1 lump (1 teaspoon) sugar
      1 dash Angostura Bitters
   Fill glass with:
      Chilled champagne *(brut* or extra dry)
   Add, if you like:
      A twist of lemon

Champagne With Fruit
>Into a champagne, or all-purpose, glass put:
>>2–3 cold, clean strawberries
>
>or
>>1–2 slices of fresh peach
>
>Fill glass with:
>>Chilled champagne (*brut* or extra dry)

>Serve before breakfast or brunch.

Dubonnet (doo buh NĀ), the darling of France, is a sweet red or white aromatized wine. Serve "up" in a six-ounce sherry glass or as below.
>Into an old-fashioned glass pour:
>>2–3 ounces Dubonnet
>
>Add:
>>A splash of soda
>>A twist of lemon

Kir (keer)
>Into an all-purpose wineglass put:
>>Several small ice cubes
>
>Add:
>>6 ounces dry white wine
>>½ ounce crème de cassis
>
>Mix gently and garnish with:
>>A twist of lemon

Kir Royale (KEER roy YAHL) is *Kir* made with champagne in place of white wine. Also see *Champagne* for service suggestions.

Lillet (lee LĀ) is a semidry French apéritif made from white wine and brandy (bottled together). Serve like *Dubonnet*.

Negroni (neh GROH nee)
>Into an old-fashioned glass pour:
>>1½ ounces Bitter Campari

    1½ ounces gin
    1½ ounces Italian vermouth (sweet)
Stir, and add:
    A twist of lemon
    A splash of soda

Pernod (pehr NOH) is a popular anise-flavored apéritif from
    France.
    Into a slotted spoon place:
        1 sugar lump
    Hold spoon over an old-fashioned glass containing:
        Several ice cubes
        2 ounces Pernod
    Pour through the spoon into the glass:
        Enough ice water to turn the Pernod cloudy (several
        ounces).
    Mix gently.

Sherry is served neat in a six-ounce sherry glass. Choose dry—
    Fino (FEE noh)—sherry only. (Sweet sherries are best *after*
    meals, unless you're a blue-haired old lady, in which case
    you can drink them anytime.)

Vermouth (vuhr MOOTH), the extra-dry French variety, is
    served like Dubonnet. (Sweet Italian vermouth is best
    served *after* meals.)

Vermouth Cassis (vuhr mooth kah SEESS)
    Into an old-fashioned glass put:
        Several ice cubes
        2 ounces extra-dry French vermouth
    Add:
        ½ ounce crème de cassis
    Then:
        2 ounces chilled club soda
    Stir, and add:
        A lemon twist

White Wine is served chilled in a white wine, or all-purpose, glass. Choose a dry wine of good, but not great, quality. (Special wines are for special meals.)

Wine Spritzer
Into a highball glass put:
   ½ cup cracked ice
Add:
   4 ounces dry or fruity white wine
Fill the glass with:
   Club soda
Garnish with:
   A twist of lemon

Cocktails

If you care about maintaining your image as a sophisticate (and who doesn't?), you must pay special attention to what you drink and when you drink it. So:

Avoid frozen, slushy, fancy drinks (except on hot summer afternoons). These drinks, and those made with colas and other sweet mixers, are the alcoholic equivalents of bubble gum. Not exactly elegant, not cherished in high society. And as if that weren't enough, they also completely demolish your appetite!

Match your drink to the season. A summer cooler like gin and tonic seems as out of place in mid-winter as a slice of watermelon.

Order as specifically as possible. "I will have Chivas neat, please" shows you know exactly what you want, and gives you a much better shot at getting it than does "A Scotch, please." Never order this way in a private home, though. What if they don't have Chivas Regal? Or even know what it is?

Drink mineral water (Perrier, Evian, etc.) if you're avoiding alcohol. Teetotalers make some drinkers uncomfortable, so why not appease them with something that looks alcoholic, tastes delicious, and promotes good health?

BAR STOCK

No bar is complete without:

Blended Canadian Whiskey
Bourbon (bottled-in-bond)
Gin
Light Rum
Scotch
Vodka

And any well-stocked bar will also contain:

Dark rum
Rye
Tequila (tuh KEE lah)

Certain liqueurs and aromatized wines are also needed to prepare many popular cocktails. They are:

Cointreau (KWAHN troh) or Triple Sec
Extra-dry French Vermouth
Sweet Italian Vermouth

Let your pocketbook guide your brand selection. When liquor is diluted, or combined with a mixer, quality differences disappear. Anyway, "blind" taste tests have repeatedly shown that significant differences between brands are few and far between.

Of course, you might have trouble convincing guests to wear blindfolds, so you had best keep expensive British gin for martini fanatics, and a twelve-year-old Scotch for straight-Scotch lovers.

Need I mention that people who plan to put cheap booze in expensive bottles are asking for trouble?

DRINKS FOR AFTERNOON AND EVENING

Enjoy any straight shot of liquor, your favorite mixed drink (like bourbon and water), or a:

Manhattan

Stir together:
> 1 jigger rye or bourbon
> ½ jigger sweet Italian vermouth
> ½ cup cracked ice

Strain into a cocktail glass and garnish with:
> A maraschino cherry
> An orange slice

Variations: A *Rob Roy* is a Manhattan made with Scotch instead of bourbon or rye.

A *Dry Manhattan* is made with dry, not sweet, vermouth and is garnished with an olive or cocktail onion.

A *Perfect Manhattan* is a Manhattan with half sweet vermouth, half dry vermouth.

Martini

To a pitcher filled with hard, dry ice cubes add:
> 3 ounces cold gin [3]
> 1 drop well-chilled extra-dry French vermouth

Stir well and strain quickly into frosted martini glasses. Garnish with:
> A twist of lemon

or
> An olive speared by a cocktail pick

Variations: A *Gibson* is a martini garnished with a speared cocktail onion.

A *Vodka Martini* is one made with vodka instead of gin.

Old-Fashioned

In an old-fashioned glass mix:
> 1 jigger bourbon or rye

---

[3] Purists keep martini pitchers, glasses, vermouth, and gin refrigerated.

1 teaspoon superfine sugar
Several dashes of club soda
1 dash Angostura bitters
Add ice and stir. Garnish, if desired, with:
½ slice lemon or orange
A maraschino cherry

Whiskey Sour

Shake together:
1 jigger bourbon or rye
½ ounce fresh lemon juice
1 teaspoon sugar
Pour into an ice-filled old-fashioned glass. Garnish with:
An orange slice
A maraschino cherry

DRINKS FOR EARLY IN THE DAY

Bloody Mary

Shake together:
2 jiggers tomato juice
⅓ jigger fresh lemon juice
2 dashes Worcestershire sauce
Pinch each of salt and cayenne pepper
1 jigger vodka
½ cup cracked ice
Pinch of horseradish (optional)
Strain into a six-to eight-ounce highball glass and garnish with:
A wedge of lime
A leafy celery stalk

Mimosa

Shake together:
6½ ounces (1 split) chilled, dry champagne
1 tablespoon *Cointreau* or Triple Sec
2 ounces fresh orange juice
Strain into a large, all-purpose wineglass.

Ramos (RĀ mohs) *Gin Fizz*

(This is the world's greatest breakfast drink—straight from New Orleans.)

Place in your blender:
  1–2 ounces gin
  1 egg white
  1 jigger light cream
  1 cup crushed ice
  Juice of ½ lemon and ½ lime
  2 teaspoons confectioners' sugar
  Several dashes Orange Flower Water
Blend a few seconds on high, then pour into a chilled highball glass after dipping its rim in:
  Lemon juice
Then:
  Confectioners' sugar
Fill to the brim with:
  Chilled club soda

Screwdriver

Fill a highball glass with ice and add:
  1 jigger vodka
  4 ounces fresh orange juice
Stir, then garnish with:
  An orange slice
or
  A sprig of mint

Variation: A *Harvey Wallbanger* is a screwdriver with a half-jigger of *Galliano* (gah LYAH noh) liqueur floating on top. (Pour the Galliano slowly onto the back of a spoon held over the drink; do not stir.)

Tequila Sunrise (tuh KEE lah)

Mix together:
  4 ounces fresh orange juice
  1 jigger tequila

Ice cubes

Strain into an all-purpose wineglass, then *carefully* add, and
let settle to the bottom of the glass:
Several dashes *Grenadine*

Let each guest stir his own with the swizzle stick you provide.

SUMMER TREATS

Beer, despite advertisers' efforts, still suffers from a negative image. As a result, many people reserve it for sporting events,
Mexican-food dinners, days at the seashore, and backyard barbecues. They usually keep several imported brands on hand,
though, in case someone requests "a brew." A few light beers,
dark beers, and lagers should be sufficient.

A liquor wholesaler friend tells me that ice-cold beer is over-
chilled, that 42 to 45 degrees is the optimum temperature. He also
says you can prevent overflows, develop a good head, and dispel
some of the beer's gas by rinsing a beer glass, mug, or stein in cold
water and leaving it wet. Then tilt the glass 45 degrees and fill it
one-third full. Return it to upright before pouring the rest.

One last note: Beer does not keep well, so buy it frequently, in
small quantities, and store it in a cool, dark place.

Daiquiri (DAK uh ree)
Place in a blender:
¾ teaspoon sugar
Juice of ½ lime
1 jigger light rum
½ cup cracked ice
If you like, add:
½ large, peeled, and sliced fresh peach
or
½ cup crushed fresh pineapple
or
3–4 large strawberries
or

1 small banana, peeled and chopped

Blend until slushy and serve in a saucer-type champagne glass or all-purpose wineglass.

Gin and Tonic

Into an ice-filled highball glass squeeze and drop in:

¼ lime

Add:

1 jigger gin

Fill glass with:

Tonic water

Variation: A *Vodka Tonic* is made with vodka in place of the gin.

Margarita "Up" (mahr gah REE tah UHP)

Dip the rim of a chilled saucer-shaped champagne glass into:

Lime juice

Then into:

Coarse salt

Let dry.

Place in your blender:

1 large jigger tequila

Juice of ½ lime

½ ounce Triple Sec or Cointreau

Cracked Ice

Add, if you like:

1–2 tablespoons frozen lemonade or limeade concentrate

Blend until slushy, and garnish with:

A slice of lime (perched on the rim of the glass)

Variation: *Margarita On-the-Rocks*. First prepare a salt-rimmed old-fashioned glass. Then, shake together *double* quantities of tequila, Triple Sec, and lime juice. Pour over ice and garnish with a lime wedge.

Piña Colada (PEE nyah koh LAH dah)

Shake together:

1½ ounces cream of coconut

3 ounces light rum
3 ounces pineapple juice
Ice

Strain into a chilled highball glass. Add a straw and a stick of pineapple.

Tequila Shooter

In Mexico, and the southwestern United States, hardy souls drink tequila straight. Should you wish to join them, know that it tastes like distilled cactus juice—with needles intact. Know, too, that the following rituals must be strictly observed: First, grasp a quarter wedge of lime with your thumb and forefinger, and sprinkle coarse salt in the "V" where the two fingers meet. Next, take a lick of salt, a shot of chilled tequila, and a good suck of lime. Then hold on.

One more thing: Tequila aficionados keep their liquor stashed in the freezer so they can serve it ice cold.

Tom Collins

In a highball glass mix:

1 teaspoon sugar
½ jigger fresh lemon juice

Add:

1 jigger gin
Ice cubes

Fill with:

Club soda

Garnish, if desired, with:

A slice of lemon
A maraschino cherry

Variation: A *Vodka Collins* (or *John Collins*) is made with vodka instead of gin.

COLD-WEATHER WARMER

Hot Buttered Rum
Place in a preheated mug:
  1½ teaspoons brown, or superfine, sugar
  1 cinnamon stick
  1½ ounces (1 jigger) dark or light rum
Add, if you like:
  2 cloves
  1 strip of orange peel
Stir until the sugar dissolves, then add:
  ¾ cup hot (not boiling) milk (or water)
Top with:
  1 tablespoon unsalted butter
  1 dash nutmeg

COCKTAIL PARTYING

What do people dread attending and criticize mercilessly? Right: the cocktail party. Here are a few thoughts on how to make your next tour of duty a more pleasant one.

HOSTING

Invite twice as many people as you want, concentrating on an interesting mix of guests: talkers and listeners, climbers and Old Guard, conservatives and liberals, rich and super rich . . .

Ask guests to RSVP so you'll know how much food, liquor, and help you'll need.

Greet, and bid farewell to, every guest. Letting your guests' arrivals and departures go unnoticed is unforgivable.

At a large party, set up a bar that is highly visible, easily accessible, away from heavily trafficked areas, generously stocked, and staffed by one bartender per thirty guests. For one hundred guests or more, add several waiters or waitresses.

Don't ever ask guests to BYOB. It's unforgivably tacky.
Serve generous portions of food. It helps guests maintain
sobriety and makes for a better party.

GUEST APPEARANCES

*Cheerfully greet your hosts when you arrive; compliment them
on the "great party" when you leave.* They have worked
hard, and spent a great deal of money, to show their guests a
good time. Let them know how much you appreciate their
efforts and skill. Even if you don't.
*When you're the guest of honor, arrive on time and help greet
guests.* Send your hosts flowers the next day.
*When you're not the guest of honor, RSVP promptly, arrive
late, and leave early.* Incidentally, if a party is scheduled,
say, from 5 P.M. to 8 P.M., one must take great care to leave
prior to 8:00. Hangers-on are seldom appreciated.

DRINKING

Alternate alcoholic drinks with non-alcoholic drinks. No one
looks attractive when he's had too much to drink.
Drink a glass of whole milk before the party. Though nothing
but abstinence will keep you completely sober and free of
alcohol's revenge, a little milk will coat your stomach and
help you cope.
Rebuild your health quickly. Have a bit too much to drink
despite your precautions? Alas, only two things will cure a
hangover: death and time. Should neither of these
alternatives appeal to you, however, you may lessen your
pain by drinking lots of water before retiring, by consuming
nourishing food and liquids upon rising, and by getting as
much sleep as possible in-between.

What about a little hair-of-the-dog-that-bit-you, i.e., more
alcohol? If it lifts your spirits, fine. But indulge with full
knowledge that you're not *curing* anything; you're simply
postponing it.

Liqueurs and Brandies

Liqueurs and brandies are served after dessert with coffee, smoking materials, and, perhaps, fine chocolates. They also make wonderful late-night soothers, and can be heavenly over ice cream or fresh fruit.

Brandy tastes best when one to two ounces are served in a four-to-eleven-ounce snifter. This size glass is small enough to cradle in the palm of your hand (thereby warming the brandy and improving its flavor), but large enough to air the amber liquid and collect its bouquet.

Liqueurs, too, require breathing space. Serve no more than one ounce at a time, using a two-to-three-ounce liqueur glass for a "neat" drink, a six-ounce old-fashioned glass for a drink "on the rocks." If you prefer a *frappé* (frah PĀ), pack one-quarter cup of shaved or cracked ice into a sherry (or small cocktail) glass, add one ounce liqueur, and finish with two cocktail straws.

BAR STOCK

Most after-dinner drinks will keep their flavors for a year or so, though fine brandies may fade more quickly. Splurge on varieties to be enjoyed straight; economize on those to be combined with sweet or sour mixes.

For a well-stocked bar, you'll need one bottle each of:

Amaretto
B&B or Benedictine
Crème de Cassis
Drambuie

You'll also need one bottle from each of the following categories:

Orange Liqueurs: *Grand Marnier, Cointreau, Curaçao, Triple Sec*
Coffee Liqueurs: *Café de Love, Kahlua, Tía María*

Mint Liqueurs: *Crème de Menthe, Freezomint, Pippermint*
Chocolate Liqueurs: Any of the *Royal* line by the *House of Hallgarten, Vandermint, Crème de Cacao*
Brandy: *Cognac, Armagnac, Champagne Cognac*

Now for the details.

Amaretto (am mahr REH toh) Almond-flavored liqueur made from apricot pits; serve over ice.

Aquavit (ah kwah VEET) Scandinavian liqueur flavored with caraway seed; serve neat and cold.

Armagnac (ahr mah NYAHK) See *Brandy*.

B&B Brandy and *Bénédictine* bottled together in France; serve neat.

Bénédictine (beh neh DEEK teen) Sweet, brandy-based liqueur flavored with plants, fruit peels, and herbs; originally made by Bénédictine monks in France; serve neat.

Brandy Cognac, the world's finest brandy and Armagnac, the second best, are made from grapes. The words "Fine (FEEN) Champagne" indicate top quality, as do stars on the label and the initials "VSOP." Serve in snifters. Fruit-flavored brandies are lesser drinks; serve them neat, on the rocks, frappéd, mixed with water or soda, or over ice cream.

Café de Love (kah FĀ duh LUHV) Exceptionally good coffee liqueur; serve like *Kahlua*.

Calvados (kahl vah DOHSS) World's finest apple brandy, from Normandy; serve in a snifter.

Chartreuse (shahr TRUHZ) Pale green or yellow liqueur developed by monks of *La Grande Chartreuse* near Grenoble, France; brandy-based, it is said to contain 130 herbs and spices; serve frappéd or neat.

Cognac (koh nyahk) A fine brandy made only in Cognac, France; see *Brandy*.

Cointreau (KWAHn troh) Fine, colorless liqueur flavored with orange peel; serve neat.

Crème Liqueurs (KREHM lee KUHR) Sweet, thick liqueurs served neat, frappéd, in mixed drinks, or over ice cream;

flavors include *d'ananas* (dah nah NAH): pineapple; *de banane* (duh bah NAHN): banana; *de cacao* (duh kah kah YOH): chocolate; *de café* (duh kah FÃ): coffee; *de cassis* (duh kah SEESS): black currant; *de fraise* (duh FREHZ): strawberry; *de framboise* (duh frahm BWAHZ): raspberry; *de menthe* (duh MAHNT): mint; *de roses* (duh RUHZ): rose; *de vanille* (duh vah NEEL): vanilla; and *de violet* (duh vee oh LÃ): violet.

Curaçao (koor ruh SOH *or* koor ruh SOW) Orange liqueur from the Dutch West Indies; made from the dried rind of small, green Seville oranges; proprietary names include *Grand Marnier, Cointreau,* and *Triple Sec;* serve neat or over ice cream.

Drambuie (drahm BOO ee) Excellent Scotch-based liqueur flavored with heather honey and herbs; serve neat.

Galliano (gah LYAH noh) Spicy gold Italian liqueur said to be made from eighty herbs, spices, and fruits; serve neat or in a Harvey Wallbanger. (See *Screwdriver* in the "Cocktail" section.)

Grand Marnier (grahn mahr NYÃ) Exceptional French cognac-based liqueur; serve neat, in a heated snifter, or over fruit.

Grenadine (GREHN nah DEEN) Syrupy-sweet red liqueur; serve on the rocks or mixed in an apéritif.

Irish Mist Whiskey-based liqueur sweetened with heather honey and served in a 6-oz. old-fashioned glass, over shaved ice, with a lemon twist.

Kahlua (kah LOO ah) Mexican liqueur made from coffee and cocoa beans; serve over ice or neat; mix in a dash of cream, if desired, or float cream on top.

Kirsch (KEERSH) Colorless brandy made from small black cherries; serve neat and cold.

Ouzo (OO zoh) Clear licorice-flavored Greek brandy; serve neat, or mix four parts water to one part ouzo and pour over ice.

Poire William (PWAHR) Colorless pear brandy; those with a pear in the bottle are generally felt to be overpriced; serve it like *Brandy.*

Pousse-Café (POOS kah FĀ) See the recipe in the upcoming
   section.
Sambuca Romana (sam BOO kah roh MAH nah) Anise-flavored
   liqueur from Italy; serve chilled, neat, with a fresh coffee
   bean.
Sloe Gin (SLOH) Ruby-red liqueur made by steeping sloe
   berries (smart tart plums) in gin; serve over ice, or shake
   with soda and cracked ice.
Southern Comfort Fine, aged bourbon flavored with peaches;
   serve neat, over ice, or as a substitute for regular bourbon.
Strega (STRĀ gah) Golden, spicy-sweet citrus liqueur from
   Italy; serve neat or over vanilla ice cream.
Tía María (TEE ah mah REE ah) Thick, rum-based coffee
   liqueur from the West Indies; serve like *Kahlua*.
Triple Sec (TRIH puhl sek) Colorless, potent, and sweet
   orange-based liqueur; serve like *Curaçao*.
Vandermint (VAN duhr mint) Thick, chocolate-mint liqueur;
   serve neat or over ice cream.

LIQUEURS +

There's one in every crowd, one person who is not content with
thirty-year-old cognac, who is devoted to Black Russians or some
other exotic concoction. Of course, *you* would never be so demanding. But others might, so perhaps you had better learn to
make some of the more popular liqueur-based mixed drinks.
Like a:

Black Russian
   Into a small old-fashioned glass put:
      1 ounce coffee liqueur
      2 ounces vodka
      Several ice cubes
   Stir.

   Variation: Shake together above ingredients with ½ ounce
      cream. Strain into a cocktail glass for a *White Russian*.

Brandy Alexander

Shake together:

   1 ounce brandy
   1 ounce brown crème de cacao
   1 ounce light cream
   1 ounce cracked ice

Strain into a chilled cocktail glass.

Variation: Use a blender instead of a shaker, and substitute a scoop of vanilla ice cream for the ice and the cream.

Grasshopper

Shake together:

   ½ jigger green crème de menthe
   ½ jigger white crème de menthe
   ½ jigger light cream
   1 ounce cracked ice

Strain into a saucer-type champagne glass or a cocktail glass.

Variation: Use a blender instead of a shaker; substitute a scoop of vanilla ice cream for the ice and the cream.

Pousse-Café (POOSS kah FÄ)

Into a liqueur glass pour:

   1 teaspoon crème de cassis

Let it rest a moment, then gently insert a thick stir stick. Pour the following liqueurs down the stick, in the order listed, to float one liquid on top of the other:

   1 teaspoon green crème de menthe
   1 teaspoon yellow chartreuse
   1 teaspoon Triple Sec or Cointreau

Remove the stick, being careful not to disturb the layered effect. Serve with coffee.

Stinger

Shake together:

1 jigger brandy

1 jigger white crème de menthe

1 ounce cracked ice

Strain into a chilled cocktail glass.

CLASS NOTES

Very Private Planes

Whereas jets owned by multinational corporations should send fear into the hearts of no one (except possibly the treasurers who pay for them), a young mogul's plane may be an entirely different matter. Ever ride in a flying MG?

If you're a newcomer to the private plane scene—and everybody is *once*—you had best read through the upcoming suggestions. At most, they'll save your life. At *least*, they'll save your reputation (which may also save your life!).

Space and weight are at a premium in small planes, so:
  Pack minimally.
  Carry soft luggage if you have it.
  Don't take a bulky coat (unless it's a really exquisite fur and you simply can't live without it).
Reduced cabin oxygen and pressure can cause many problems, so:
  Refrain from drinking alcoholic cocktails before or during flight (because one drink can feel like three).
  Refrain from smoking.
  Tighten all caps and tops on toiletries so they won't leak.
  Leave air space in thermoses as liquids may expand and spew out.
  Do not bring carbonated beverages (which may also spew).
Turbulence may cause unexpected bumps, so:
  Take nothing into the cockpit that might spill.
  Drink nothing that will stain if overturned.
  Take a Dramamine or other motion-sickness preventative thirty minutes before departure.

Your pilot will be busy during take-off and landing, so:
   Don't bother him.
   Do what he asks—immediately!
Women should wear trousers and low-heeled shoes. They may
   have to crawl over something. Or someone.
*When traveling strictly for fun, offer to contribute your share
   of expenses.* Flying a private plane can be very expensive,
   and although your host will more than likely decline your
   offer, he or she will greatly appreciate your generosity.
Don't fly with anyone you don't trust. If your pilot is
   irresponsible or reckless on the ground, he will probably be
   worse in the air. So have your chauffeur drive you instead.

You need not be a professional chef, like the gentlemen above, to serve professional-looking food. The delicacies, and this photograph, are courtesy of The Plaza.

8

· CULINARY CHICANERY ·

A gourmet is just a glutton with brains.

—PHILLIP W. HABERMAN, JR.,

VOGUE

If you think keeping up with the Joneses is tough, try *cooking* for them. Having recently discovered Julia Child and James Beard, they may be looking for more than you were planning to offer.

So what do you do when Cook goes on vacation? Try those recipes printed on soup cans? Chain yourself to a stove? Or—heaven forbid—enroll in a cooking class?

Instead, maybe you should:

Get others to do any, or all, of the cooking while you take the credit.

Take advantage of little-known services offered by specialty shops and restaurants.

Use *ingredients*, not complicated techniques, to make ordinary meals extraordinary.

Prepare glamorous meals from what you have on hand.

Decorate and garnish your dishes like a professional chef.

Interested? Then get moving. The best time to make, fake, and delegate your way to culinary (KYOO luh neh ree) stardom is long before Cook starts planning her next trip!

Gourmet Feasts for Non-Cooks

Cooking when you're less than inspired isn't hospitality: It's sadism. So if you cannot, or will not, devote yourself completely, do your guests a favor and stay away from the food. Delegate the work and get the job done right.

In business and government, delegating and subcontracting are everyday occurrences. How better to offer a wide variety of goods and services despite limited talent, time, and experience? Of course, responsibility for the job remains with the delegator. But that's all right, because the credit does too!

Is it dishonest to take credit for work you didn't do?

You worked to earn the money to pay for it, right?

And your guests will like thinking you've been slaving away for weeks, right?

Then, viewed this way, isn't it almost un-American to reveal the sordid details?

Undercover Work

Clandestine activities require careful planning, but if you follow these suggestions, you won't have any problems.

Contract to have everything done—from shopping to cleaning up; then stay out of the way. You know about too many cooks and what they do to the broth!

Pay by the job, not the hour. When every passing minute means a few more coins, you can count on more minutes passing than are absolutely necessary.

Have the cook prepare one of his specialties, something that excites you gastronomically without flooring you economically. Never let anyone short of a professional chef do any experimenting. Terrific ideas often become disasters.

If at all possible, have the work done in your own kitchen. An absentee cook can make you really nervous. Besides, if he's working in your home, you might learn something by osmosis.

Get the cook out of the house long before guests arrive. A stranger sneaking out the back door with a Cuisinart (KWEE zeen ahrt) under his arm, and flour all over his clothes, could make guests suspicious.

If you're planning to have food delivered, make certain everything travels and reheats well (no soufflés, no egg-based sauces).

Make sure, too, that the food arrives early. Dinner should be announced by a maid, not a honking horn at the back door.

Get complete instructions for heating, garnishing, serving, and eating each dish. Discuss condiments, wines, and order of service. Ask questions about everything. Think of how embarrassed you'll be if you forget something—like removing concealed toothpicks or the string around the roast!

Understand each dish. You should never serve Chicken Marengo if you cannot pronounce it (mah REHN goh) or explain that its lovely flavor comes from olive oil, white wine, garlic, and brandy.[1] And should your dish have an interesting past (Chicken Marengo was first served to Napolean after the battle of Marengo), you should know that too. Consult any good cookbook for details.

Get recipes in writing, in advance, for every dish. When an awestruck guest begs for a recipe, you will want to be gracious.

Keep guests out of your kitchen. Say there's a curse on it, or that it's a mess, but keep them away from your kitchen—and your secrets.

Surrogate Cooks

Now, let's take a look at the people who are going to make you a star, baby. For those of you with temporary cash-flow problems,

---

[1] Marengo also contains tomatoes, mushrooms, poached eggs, seasoning, and, of course, chicken parts.

I'll start out slowly. But watch out! The speed and the cost accelerate quickly.

A discreet friend or neighbor who cooks like a pro, and has plenty of leisure time, can be a perfect stand-in. Pay your cook or offer to baby-sit, clean house, or do whatever it takes to make an equitable exchange. If someone offers free assistance, refuse. What you save in money, you lose in control.

Another caution: Be sure to check references. If you have no personal knowledge that your stand-in is both a kitchen virtuoso and basically reliable human being, do a little detective work before asking for help.

The chef at your favorite restaurant, who may well be bored to tears, overworked, and underpaid (who isn't?), will probably jump at the chance to moonlight.

Tell him you want a glorious meal, a spectacular meal, something guests could not get elsewhere. If he is busy the day of your party, ask him to prepare dishes that refrigerate well. Better yet, request courses you can freeze. And have him make two or three batches; that way, you'll get several parties for the price of one cook.

Contact your chef when he isn't busy working; midway between lunch and dinner should be safe. Explain what you want, ask what he'll charge, then start negotiating.

The proprietor of a specialty food shop either employs, or *is*, a fine cook. You will have found the right person if his shop carries unusual tarts and cakes, fresh pâté, marinated mushrooms, and an exciting variety of side dishes (like stuffed artichokes or *ratatouille*[2]).

To secure his services, just ask. Wealth does a marvelous job of eluding most merchants, so he will probably be more than happy to help.

---

[2] Ratatouille (rah tah TOO ee) is chopped zucchini, onions, tomatoes, eggplant, and green peppers stewed in olive oil and garlic.

The owner of a gourmet cooking school, or one of his pupils, might be just the person to help. To find a good school, call a gourmet shop or the food editor of the local newspaper.

Caterers are expensive, but they'll do absolutely everything for you: plan, cook, serve, clean up, decorate, even supply tables, glasses, silverware, tea services, and chairs.

The larger ones will bring oil derricks for Texas shindigs, Eiffel Towers for Parisian *soirées,*[3] and almost anything else for any other parties. You may have to mortgage your home to pay for them, but what is money compared to social immortality?

The food editor of your city's largest newspaper, or the chef from a local television cooking show, will recommend several reputable firms and tell you how much to tip. (Note: The entire catering staff, with the exception of the owner, will expect gratuities. See "Tips on Tipping," page 39, for details.)

Restaurants may package entire meals "to go" if you ask nicely. Some even offer a full catering service. The maître d' will supply details. (See Chapter 2 for more information.)

Gourmet Feasts for Everyday Cooks

If you like to cook a *little,* this section's for you.

First, we'll look at help available on a piecemeal basis. We don't want you to overdo, do we? After that, we'll see how the choice of ingredients, and the adoption of a few European customs, can turn an average meal into something really special.

A Little Help

Anything you *want* done, you can *have* done. Just find the right people, charm them, and pay them.

Expect a great deal from these people. Tell them what you

---

[3] Soirées (swah RĀ) are parties.

want, and what you don't want. When they do a marvelous job, lavish them with praise. Give them all the business you can—and an occasional bottle of Scotch.

Bakers will prepare bread in the shape of a turtle, a crocodile, or whatever. But don't try rattlesnakes. My sister ordered some for a big Texas party, but they looked so fearsome no one would eat them. In fact, a few timid souls wouldn't even go near them.

For less whimsical occasions, your baker will supply giant popovers or hard rolls, or will braid rye, wheat, and white dough for a tri-color loaf. He might even work from your favorite recipe.

If you like, you can buy raw dough to take home and bake yourself. Get bread dough from any baker, *choux*[4] and puff[5] dough from pastry specialists, and phyllo[6] dough from Greek bakeries or grocers who carry imported foods.

Butchers—the ones in private shops, not supermarkets—will sell you special cuts, unusual or hard-to-find items like venison, suckling pig, and baby goat, and made-to-order items like crown roasts and racks of lamb. They will do your boning and slicing, and can show you the difference between old pheasants and young ones. Many of them will marinate or cook the meat for you. Some will hunt down the last *châteaubriand*[7] in town or clean the game from your last hunting trip.

Fish-market merchants will clean and filet fresh fish for you, even if *you* caught them. They will open clams and oysters, prepare lobster tails, and clean and cook your shrimp. When you need soft-shell crabs, bay scallops,[8] rock (or stone) crabs, or Maine lobsters, they'll find them. They'll also sell fine chowders[9] and cocktail sauces.

---

[4] Choux (SHOO) is the dough used for cream puffs.

[5] Puff pastry is flaky French pastry dough made in thin, buttery layers.

[6] Phyllo (FEE loh), or fillo, is multi-layered dough used in making strudel.

[7] Châteaubriand (shah toh bree AHn) is a large cut off the beef tenderloin, usually served with a sauce.

[8] Bay scallops (SKAH luhps) are tiny East Coast shellfish.

[9] Manhattan chowder is tomato-based; New England chowder is cream-based.

Gourmet shop merchants stock wonderful ingredients to glorify your meals: truffles, crèpes, chocolate leaves, candied roses. Befriend the owner and memorize every shelf. Have him show you short-cut foods (like a decent canned soup). Ask him to specially order what he doesn't keep on hand, and have him recommend appliances, cooking schools, and other stores offering quality goods and services.

Mail-order houses specializing in food sell almost everything from practically everywhere. Most have catalogs for the asking; others charge a small, usually refundable, fee. For a list of firms, see "Gourmet Goodies by Mail," page 214. For other opportunities, see the back pages of *Bon Appétit* (bon nah puh TEE), *Gourmet,* and other cooking magazines.

Some *restaurants* will prepare the ducks you shot, follow your recipes, and cook special take-out dishes. They will sell one course, or five, and will deliver them via taxi. And you already know, don't you, that they'll sometimes divulge the recipe for your favorite concoction? Unfortunately, they occasionally leave out the most important ingredient, so test the dish before serving it to guests.

Specialty food shop proprietors sell beautiful desserts and side dishes. Many will cook to order and offer suggestions for completing your meals. Get a list of foods prepared regularly, and ask them to call when they have made something special.

Wine merchants can be surprisingly helpful. In addition to finding the perfect bottle to complement your dinner, many will stage wine tastings in your home for a group of six or more. Arrange to have them on a regular basis and you'll probably receive a substantial discount.

Caterers and party suppliers will rent dishes, glasses, tables, chairs, tents, even dance floors, at surprisingly low rates.

Florists, if you call several days before your party, will prepare lovely fresh, dried, or silk flower arrangements to enhance your dining room.

Before each party—or every week, if you like—have your florist pick up your vases and return them full of flowers. Ask him to deliver dried or silk arrangements as soon as possible, but have him hold fresh flowers until the morning of The Big Event.

Course-by-Course Magic

Now you know *where* to find what you need to turn simple suppers into epicurean feasts. But do you know exactly *what* to serve? And *when* to serve it? And do you know *how* to make glamorous last-minute meals without convenience foods?

You soon will, though you'll pay dearly for the privilege. If you want *cheap,* you'll have to become an expert cook. Of course, you will still want expensive ingredients. And you'll have to pay for cooking lessons. And kitchenware. And cookbooks. And . . .

Apéritifs. When great food is to be served, an apéritif precedes dinner. A single glass of the driest champagne, sherry, or vermouth whets the appetite, as do Campari and soda, and Dubonnet on the rocks. And there are other benefits as well: Your liquor bill will lose its resemblance to the national debt and guests will think you're divinely chic. (See Chapter 7 for details.)

Hors d'oeuvres. [10] If cocktails spoil the appetite, hors d'oeuvres demolish it.

Should a delay cause guests to start knawing on the furniture, put out carrot sticks or slices of mild cheese. Better yet, serve the first course early, in the living room.

Of course, you will want to serve hors d'oeuvres at cocktail parties and before the theater—to stave off hunger. So, for these occasions, here are a few favorites.

Mushroom caps, stuffed with snails or smoked oysters, are

---

[10] Hors d'oeuvres (or DERV *or* DUH vruh) differ from canapés only in that the latter are always served in small pieces of toast or bread.

positively ambrosial. Buy three or four jumbo mushrooms per person, twist off and discard the stems, and clean with a damp cloth. Rinse and dry the delicacy of your choice and insert one into each cap. Drizzle liberally with melted sweet butter lightly laced with pressed garlic. Broil close to the flame until sizzling, and serve on a platter garnished with curly parsley and scallion flowers. (Trim scallion root and top; make five to six lengthwise slits in white portion; chill in ice water two to three hours.)

Raw, chilled mushrooms are also divine. Fill each one with a dollop of sour cream, a spoonful of caviar, and a squeeze of fresh lemon. Or mix a filling of one part cream cheese, one part blue cheese. Or stuff each cap with a dab of steak tartare, made by combining fresh chopped sirloin with a dash of Worcestershire sauce and diced Bermuda onion. For variations, trade the mushrooms for canned (and rinsed) artichoke bottoms. Garnish with capers.

To make a delicious canapé that will intrigue your guests (no one will know what it is), start by cutting bread into two-inch rounds using a canapé cutter or a shot glass. Spread each round generously with three parts mayonnaise and one part diced white onion. Sprinkle well with grated *parmesan* (PAHR mah zahn) cheese, and broil a few minutes till they're golden and puffy. Serve immediately on a tray garnished with black olives and pretty cherry tomatoes stuffed with blue cheese.

Keep your calorie-conscious friends happy with *crudités* (kroo dee TĀ)—a selection of carrot and celery sticks, cauliflower and broccoli flowerettes, cherry tomatoes, mushrooms, and endive. Arrange the crisp, raw, and well-chilled vegetables around an attractive bowl filled with a good dip. One of my favorites is made by stirring together three-quarters cup sour cream, one-half cup mayonnaise, one tablespoon each of minced onion, minced parsley, lemon juice, *Beau Monde* (boh MOHND), and fresh chopped dill (or one teaspoon dried dill). Cover and refrigerate at least eight hours before serving.

The First Course. Unless you have a house full of hungry lumberjacks, precede the entrée with only a light soup or appetizer.

Have it waiting on the table before seating your guests, along with utensils and glasses for the first three courses, one or more bottles of opened wine, and a basket of breadsticks, crackers, or toast points (crustless dry toast cut into two or four triangles). Call your guests to the table with "Dinner is served."

Appetizers. Fish before fish is boring. Beef or pork before fish is overwhelming. But shellfish before fish is nice, as is a mild pâté. In fact, both work well before almost any main course, and are as easy to prepare as they are wonderful to eat. (Note: Both also make excellent luncheon entrées.)

Serve pâté sliced, with a basket of toast points. To eat, spread a little on the toast leaving pastry, if any, behind.[11] Buy quality pâté at a specialty food store or from a mail-order house. Better yet, prepare it yourself.

For an easy, delicious seafood appetizer, try marinated scallops, ready-to-heat stuffed clams, or escargots. Or sweet-talk your fish merchant into preparing clams or oysters on the half-shell. Or try crab fingers (cooked claw meat with pincers still attached). Serve on cracked ice with lemon wedges and homemade cocktail sauce.[12] Provide seafood forks.

When you're really out to impress, try caviar. Add a spoonful to oysters on the half shell, or nestle several spoonfuls into an avocado half (see page 265). Or serve as purists do: straight out of a tin ensconced in cracked ice. Offer bowls of diced Bermuda onion and chopped hardboiled egg. Add melba toast or toast points, lemon wedges, and a bottle of cold vodka. For extra drama, encase the vodka in ice (see page 265) and season each with a grind of black pepper.

Soups. There are few better ways to begin a meal than with the subtle flavor and creamy texture of a fine soup. *Vichyssoise,*[13] lob-

---

[11] Pastry-wrapped versions are called pâté en croûte (pah tä ahn KROOT). The crust is there to keep the pâté moist and is edible only if it's light and buttery.

[12] Add one-quarter cup prepared horseradish, the juice of one lemon, and a dash of tabasco sauce to one cup of the best ketchup you can buy.

[13] Vichyssoise (vee shee SWAHZ, *not* vee shee SWAH) is cold cream of potato and leek soup. Serve with a fresh chive garnish.

ster *bisque*,[14] cream of celery, cold cherry or strawberry are all
wonderful choices. But heartier soups, like French Onion and
Clam Chowder, are best left for lunch.

Buy soup ready-made from a restaurant or make your own.
You'll find a recipe on page 251 that takes only minutes to prepare.

For emergencies, keep a good canned *madrilène*[15] in your pan-
try. Serve it hot, spike it with a tablespoon of dry sherry per serving, and float a lemon slice on top. If possible, add a bit of red
caviar.

Keep the course light by limiting portions to four ounces.
When serving hot soups, use warm bowls. For cold soups, use
chilled bowls and pass frosty soup spoons on a napkin-covered
dish.

Set each bowl on a liner plate, and slip a colorful napkin flower
in-between for drama (see page 235). When the course is over,
remove plates, bowls, and any special wineglasses.

Entrées. Reputations are made or lost on the choice of entrée.
Some cooks attempt to play safe by serving a classic like *coq au
vin*,[16] but I think this borders on culinary suicide.

Everyone knows how classics should look and taste. Worse yet,
they may well know a *great* version from an *ordinary* one. Now,
wouldn't you be happier avoiding such pressures?

If so, choose exciting cuts and varieties of meat, fish, and poultry, then prepare them as simply and elegantly as possible. You
may run up an impressive bill at the butcher shop, but you'll be
rewarded with improved results and, occasionally, reduced work.

So forget *coq au vin*. And bid *adieu* (ah DYUH) to plain old
chicken. Instead try plump, oven- or spit-roasted pheasant,
capon,[17] squab, or boned Rock Cornish game hen. And turn in
those boring chops for legs of lamb studded with garlic, or racks

[14] Bisques (BISKS) are rich cream soups, usually with a fish or shellfish base.

[15] Madrilène (mah druh LEHN) is a tomato-based broth which may be served
hot, or cold and jelled.

[16] Coq au vin (kah koh VA*n*) is chicken cooked with wine, cream, and diced
pork.

[17] Capons (KĀ pahns) are castrated roosters, which are larger and tastier than
other chickens.

of lamb seasoned with breadcrumbs (see page 252), or crown roasts of pork or lamb constructed by that wonderful butcher of yours.

In place of the ubiquitous sirloin steak, try scallops of veal pounded and sautéed in butter, olive oil, and garlic. Or serve *tournedos* (toor nuh DOH), pieces of tenderloin so small they are cooked before a Frenchman turns *(tourne)* his back *(dos)*.

Fresh fish, baked, broiled, or sautéed (fish free of heavy batter), is always a lovely choice. Top with almonds lightly sautéed in sweet butter, or with paper-thin slices of lemon and sprigs of curly parsley.

Try giant shrimp, marinated in garlic-spiked olive oil and broiled to perfection. Or try ready-to-cook king crab legs, or cooked and stuffed lobster tails, or jumbo shrimp—all from your favorite fish merchant's shop.

Forget such family favorites as spaghetti, chili, fried chicken, casseroles, skillet dinners, and pot roasts unless you're having a theme party (as suggested in an upcoming chapter.) *You* can do better.

Side Dishes. Side dishes add color, variety, and nutrients to the main course. Americans seem to prefer the combination of one colorful vegetable and one starch or grain, but there is no set rule.

In fact, calorie counters and warm-weather diners usually welcome a bright *mélange*[18] of vegetables in place of buttered or cream-soaked starches. Try *juliennes*[19] of zucchini and carrots gently sautéed in equal parts of oil and butter, with a pinch of tarragon or thyme (TĪM). Or try groupings of baby carrots and pearl onions, separately steamed.

Green beans, asparagus, and broccoli, when cooked properly to retain their colors, make excellent additions to any meal. Serve cold, or at room temperature, with an oil and vinegar dressing. Or serve hot, tossed with melted sweet butter. Or cover hot broccoli and asparagus with lemony *hollandaise*.[20] (See page 252 for instructions.)

---

[18] Mélange (mā LAHnZH) means "medley" or "mixture."
[19] Juliennes (zhoo LYEHN) are thin strips.
[20] Hollandaise (ah lahn DEHZ *or* HAHL uhn dāz) is a rich sauce made with egg yolks, lemon, and butter.

Steamed fresh spinach, buttered or creamed, makes a wonderful side dish, especially when packed tightly in a ring mold for a few moments before being unmolded on a warm platter. Try plain steamed spinach as a bed for sauced entrées. Or *sauté* (soh TĀ) fresh, whole leaves—just until wilted—in butter and a bit of garlic; for variety, add sautéed mushrooms, toasted almond slices, or white truffle pieces.

Serve *fresh* vegetables whenever possible, selecting them for their color and beauty. And always be on the lookout for the unusual: miniature zucchini and eggplant, squash blossoms, purplish-black peppers, yellow peppers, miniature yellow tomatoes, a French sea plant called *pousse-pied* (poos PYEH).

If in the dead of winter you encounter only wilted broccoli and make-believe tomatoes, try a top brand of frozen carrots, peas, artichoke hearts, or cauliflower. But avoid those packed in sauces; they seldom taste homemade. Or good.

You might consider puréeing (pyoor RĀ ing) frozen vegetables to disguise their icy origins. *Purées* have recently been quite the rage, probably because the advent of home food processors makes their preparation so easy. You simply pop chopped-and-cooked vegetables (carrots, broccoli, asparagus, squash, etc.), seasonings, and a few spoons of cream into the machine and process to the consistency of mashed potatoes. Pile onto lettuce leaves or decorate with a sprig of parsley or dill.

About canned vegetables: With the exception of imported mushrooms, hearts of palm, pimentos, white asparagus, Italian plum tomatoes, artichoke bottoms and hearts, and other canned items specifically pardoned in this book, *avoid them*. Like the plague.

Also steer clear of the more mundane versions of starchy vegetables and grains. Think beauty. Be original.

Potatoes *à la Duchesse* (ah lah doo SHESS), those lovely swirls of potato piped from a pastry tube, are elegant, versatile, and simple enough for a patient beginner. Use the recipe in your favorite cookbook.

Pretty little new potatoes, buttered and topped with snipped chives or dill, are a lifesaver when you're in a hurry and are always delicious. And baked potatoes, split and packed with sour cream and a spoonful of caviar, add a lovely new dimension to any dinner.

What potatoes do for beef and lamb, rice does for everything else. Serve it under any entrée with a sauce, or in a chafing dish or ring mold. (Pack hot buttered rice into the ring, then carefully unmold onto a warm platter one minute later.)

With roasted fowl or game, try wild rice. Brown rice is both aesthetically and nutritionally superior to plain or converted white rice. Serve plain or add one or several of the following: butter, parmesan cheese, almond slivers, pimentos, sliced water chestnuts, sultana raisins, sautéed shallots, toasted pine nuts, or sautéed mushrooms—*cèpes*, morels, or any of the Chinese or Japanese varieties.

Noodles (from your kitchen, an Italian grocer, a restaurant, but never a supermarket) are lovely with meat, poultry, or game. Cook till *al dente* (ahl DEHN tā)—somewhat firm to the bite; then toss with butter and a sprinkling of poppy seeds or sautéed pine nuts.

Salad. Serve greens after the meal, European style, to prepare the palate for dessert. Or serve salad with the main course. Or omit it. Or, if you must, begin your meal with salad—like the rest of America.

Save Caesar and chef's salads for lunch and family dinners. With a multi-course meal, a nonfilling portion of mixed greens is more appropriate.

But do choose interesting ingredients (never boring iceberg lettuce). Try watercress or spinach. Or combine *rugula* (ROO goo lah), *endive* (ahn DEEV), *mâche* (mahsh), or *escarole* (ESS kah rohl) with milder greens like Bibb, Romaine, or Boston lettuce.

On the day of the meal, rinse the greens well and pat or spin them dry. Tear (do not cut) into bite-sized pieces; bag and refrigerate. Then, just before serving, add no more than one or two of the following: crumbled blue cheese, sliced imported mushrooms or truffles, rings of red onion, sliced water chestnuts, chunks of pâté, or homemade croutons (small cubes of bread sautéed in butter and a touch of garlic and dried herbs). Toss with freshly made dressing. Lemon and oil is excellent with seafood; oil and vinegar is good otherwise.

Serve salad on a small, chilled plate and offer cold forks from a napkin-covered dish. If it precedes the main course, add breadsticks, melba toast, or toast points. Other times, bread is optional.

Cheese and Fruit. A cheese course is chic, French, and very easy. Try it before—or instead of—dessert, choosing fine, ripe cheeses from a specialty shop and accompanying them with unsalted cheese biscuits. (Processed cheeses, and flavored or salted crackers, are for family use only.)

When cheese *precedes* dessert, let the main-course wine guide your selection. If you're serving a dry white wine, or a light red *Bordeaux* or *Beaujolais,* offer a ripe *Camembert* (kah mehn BEHR) or *Brie* (BREE). With heavier wines, like red Burgundies, try cheddar or *Edam* (ā DAHM).

If cheese *ends* the meal, try the classic combination of Stilton cheese, peaches or apricots, and Vintage Port. Or try a fine French *Sauternes* with blue cheese and ripe pears. Add cheese biscuits and, perhaps, walnuts.

Serve your cheeses on an attractive cheese board, allowing a slicer or knife for each variety. Guests will need elegant little plates, clean utensils, and fresh glasses (if you're changing wines).

Dessert. As Mother said when she confiscated your Twinkie, sweets spoil the appetite. Of course, at the end of the meal, you *want* appetites ruined. So serve something light and luscious after a heavy meal, or something gooey and rich after spartan fare. Guests may insist that they are too full to keep eating, but don't take them seriously. Set dessert out, and have plenty for seconds. (Don't push, though; just offer.)

Do you cook? Even a little? Then try either of the show-stopping desserts in this book. Or, if the idea of cooking sounds too exhausting, call your favorite bakery, specialty shop, or restaurant—you know, the ones you've been haunting all year? Ask the owner to prepare a delectable dish that looks homemade: no perfect cheesecakes, no classic *éclairs* (ā KLEHR), no too-fancy cakes. If the owner will make it in *your* serving dish, so much the better.

Frequently set upon by last-minute guests? No problem. Fill

the freezer with hand-packed ice cream; the bar with fine liqueurs. Then, when unexpected guests arrive, improvise.

Pour coffee liqueur over praline ice cream; or crème de menthe over chocolate chip; or half crème de menthe, half crème de cacao over vanilla; or Amaretto over peach.

Top your creation with a compatible decoration of blanched almond slices, chocolate shavings or leaves, chopped walnuts or pistachios, candied flowers or fruits, a sprig of mint, a fresh blossom, or fruit slices. Your favorite gourmet shop should have what you need.

Do you enjoy making layer cake? Why not try a French *gâteau* (gah TOH) instead? Bake and cool one thick layer of cake, then frost it smoothly with butter cream icing. Arrange candied flowers or chocolate leaves on top, or press chopped walnuts around the side. Add whipped cream, if you like, for French pie *à la mode* (ah lah MOHD).

In the interest of interesting food, avoid gelatin-fruit rings, desserts made with marshmallows or artificial whipped cream, and any recipe that is part of an advertisement. Ditto frozen cheesecakes, layer cakes, and other convenience desserts.

Coffee, Tea, and Liqueurs. End your meal with freshly brewed coffee and tea, and offer an assortment of liqueurs. When dessert is simple, try a special coffee like *Café Diable* (kah fä DYAH bluh) or *Brûlée* (broo LÄ). When dessert is rich or complex, serve only *demitasse* (deh mee TAHSS) or *espresso* (eh SPREH soh).

If you're not serving an alcohol-laced coffee after dinner, offer brandies and liqueurs. If your guests smoke, set out smoking materials and ashtrays. *Montecristo* (mahn tä KREES toh) cigars are of the highest quality; loose cigarettes in a silver cup add a *chichi*[21] touch. When you're really out to impress, add Godiva chocolates.

Accompaniments

Beverages. A dinner without one or more good wines should be illegal. At the very least, it is unpalatable and unwise. So serve

---

[21]Chichi (shee shee) means elegant or sophisticated.

wine with every course unless all guests are teetotalers, or unless the *vino* clashes with a particular food (like chocolate or vinegar).

As man does not live by wine alone, you should serve ice water, too, and have milk and soft drinks available for youngsters. Do not, however, offer cocktails at the table; they're even more damaging *with* dinner than they are *before*.

Bread. If a cook doesn't bother to heat the breads accompanying his meals, what other shortcuts is he taking?

Attention to detail can make all the difference, so always accompany dinner with steaming hot bread. Foil-wrapped, it requires only about twenty minutes in a preheated 350°F oven. Remove the foil to serve, and pop the bread into a napkin-lined basket. Better yet, keep it hot in a heated warmer.

For breakfast or brunch, offer fresh muffins, *croissants*, or *brioche*[22] with exotic jams and honeys. For the main course of other meals, try a braided loaf, hard rolls, oversized popovers, or French bread.

Soup and appetizer courses call for homemade toast points, melba toast, or gigantic breadsticks (all served at room temperature). Cheese and fruit need only unsalted biscuits.

Make colorful napkin flowers (see page 235) to display breads attractively. Put out lots of creamy sweet butter. And don't forget to remove one bread before serving another.

Purchase breads from the best bakery in town on the day of your party. (Only saints bake their own.) Always buy extras and freeze any leftovers. That way, you'll never have to resort to brown-and-serve rolls.

Condiments, Seasonings, and Sauces. If you wish to be known as a fantastic cook, you must use only the freshest garlic, onions, chives, and shallots; powders, flakes, and juices are completely unacceptable. Take the hassle out of their preparation with well-made equipment and proper techniques.

Peel onions under cold, running water; dice in a food processor or small chopper. Snip chives with your kitchen shears.

[22] Croissants (krwah SAH*n*) are crescent-shaped rolls; brioche (bree OHSH) are buttery-rich buns. Both are served at breakfast and brunch only.

Loosen the skin and sections of garlic and shallots by smashing with a heavy object or the side of a large knife. The skin will fall off, sections will separate, and you can dice them with ease.

Herbs, too, should be chosen for their freshness. Grow your own, buy them from a produce market, or purchase recently dried herbs at your favorite gourmet shop. (Note: One *tablespoon* fresh equals one *teaspoon* dried.)

For your table spread, choose whipped *un*salted butter. Whipping makes it spread easier, decreases calories by one-third, and facilitates formation of pretty little balls: Dip an ice cream scoop or melon baller in warm water, scoop up some butter, drop in ice water to harden, then drain.

Bag and freeze balls you won't use within twenty-four hours; unsalted butter spoils quickly. Just before serving, arrange on an attractive dish with a parsley garnish.

Use sweet *stick* butter for cooking. (Whipping prevents accurate measurement.) Impart a lovely flavor in sautéed foods, while increasing heat resistance, by adding one part oil to each two parts butter.

Buy your oil in health-food stores or gourmet shops. Purchase only a two- or three-month supply; oil turns rancid quickly. Store in a cool, dark place.

Use cold-pressed corn or safflower oil in sweet foods; in special salads, try walnut oil; for all other purposes, use light French virgin olive oil.

Fine salad oils call for exotic wine, fruit, or herb vinegars. (Raspberry is heavenly with walnut oil.) When you need soy sauce, buy the light variety available only in gourmet shops and Chinese markets. For mustard, try *Dijon* (dee ZHOHn) or *Meaux* (MOH).

Grate parmesan cheese yourself using a food processor or small grater. When you want mint jelly for lamb, chutney for curry, cocktail or tartar sauce for seafood, or horseradish for roast beef, make it or buy the best you can afford. When you need jams, preserves, or honey, choose local brands (if possible) and offer an exotic assortment. Hollandaise, *béarnaise*,[23] and other fine sauces should always be homemade.

---

[23] Béarnaise (behr NĀZ) is a lovely sauce made with egg yolks, wine vinegar, shallots, and tarragon. Enjoy it over meat or grilled fish.

Ordinary table salt is too, too boring. Instead, try coarse sea salt in a sturdy grinder; or use kosher salt in little dishes called salt cellars. If you simply *must* be conventional, fill beautiful shakers with ground kosher salt.

The only acceptable way to serve pepper is freshly ground from a pepper mill. Use white peppercorns to season light-colored foods; otherwise, use black. Just be sure to have the butler do all the grinding. You'll need your strength to handle all the compliments your meals will elicit.

The Coordinated Meal

Now you know how to plan each element of an elegant repast. But wait. Before lulling yourself into a false sense of security, you should know that you can't just put together a series of sensational courses and end up with a marvelous meal. You must coordinate the parts and consider the effect of the whole. And you must avoid all sorts of nasty little traps that can ruin even the best efforts.

So when you plan that special meal:

Consider the time of year, but don't be a slave to the seasons.
   Although most of us like hot, rib-sticking food in winter, and
   light, cool food in summer, sometimes the reverse can be
   refreshing. A springtime extravaganza, complete with all the
   trimmings, can be just what your guests need to zap the
   winter doldrums.

Adapt the size of the meal to the time of day. Generally, meals
   should increase in size as the day wears on. Except for
   elegant Sunday brunches, most early meals should be
   limited to an appetizer or salad course, a main course, and,
   perhaps, dessert. For dinner, portions need not be larger,
   but you may want to add one or more dishes. When in doubt
   about the size or heaviness of a meal, err on the light side.
   But keep seconds available, and in plain view.

Avoid too many "star" dishes. Each part of a meal should
   complement, not compete with, all other parts. So don't use
   too many rich, or fancy, dishes at one time. For instance, a

stuffed lobster appetizer, plus Veal *Cordon Bleu,* [24] plus
potatoes in a cream sauce, plus Bananas *Flambé* (flahn BĀ)
would overwhelm anyone—and I do mean overwhelm.

Avoid duplication of textures or ingredients. No meal should
have more than one dish that is flambé, puréed, molded, or
sauced. (Salad dressings and dessert sauces don't count.) And
never repeat a main ingredient; for example, you wouldn't
want to serve a potato-based soup when you're also serving
potatoes. If you did, guests might think you had run out of
ideas.

Don't serve a foreigner one of his country's specialties. You
may think you are flattering an Italian visitor by serving him
lasagna, or an Indian visitor by serving him curry. But you're
not. He will want to experience American cuisine, just as
you would want to try his country's best cooking. Besides, do
you really think you could do a better job with the dish than
his mother did? Talk about unfair competition!

Make every new dish for yourself before serving it to guests.
Recipes can be inaccurate or incomplete. In fact, recipes can
be absolutely useless. Unless you are prepared to have your
company discover the resemblance between your terrific
new soup and dishwater, hadn't you better discover it first?

Keep anything mundane off your table. Included in this
category are toothpicks (except frilly ones for canapés);
instant coffee; tea bags; cardboard containers; cooking tools;
paper plates and plastic utensils (even outdoors); ash trays;
milk cartons; pop or liquor bottles (wine bottles are fine);
bottles or packets of sugar substitute (they belong in a sugar
bowl); tubs, jars, or bottles of ketchup, mustard,
mayonnaise, butter, etc.; dogs, cats, children; and, of
course, elbows.

The Beautiful Meal

Dahling, you aren't one of those people who would send a poor
defenseless meal out to face the world without so much as a sprig

---

[24] Veal Cordon Bleu (kohr dahn BLUH) is veal stuffed with ham and Swiss
cheese, then breaded and sautéed.

of parsley to hide behind, are you? A few minutes spent on food beautification could win you more compliments than you would ever believe. Here are a few hints:

Consider the color. Your best chicken in cream, nestled on a bed of snow-white rice, and lovingly served on your finest bone china, is about as appetizing as a saucer full of paste. You need tomato slices sprinkled with dill, fresh broccoli or carrots, or perhaps just a handful of curly parsley to break the monotone and the monotony.

Vary the shape. A filet mignon, discs of zucchini, and a broiled tomato add up to a boringly round dinner. Balance the plate and give it new interest with long slender green beans or asparagus.

Vary the Shape

Create a Pattern

Create a pattern. Think of the plate as your canvas; the food, as your artistic medium. Lay out asparagus spears like the spokes of a wheel, or bundle them up with long strips of pimento. Encircle roasts or chops with Potatoes *à la Duchesse*. Create rows, squares, crosses; the patterns are endless; the results, sensational.

Add some fantasy. A wedge of lemon and a sprig of watercress do not excitement make (though they can't hurt). You need some whimsy, something to set your meal apart from all others, something to add a memorable touch.

You need "Shindig Chic" (that's Chapter 10) coming up soon.

CLASS NOTES

Gourmet Goodies by Mail

Is Cook having problems meeting the many demands of your discriminating palate? Is your estate so secluded that you have to crank up the helicopter just to get some more caviar? Not to worry. Relief is in sight.

ARTICHOKES

Mr. Artichoke
11000 Blackie Rd.
Castroville, CA 94102
(408) 633-2486

CONFECTIONS

Godiva Chocolates
701 Fifth Ave.
New York, NY 10022
(212) 361-2781

Krön Chocolatier
506 Madison Ave.
New York, NY 10021
(212) 486-0265

Plumbridge Confections & Gifts
33 E. 61st St.
New York, NY 10021
(212) 371-0608

CAVIAR AND DELICACIES

Caviarteria
29 E. 60th St.
New York, NY 10022
(212) 759-7410

Pâté and Quiches
267 W. 17th St.
New York, NY 10011
(212) 219-1230

CHEESE

Cheese of All Nations
153 Chambers St.
New York, NY 10007
(212) 732-0752

Cheeselovers International
Cheeselovers Building
P.O. Box 1205
Westbury, NY 11590
(516) 997-7045

COFFEE AND TEA

McNulty's Tea & Coffee Co.
109 Christopher St.
New York, NY 10014
(212) 242-5351

EQUIPMENT

The Chef's Catalog
725 County Line Rd.
Deerfield, IL 60015
(312) 480-9400

Colonial Gardens Kitchens
270 W. Merrick Rd.
Valley Stream, NY 11582
(516) 561-8800

Williams-Sonoma Catalog for
Cooks
P.O. Box 3792
San Francisco, CA 94119
(415) 982-0295

FRUIT

Fruit-of-the-Month
Harry & David Co.
2518 S. Pacific Highway
Medford, OR 97501
(503) 776-2121

FRUITCAKE

Collins Street Bakery
401 W. 7th St.
Corsicana, TX 75110
(214) 872-3951

Mary of Puddin Hill
P.O. Box 241
Greenville, TX 75401
(214) 455-2651

MEAT, FISH, AND FOWL

Alaskan Seafood Gift
Company
P.O. Box 2211
Anchorage, AL 99510

Fin 'n' Feather
RFD 2
Dundee, IL 60118
1-800-323-6895

Hegg & Hegg, Inc.
801 Marine Dr.
Port Angeles, WA 98362
(206) 457-3344

Legal Seafoods Market
33 Everett St.
Boston, MA 02134
(617) 783-8084

New Braunfels Smokehouse
P.O. Box 1159
New Braunfels, TX 78130

Omaha Steak International
4400 S. 96th St.
Omaha, NE 68127
(402) 391-3660 (in Nebraska)
    or 1-800-228-9055

Pfaelzer Bros.
4501 W. District Blvd.
Chicago, IL 60632
(312) 927-7100 (in Illinois
    and Alaska)
or 1-800-621-0226

Virginia Veal Farms
P.O. Box 96
Stanardsville, VA 22973
1-800-446-1749

WINES

Wines by Wire
34 Exchange Pl.
Jersey City, NJ
1-800-223-2660
($40 minimum)
    *(They will ship throughout
    the U.S., including Hawaii
    and the Virgin Islands, and
    to London.)*

Caretakers

Babies have nurses; children have nannies; grandparents have faithful family retainers. But *dahling*, who will take care of you?

Successful men and women need a network of caretakers to help them look great and to save them time, energy, and money. Of course, in the absence of recommendations from trusted friends and associates, you'll need to be clever to find really great people. To help you get started, here are a few ways to find your:

Automobile mechanic. Join the Owners' Club for your make of car (Mercedes, Rolls, whatever); an authorized service center should have all the information you need. After joining, ask the club's technical representative to name a few good mechanics. Visit each shop and look for signs of inspired management: helpful personnel, a garage full of expensive cars and smiling clients.

Cleaners. To find someone to clean or press particularly fragile garments, call your local opera or Shakespeare company. Find out who they trust with their costumes.

Cobbler. Ask the managers of several stores selling expensive men's shoes for recommendations.

Movers. Call your favorite antique store or museum and see who transports their valuables.

Tailors (and seamstresses). Pull out the Yellow Pages and find four or five tailors in your area. Visit each of them, saying you are looking for *two* tailors to handle your many needs. Ask who, in addition to themselves, they would recommend. It shouldn't take you long to find out who's best.

Tiffany & Co.'s beautiful octagonal-pattern silver service includes sterling coffee pot, teapot, waste bowl, creamer, and sugar bowl.

9

· COFFEE, TEA, AND YOU ·

You may tempt the upper classes
With your villainous demitasses
But
Heaven will protect the working girl.

—*EDGAR SMITH, 1857–1938*

Most people can count the times they've been served flaming coffee or an exotic blend of tea. This is significant for several reasons.

For one thing, it's interesting that those occasions are so memorable, that the sight, smell, and taste of those drinks stick in the mind while thoughts of the preceding meals have completely disappeared. It is also of interest that these occasions are so rare. Preparing exotic coffees and teas requires little in the way of expense or skill. In fact, your basic butler (or basic host or hostess) can whip them up with no trouble at all.

So why in the world don't they do it more often?

So why don't you do it? Here's all you need to know.

Classy Coffee

Selection

Buy coffee at a specialty store or gourmet shop. No exceptions!
Experiment with beans and blends from various locations.

Armenian beans are full-bodied; Maracaibo beans are delicate; numerous coffees fall in-between. Ask your vendor for recommendations. And do some experimenting on your own. Then, when guests start raving about your coffee and asking about the brand, you can say: "No brand, *dahling*. I use a private blend."

Select roasts carefully. American Roast, with its light color and mild flavor, makes wonderful breakfast coffee, as does the stronger New Orleans Roast. French Roast is dark, rich, and perfect for *demitasse;*[1] use it, too, as a base for exotic coffee-based drinks. Choose Italian Roast, the darkest and most bitter, for preparing *espresso*.[2]

Use freshly ground coffee to ensure full taste. Have your merchant grind the beans for you. Better yet, do it yourself using a well-cleaned grinder. Whole beans stay fresh about one month; ground coffee, even in an unopened, refrigerated container, starts deteriorating within two weeks.

Keep decaffeinated coffee on hand for guests who cannot tolerate regular blends. (Note: French and Italian roasts contain less caffeine than lighter roasts.)

Making It

Whether you use a vacuum pot, percolator, or drip pot is primarily a matter of personal preference, though drip pots that brew tea and coffee simultaneously, and that work on timers, are wonderfully convenient.

Whatever pot you use, keep it scrupulously clean, store it where it will air properly, measure ingredients accurately, and use bottled water (unless you have *naturally* soft, good-tasting tap water).

Never make coffee more than one hour before use; never let it boil, even for a moment; and never reuse grounds. Did I mention the biggest never of all? Never serve instant coffee to guests!

---

[1] Demitasse (deh mee TAHSS) is French for "half cup," so never say "demitasse cup." It refers to the small cups in which many after-dinner coffees are served, as well as to a special coffee.

[2] Espresso (eh SPREH soh, *not* ex SPRESS oh) is a strong, dark Italian coffee.

Serving It

Morning and afternoon coffees are served in china cups (or mugs on very casual occasions). After-dinner coffees are generally served in china cups or *demitasses*. Each should rest on a saucer, the handle facing right, with a spoon under it. Either may be set on the table before dinner or brought out on a tray with, or after, dessert.

Though the most elegant way to pour coffee is from an antique silver pot, any attractive pot will do. If the one you own is less than beautiful, fill cups in the kitchen—not so full that they might spill—and pass them to your guests on a lovely tray.

Choose your condiments carefully; they are every bit as important as the coffee itself.

Use instant-dissolving superfine sugar (or lumps, if you have tiny silver tongs), granulated artificial sweetener, and fresh, room-temperature cream. For a special touch, whip the cream and offer orange and lemon twists.

Place all accompaniments in lovely serving bowls and pass them around on an attractive tray, always serving from the left. Better yet, have the butler do it. You don't want to miss any gossip!

Show Stoppers

Want to really dazzle your guests? Try one of these:

Café au Lait (kah fã oh LÃ), the traditional English breakfast drink, is half scalded milk, half very strong coffee, poured simultaneously into a china cup. (If you like, add 1 ounce ground chicory to each cup of ground coffee before brewing.)

Café Brûlée (kah fã broo LÃ) is prepared by pouring seven parts strong, hot coffee and one part cognac into a large, heated wineglass whose rim has been dipped first into lemon juice, then into powdered sugar. Carefully set the coffee ablaze just before serving.

Café Diable (kah fã DYAH bluh) is six lumps of sugar, six cloves, a strip of lemon or orange rind, and one-third cup cognac placed (but not mixed) in a chafing dish and flamed. One quart strong French roast coffee is then added and heated for a moment. Finally, the hot mixture is ladled into demitasses and garnished with cinnamon sticks.

Café Espresso (kah fã eh SPREH soh) is thick, strong coffee made in a special pot by passing steam under pressure over Italian espresso grounds. Follow pot directions exactly; serve in espresso cups or demitasses. Add a lemon twist to each serving.

Café Royal (kah fã roy YAHL) is prepared as follows: Place a sugar lump in a demitasse spoon balanced over a demitasse, cover with cognac, and apply a flame; when dissolved, stir into cup filled with strong, hot French roast coffee.

Cappucino (kah poo CHEE noh) is equal parts of espresso and scalded milk flavored with a dash of nutmeg or cinnamon, and served in cappuccino cups or demitasses.

Demitasse (deh mee TAHSS) is thick, strong French roast coffee served *after* dessert at formal lunches or any dinner. *Devotées* (dā voh TĀ) drink it black, no sugar, in demitasses, with a twist of lemon.

Iced Coffee is made by pouring cool, strong coffee into a tall, chilled glass filled with ice; add sugar and cream to taste; or pour the coffee into a tall glass with a scoop of vanilla ice cream. Top with fresh, sweet whipped cream and supply a saucer and a long spoon.

Irish Coffee is one jigger of Irish whiskey mixed with four to five ounces strong hot coffee and one teaspoon Demerara (a light-brown sugar) or superfine sugar; float cream on top[3] and serve in a preheated goblet.

---

[3]To float cream: Pour heavy cream onto the back of a spoon so carefully and slowly that it remains on top. To simplify the process, whip the cream *lightly;* sweeten it if you like.

Mocha (MOH kah) is half strong, hot coffee, half hot cocoa, poured simultaneously into china cups.

Tasteful Tea

Tea would probably be our national drink were it not for the high-handedness of the British East India Company in the days preceding the Boston Tea Party.

Too bad. Tea is so civilized. It comes in a wide variety of flavors and colors, has half the caffeine of coffee, and is blessed with the most endearing quality of being just a touch highbrow. And it's delicious.

You'll want to keep several varieties of fine *loose* teas on hand, sealed in airtight jars. (They will keep about six months.) Try one or two black teas, one *oolong* (oo LOHNG), one green, and one herbal.

Selection

Surprisingly, the same basic plant produces black, green, and *oolong* teas. Differences in color and flavor are attributable to variations in soil, region of growth, plant age, blend, and method of processing.

> *Black Tea,* so named because its green leaves turn black when fermented, produces the amber teas so popular in America. Leaves are graded in four sizes, listed here in order of decreasing size: *souchong* (soo shahng), orange pekoe (PEE koh), broken orange pekoe or broken pekoe *souchong*, and fannings (used in tea bags). The more famous black teas, found in the best tearooms everywhere, include:
> *Assam* (as SAM): robust tea from northeast India
> *Darjeeling* (dahr JEE ling): wonderful, delicate tea from Himalaya
> *Earl Grey:* famous, full-bodied tea from Taiwan
> *English Breakfast:* mellow blend of tea from India and Ceylon

Keemun (KEE muhn): one of the best black teas of China

Lapsang souchong (lap sang soo shahng): hearty, smoky, distinctively flavored tea from Taiwan or China

Green Tea, made from unfermented leaves, produces elegant pale-green brews. Choose among teas marked *Japanese panfired, imperial gunpowder,* and *young hyson*.

Oolong Tea, made from semifermented brown-green leaves, produces a light brew and is the perfect foil to a heavy meal.

In general, the paler the color, the finer the grade. Try *Formosa oolong* (considered by many to be the world's finest tea). Or try one of the *oolongs* scented with herbs and flowers: *Jasmine*, from Formosa, is a well-known complement to spicy foods; *Lichee* (lee chee), from Taiwan, is a faintly sweet tea flavored with lichee blossoms.

Some Like It Hot

THE PREP

The boiling-tap-water, stale-tea-bag method of preparation no doubt accounts for the low incidence of tea consumption in America. Savvy hosts and hostesses, however, offer their guests the very best; they brew tea as follows. Every single time.

Step 1. Bring *cold, bottled* drinking water to a brisk boil using six cups water per four-to-six servings.

Step 2. Pour one cup of the boiling water into any *clean, nonmetal* teapot. Swish it around to scald the pot, then discard.

Step 3. Dry the scalded pot and insert one teaspoon of *loose* tea per serving, plus an additional spoonful per three to four cups. Add six ounces boiling water per serving. Stir and cover.

Step 4. Let the tea steep (that is, pass its flavor into the water) for three to five minutes; no less, no more.

Step 5. Scald a second teapot for serving—one that's pretty and nonmetallic (unless it's silver). Stir the tea quickly, then pour through a strainer into the serving pot. Serve immediately.

Note: Keep your perfect brew hot with a small burner or a tea cozy (a pretty padded cover in a style compatible with your general decor).

THE SERVE

Hot tea is poured straight from the most attractive teapot you can afford; it is *never* passed on a tray. Serve the brew in pretty cup-and-saucer sets and provide silver spoons.

Offer bowls of superfine sugar (or lumps, if you have tiny silver tongs) and granulated sugar substitute, a pitcher of plain, steaming hot, bottled water (to dilute too-strong tea), and a plate of lemon wedges (accompanied by a small serving fork). For black teas add fresh mint, cinnamon sticks, and a server of room-temperature milk (never cream). Pass everything on a pretty, uncovered tray.

Some Like It Cold

THE PREP

In a glass jar, combine one cup cold *bottled* water and one teaspoon loose (non-instant) tea per serving. Cover and refrigerate overnight. Strain and serve.

or

Make double-strength hot tea, let it cool (if possible), and pour over generous amounts of ice.

Do not add lemon or sugar to your guests' tea; let them add their own.

THE SERVE

Iced tea is lovely at lunch or as an afternoon refresher, but omit it at dinner parties (except, perhaps, barbecues) and at meals where hot tea will be served.

Offer the tea in tall, clear glasses packed with ice (preferably crushed). Garnish with a sprig of mint and a lemon wedge; pass sugar, sugar substitute, and extra lemon (as previously described). Provide a long spoon.

High Time at Tea

Not long ago, only debutantes and blue-haired grandmothers took tea in the afternoon. But that's all changed. Today these ladies have to fight for a table. You see, moguls are making deals over tea. Lovers are making plans over tea. And a few newcomers are making big mistakes over tea.

But not you. You will soon know all there is to know about this most civilized of customs.

To find a lovely place for tea, check with the most elegant hotel in your city. If they don't have a tearoom, they'll probably know who does.

Expect to be seated between 3:30 and 5:00 P.M. You'll generally be there for one to three hours.

Dress is chic business attire. Ladies should not hesitate to wear furs or expensive jewelry.

Afternoon tea is served in a series of courses, the first of which, not surprisingly, is the tea. Order one of your favorites: Darjeeling, Earl Grey, Assam, Jasmine, whatever.

When the teapot arrives, look about the table for a small silver tea strainer. If you see one, presume that the pot contains loose tea which must steep three to five minutes before serving. (If no strainer is in sight, the tea no doubt has already been strained.)

Sometimes your waiter will pour the tea for you; sometimes not. A quick glance around the room should provide the answer. If you must serve yourself, place the strainer (if any) over your cup and pour. As leaves collect, dump them into the little silver dish that holds the strainer. Hide the used leaves by replacing the strainer in its holder.

Flavor your tea, as desired, with sugar (using the sugar tongs, if any), lemon (using the lemon fork, if any), and milk.

You will more than likely be served a delicious assortment of finger sandwiches (so named—now this is really clever— because you eat them with your fingers!) Expect the sandwiches to be filled with watercress, salmon, cucumber, pâté, and the like.

Next come the sweets. Partake of cookies and other easy-to-eat items with your fingers, but use your fork for messy pastries. (Note: If you wish to use butter, bring a small amount to your plate.)

Toward the meal's end, you may wish to order a glass of dry sherry to fortify you for the check. Which may be quite substantial. But worth every penny!

Spas for the Sybaritic

Poor baby. Is your neck stiff from counting all those Krugerrands? And has coupon clipping brought on socialite's spread? Well then, it's obviously time to wing off to your favorite spa, someplace like:

Maine Chance, Elizabeth Arden's legendary retreat in Phoenix, Arixona.

The Golden Door, Oriental-like refuge in Escondido, California.

The Greenhouse, the super temperature-controlled spa just outside Dallas in Arlington, Texas.

La Costa Hotel and Spa, resort *extraordinaire* just north of San Diego in Carlsbad, California.

The Spa at Turnberry Isle, the glamorous oasis in North Miami, Florida.

The Spa at Palm-Aire, that incomparable spa and resort in Pompano, Florida.

One more thing. Do not forget, in your haste, to pack a few coins. Twenty-five hundred dollars or so should handle a week's worth of pampering at even the most expensive spa. A few will even leave you with change.

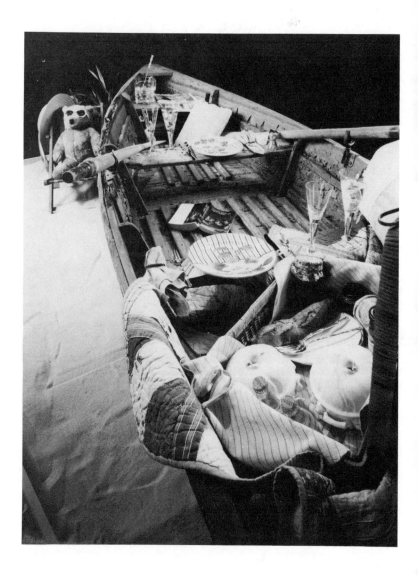

Shindig Chic is a "Lunch Encounter in Central Park" by Mario Buatta.
Photo by Billy Cunningham courtesy of Tiffany & Co.

10

· SHINDIG CHIC ·

Drink and dance and laugh and lie,
Love, the reeling midnight through,
For tomorrow we shall die!
(But, alas, we never do.)

—DOROTHY PARKER

Well, you've had your kitchen staff scouring the town for the finest ingredients and spent hour upon hour supervising their work. Now, can you in good conscience let your beautifully dressed dinner sit on a plain table in a plain room?

I thought not.

House Rules

Start with a clean house, send uninvited relatives to the movies, and hide your perfectly adorable dogs, cats, and children; lock up the kids' artwork, *your* work, home computers, television sets, home movies, video games, and snapshots of your last trip to anywhere. Lose the key.

While you're at it, lock away all musical instruments and forget you know anyone who plays, sings, juggles, or does anything that might be considered even remotely entertaining. Because they seldom are.

Then start on the decorations.

Shindigs

Only the most elegant (otherwise known as expensive) ingredients will do when you're entertaining moguls, magnates, and mothers-in-law. Other times- —when a group of peers have been invited over—down-home cooking can be a real hoot!

So attention y'all! It's time to turn your world-famous chili (lasagna, tacos, or whatever) into a gala event. All you have to do is beg, borrow, and steal until the party area looks fantastic. (Note: Anything short of overdone is totally unacceptable. After all, we can't have friends thinking we eat food like this *every* day!)

Start with *objets d'art* (oh zhā DAHR)—objects of art—from your local museum; you can sometimes rent amazing things for a pittance. Coax posters from foreign airlines or tourist bureaus. Better yet, ask your travel agent for help. After making a fortune on your last trip to Europe, she owes you a few favors.

Now some party ideas.

To show off your Texas chili, you need Stetsons for both host and hostess, and imaginative invitations. You also need a few pots of cactus, a Texas state map to mount on the wall, and, if you really want to splurge, masses of yellow roses. And don't forget the toe-tapping music, piping-hot corn bread, Lone Star or Pearl Beer, and bread in the shape of some varmint.

For a south-of-the-border fiesta, you'll need a map of Mexico, sombreros, pitchers of margaritas, tequila shooters, and bunches of colorful crepe-paper flowers. To put guests in a festive mood, play appropriate music, or splurge on *mariachis* (mah ree AH chees)— Mexican musicians. (Note: If you augment your menu with selections from a Mexican restaurant, you can no doubt enlist the owner's help in finding your props.)

If Italian food is your specialty, turn your dining room into a cozy *ristorante* (ree stoh RAHN tā). Set the mood with red-and-white checked tablecloths, giant baskets of Italian bread, glass jars overflowing with different pastas, candleholders made from empty straw-wrapped *Chianti* (kee YAHN tee) bottles; well, you get the idea.

Extravaganzas

If you'll throw a party for chili, what will you do for Dover sole? Get out the Waterford and Wedgwood and wait for rave reviews? Not enough. You need dazzle. Not too much, mind you, just enough to keep people discussing your party for the next five years or so. Of course, such pizzazz doesn't just happen; it must be created.

Bring excitement to the dining room by repeating a theme. Instead of your usual candlesticks, try *twenty* small white candles planted in sparkling glass holders, and reflected in a mirror (on the wall? behind the buffet?). And if you're really feeling spirited, weave strings of tiny white lights through sturdy house plants. The room will come alive.

Here's another idea. Create an indoor garden by repeating a nature theme. You'll need a floral centerpiece, flowered tablecloths and dishes, and perhaps a gigantic chintz screen. Add lots of plants and suddenly it's spring.

Now, about those floral arrangements. Because you and your guests will be staring at them throughout dinner, they had better be interesting (and low enough to see over).

For elegance and simplicity, place a single perfect blossom at each guest's seat. Float magnolias or camelias in shallow crystal bowls; or slip tea roses, tiger lilies, or jonquils into tiny bud vases.

Perhaps you would prefer a centerpiece. Ask your florist or interior decorator to match the flowers on your wallpaper, draperies, or dinnerware. Or have him incorporate some of your favorite objects into the arrangement.

One of the most exciting centerpieces I've seen consisted of a generous bouquet of daisies and baby's breath, with tiny white porcelain birds and rabbits peeking out here and there.

Small wooden birds arranged with driftwood and cattails could also be effective, as could a collection of tiny antique dolls and complementary flowers (for a women's luncheon), or a grouping of seashells—with or without flowers. Use your imagination and your favorite things to come up with something you really love.

Dinnerware should complement favorite centerpieces and

themes. If you entertain extensively, you will need several sets; pick patterns and styles that can be interpreted many ways. Should one set have to suffice for the time being, pick something elegant but simple so you can change the look by changing flowers and linens.

I have a set of semi-transparent Swedish glass dinnerware that looks different on each new surface. Friends have achieved similar versatility by combining several sets of brightly colored art deco.

What if you are already burdened with a set of plain ol' $300-per-place-setting bone china? Don't despair; quality is *always* stylish.

But remember the wonderful earthenware your mother gave you? And the colorful plastic dishes? And those decorative paper plates? Forget them. Fine food deserves fine dinnerware, even at lunch, even outdoors, even if you fear breakage. China and stemware are meant to be enjoyed—and destined to be destroyed. So purchase no better quality than you can bear to see shattered.

Choose silverware to complement your dishes; use modern with modern, traditional with traditional, and so on. Select linens to reflect the style of tableware and of the food you'll be serving. You would not, for example, want a checkered tablecloth with either outrageous art deco dishes or delicate French cuisine.

If you had a large wedding, you are probably loaded with *silver* platters, tureens, punch bowls, and chafing dishes. If not, you might want to consider buying *copper* instead. Its lovely, warm color enhances the beauty of food, it is appropriate for all but the most formal occasions (like state dinners), and you can use it for cooking as well as for serving. Choose heavy pieces lined with another metal (usually tin or stainless steel), and always keep copper cookware away from high heat.

Do you want to decrease your work load while adding a touch of professionalism? Invest in a serving cart. It will extend your table or buffet area, display hors d'oeuvres, hold bar items, and transport food between table and kitchen. It may be expensive, though, so if your funds are tied up in the stock market (or the supermarket), use several beautiful trays instead.

Now, about napkins. Because you'll want to use them for

effect, as well as for keeping stray morsels off your guests' Paris originals, buy enormous squares of fine, sturdy fabric. (No paper napkins. Ever!) Select colors to complement, but not necessarily match, your tablecloth, checking to see that patterns look attractive on both sides. Then try folding your napkins as shown below.

NAPKIN FLOWERS

Use these pretty flowers to line serving bowls, display dinner napkins, or separate soup or salad bowls from their liners.

Place a starched *square* napkin on a flat surface; smooth out any ripples. Fold all corner points toward center and crease.

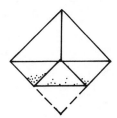

Repeat, folding newly formed corners to center. Crease. Holding center points together, carefully flip napkin over.

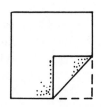

Once again, fold points to center and crease. Holding center carefully with one hand, reaching underneath with the other, pull corner flaps halfway out.

When corners are out, pull out the
four side flaps. Use the finished
napkin in a basket or bowl.

GOBLET FLOWERS

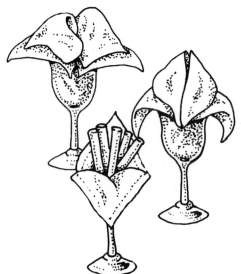

The napkins at left were folded us
the basic technique below. Use to
display dinner napkins or to hold
breadsticks, cigarettes, etc.

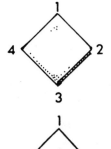

Fold a new or starched napkin
square in half, then in half again.

Fold up corner 3 to center.

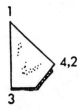

Fold corner 4 across to corner 2.

Fold back corner 4 in accordian pleats.

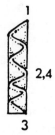

Flip napkin over and pleat back corner 2.

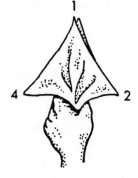

Grasp end 3 and fan out napkin. Separate points at end 1, shape as you like, and insert in a goblet.

Attitudes, Etiquette, and Atmosphere

The best parties are given by people who truly care about their guests.

They anticipate the hundred and one things that could go wrong at the last minute. They make lists (like the Party Checklist and Dinner Countdowns in Chapter 11). They consult a good etiquette book before every party. And they:

Call or send written invitations, ten to fourteen days before the big event, requesting that guests RSVP. Then, several days before the evening in question, they send a small card reminding the guests that they are looking forward to the pleasure of their company. By doing so they never serve a sit-down dinner for twelve to the scant six people who show up!

Invite guests for 7:30 if dinner will be served at 8:30. Because so many people think arriving late is fashionable (it is at cocktail parties, but not at sit-down dinners), clever cooks plan the meal for an hour or so after friends are scheduled to arrive. That way, prompt guests have time for apéritifs, and late comers show before the soufflé falls.

Thomas Wolfe, *concierge* (kahn SYEHRZH) *extraordinaire* at San Francisco's chic Meridian Hotel, says most of his clients prefer to dine at 8:00 P.M. (He should know; he's the magician who makes their impossible-to-get reservations!) Of course, when planning an evening around a special event—a play? a movie?—he books them for the earliest or latest seating.

Attend to guests, but don't push, hover, manipulate, or intimidate. There is a fine line between being attentive and being a pain. Learn it. This line is most obviously, and obnoxiously, crossed by the guilt-provoking cook. You know the type: He or she "slaved all day" making that dessert, so how can you not eat it? Closely related, and almost as bad, is the host who *asks* if you want something, then *makes* you take it whether you want it or not.

Keep culinary secrets secret. Hosts must never cheat guests, or themselves, by revealing how little they cooked, planned, suffered, or paid.

Handle failures and disasters with aplomb. No one needs to know that the dog played fetch with the potatoes, or that your youngest child licked half the icing off the cake. If you can safely repair the damage, do so (and say nothing). If you can't repair it, make a last-minute substitution (and say nothing) or omit it (and say nothing). If you've managed to ruin the whole dinner, quietly make reservations at a good restaurant, then invent a wild story about how dinner burned because Julia Child just wouldn't let you off the phone, or how you suddenly had this craving for Hungarian food and does that mean you're pregnant? Laugh.

Never make excuses or apologize for shortcomings. Why draw attention to a hole in the rug, chipped dishes, or curdled sauce by making excuses or by telling everyone how sorry you are? In the first place, excuses excuse nothing. In the second place, alibis and apologies only embarrass all concerned. And, in the third place, probably nobody noticed in the first place!

Handle guests' accidents graciously. Salt thrown on spills helps to soak up liquid and discourages stains; a napkin tossed over a spill helps to conceal it. The gracious host makes light of any damage, attends to it quickly, and resigns himself to any resulting expense.

Don't let guests help with cooking, serving, or cleaning even if they truly want to help. Guests are invited to enjoy themselves, not to work. If you require assistance, you must engage help. Sorry, but that's the price you pay for giving your staff the evening off!

Anyway, if you allow guests to help, they may discover your darkest culinary secrets. And then there's the age-old problem of women getting stuck in the kitchen while men chat in the living room. It doesn't make for a very liberated, or interesting, evening.

Use place cards to facilitate the seating of large groups. Beautifully inscribed cards in pretty little holders, diplomatically placed, free hosts for more important duties.

Treat arrivals and departures as major events. Both host and hostess must welcome guests at the door, offer them drinks, and introduce them to everyone at a small party, or to a few interesting people at a large one. At evening's end, both host and hostess must escort guests to the door, praising each one for his contribution to the evening and expressing a desire that he return again soon.

Only kitchen fires, earthquakes, or labor pains should divert hosts and hostesses from this duty. Even then, I'd think twice before being so rude as to ignore the arrival and departure of friends.

Play soft, uninterrupted music all through the evening. Try classical, semi-classical, or mood music, anything with no commercials and requiring no adjustments. Note: Sticking records and dog food commercials do little to improve digestion.

Plan after-dinner amusements carefully. I would like to go on record as being totally opposed to anything that requires guests to exhibit talent or brains—unless said happening is announced on the invitation. Impromptu Trivial Pursuits, card games, and the like seldom do more than divide guests into two divergent groups: the obnoxious winners and the sulking losers. This, to my way of thinking, is not the best end to an otherwise smashing evening.

Pre-announced fun and games are quite another story. Card games (bridge? poker?) can be wildly entertaining among players of roughly equal skill. And who doesn't enjoy a good play or movie? But please forgo dancing in the den or charades in the salon; even with warning, such amusements rarely work.

As for after-dinner drugs, well, as it is unlikely that all of your guests will be interested (if you've chosen your friends wisely), don't embarrass the non-users by either offering, or allowing, contraband.

What happens if you simply let things drag on after dinner?

Invariably, the most interesting guests leave too soon and the *least* interesting ones seem to stay forever. Some fun.

Relieving the Burden

Time and Money Savers

Entertaining can be difficult, expensive work, but you can eliminate some of the hassle and expense if you:

Give parties on consecutive nights. You can cut your staff's work almost in half, and save money, by entertaining two nights in a row. Change the guest list from night to night, but don't change the menu or decorations. Then your people need shop, cook, decorate, and clean house but once. On the second night, you simply straighten up, then begin again. Just don't divulge your strategy. Guests invariably invent ulterior motives for your inviting them one night instead of another.

Serve buffet-style. You won't need extra help, nor will you have to keep leaving your guests to supervise things. Arrange the food on a table decorated with baskets of fresh fruit and vases of flowers.

Hire inexpensive assistants for behind-the-scenes duty. Only professionals will ever be allowed to serve your guests; after all, you have an image to uphold. But why not hire a teenage friend to help with bothersome tasks *before* and *after* dinner?

Choose someone who is honest, conscientious, and not overly clumsy. Give your assistant complete written instructions on what to do, and when to do it, then turn him or her loose to do your dirty work. Pay this helper as you would a good baby-sitter; offer dessert as a bonus.

Do a party swap with a friend. You'll ease the work load, and save money, by being each other's slave-for-a-day. Help with shopping, cooking, decorating, and cleaning up—but stay out of sight.

The World's Easiest Parties

If just reading this chapter has exhausted you, forget about entertaining at home.

Caterers will throw shindigs for you in a football stadium, a rented Rolls Royce, a hay wagon, a yacht, a leased country mansion, and practically anywhere else. Your contribution? Just help plan the menu and pay the bill.

Public and private airplanes, trains, buses, ships, and charter boats are wonderful places for parties and many have large staffs to attend to your wishes. How about a champagne supper a few miles off shore? Or thirty thousand feet up? To get things rolling, flying, or sailing, just pick up the phone.

Restaurants can be exciting places to entertain, if you take the time to do things correctly. Refer back to "Restaurant Resourcefulness" for more information.

Hotel concierges plan marvelous parties. An intimate dinner for two? Right away. An outlandish blowout for five hundred? No problem.

And we're not talking creamed chicken in a stuffy banquet room. We're talking Big Time: caviar and scrambled eggs at Regine's (reh ZHEENZ), lobster and chocolate soufflés at The Bistro (BEE stroh). Just ring up your concierge when staying at a fine hotel and the party of a lifetime is but a moment away!

Houseguesting

Weekending at someone else's house can be such a trying experience! There you are, away from your upstairs maid, your downstairs maid, your valet; the entire situation is simply too primitive to bear!

Obviously, your biggest concern is: Who is going to attend to domestic matters? And well it should be. Alas, here is the unfortunate answer:

After using your host's powder room, *you* must wipe off the sink and counter and fold your towel neatly, but in such a way as to indicate that it has been used.

On Saturday morning, *you* should put the spread on your bed and leave the room looking as though an aristocrat had come to visit.

On Sunday morning, if your host has the good taste to have a large staff, you need only put the spread on your bed again and pack.

If (heaven forbid!) your host has a small staff or (worse yet!) no staff at all, I'm afraid *you* are going to have to strip the bed, fold the used sheets, and ask the hostess for fresh linens with which to remake the bed. With a little luck, she'll refuse your offer to help (as you would in her place). If she actually supplies the linens, go ahead and make the bed as neatly as someone of your good breeding and obvious lack of experience in such matters can.

By the way, if you're off to Paris at dawn, you need only pull the bedspread up over the pillows. Your hostess will make it herself—at a more civilized hour.

Even though you worked your fingers to the bone all weekend, you really must send your hostess a little something in the way of a "thank you." Flowers, maybe. Or wine. Or a maid. (Maybe not a maid.)

11

· BLUE-BLOODED MEALS FOR RED-BLOODED COOKS ·

*Cooking is like love. It should be entered
into with abandon or not at all.*

—HARRIET VAN HORNE,

VOGUE

Don't you just adore poking around the kitchen, that is, once you get Cook and her staff out from underfoot? This is the time for you to be you: free, creative, positively sensational. And don't you just love it when the butler lets it slip that you did everything yourself? Imagine: brains, good looks, *and* culinary talent—all in one perfect person. Surely your guests will find a way to reward you. A promotion? A signed contract? A Maserati? You deserve whatever your little heart desires, you talented devil, you!

Get Ready

I recently viewed a most impressive demonstration of Chinese noodle making. The young chef, I was told, had studied four years to perfect his technique.

You will be pleased to learn that the recipes in this chapter require considerably less dedication.

You may also be pleased at the completeness of instructions. Everything from shopping lists to timetables has been provided. So pick up the phone and invite over a few of your closest friends

What a way to set a table! "Dinner for Four" by Donghia Associates, Inc.
Photo by Billy Cunningham courtesy of Tiffany & Co.

(the ambassador, her husband, several assorted billionaires). You'll adore the way they adore your cooking!

The Great Divide

The upcoming meals are planned for four. This allows for easy conversion to two (divide everything in half), to six (add half), to eight (double), etc. Do *not* increase herbs or garlic in this manner, though. For six servings, increase seasonings by one-quarter; for eight, by one-half; well, you get the idea. Remember, you can always add more, but *unspicing* can be tricky.

One last word. Read the recipes completely before proceeding: You don't want any last-minute surprises.

Party-Planning Checklist

Lest you forget a few little details, like inviting your spouse or buying the food, here's a general checklist for planning your next gala. Use it in conjunction with the "Cooking Countdowns," which follow the recipes for each meal.

If possible, pull out both lists a week or so before the big event. Place them in the hands of your housekeeper, then check into a spa for a few days while she handles the preliminaries.

Or, if worse comes to worst, use them yourself. These checklists will cut down significantly on the time and effort required to treat your guests to perfection. And you know how much your guests adore perfection!

14 DAYS BEFORE

___ Select a date and check your calendar for conflicting engagements.

___ Clear date with your spouse/lover/friend/mother.

___ Send out invitations.

2–7 DAYS BEFORE

___ Make a copy of this checklist and fill in the details.

___ Arrange for help (if any).

___ Copy the "Countdown" checklist for the meal.

___ Check utensils, cookware, dishes, etc. Purchase or rent anything needed.

___ Purchase wine, liquor, liqueurs, mixers, condiments, etc.

___ Shop for hard-to-find ingredients and decorations.

___ Prepare dishes that can or must be made ahead.

___ Prepare and freeze butter balls and herbed butters.

___ Order baked goods.

___ Order flowers.

___ Order special meat, seafood, poultry, etc.

___ Select clothing.

___ Make appointments to have hair styled, makeup applied, etc.

ONE DAY BEFORE

___ Buy ice.

___ Do marketing for everything but baked goods and seafood.

___ Pick over parsley. Rinse and refrigerate pretty sprigs for garnish. Mince the rest and freeze.

___ Prepare, bag, and refrigerate condiments: lemon curls, grated orange rind, chopped onion, etc.

___ Clean house and decorate.

___ Prepare food that must be made one day in advance.

THE NIGHT OR MORNING BEFORE

___ Thaw food that needs defrosting by placing in the refrigerator overnight.

___ Chill wines and their glasses, serving plates, dishes, and silverware for cold dishes.

___ Set the table (omitting dishes and silverware requiring heating or chilling).

___ Set up buffet area or trays for cocktail and hors d'oeuvres service, meal service, and dessert and coffee service.

___ Pick up baked goods and seafood.

___ Place platters, plates, etc., in one oven to be warmed later.

___ Check on flower delivery.

___ Assemble nonperishable ingredients, skillets, bowls, mixers, etc.

JUST BEFORE GUESTS ARRIVE

___ Dress.
___ Fill ice bucket.
___ Assemble ingredients and garnish for special cocktails.
___ Put your feet up, have a small glass of wine, and relax.

Get Cooking

And now, the food: two meals and a pre-theater refresher designed to reserve you a special seat in the Culinary Hall of Fame.

You'll note that the ingredients used in these meals are not altogether inexpensive. But when you're going to go all out, you might as well go all out!

Dinner

I served this meal recently to a motley group which included an artist, a salesperson, a television news "anchor," and the Field Master[1] of our hunt. Every last morsel was devoured and a good time was had by all. I think your guests will enjoy it, too.

Iced Pink Cucumber Soup
Chablis

Twin Racks of Lamb
Asparagus with Hollandaise Sauce
Buttery New Potatoes
Bordeaux

Crème Caramel
Coffee
Tea

Brandy and Liqueurs

---

[1] The *Field Master* is a member of a Hunt Club who leads riders (who are called "The Field") in their search for a fox. The *Hunt Master* controls the hounds. *Whips* assist the Hunt Master.

MARKETING LIST

Dairy:

   14 ounces plain low-fat yogurt
   1 pound sweet butter
   1 quart whole (or low-fat) milk
   1 dozen large eggs
   5 ounces half & half or light cream

Meat:

   2 racks of lamb, fully trimmed, bones frenched, backbones removed

Produce:

   12–16 pretty new potatoes
   4 bunches curly parsley
   1 cucumber
   1 lemon
   2 pounds fresh green asparagus

Herbs, Spices, and Seasonings:

   1 cup granulated sugar
   Vanilla
   Salt
   Cayenne pepper (optional)
   1 bunch fresh dill weed
   1 clove garlic

Bread:

   ⅓ cup plain bread crumbs

Miscellaneous:

   5 ounces tomato juice
   Dijon mustard
   15 ounces chicken broth

Wines and Liquors:

   Chablis (good quality)
   Bordeaux (good quality)
   Brandy and liqueurs as desired

SPECIAL EQUIPMENT

Instant meat thermometer
Double boiler or blender

Wooden spoon
Custard dishes
Timer
Basting brush
Strainer
Aluminum foil
Wax paper

DINNER RECIPES

ICED PINK CUCUMBER SOUP

Even people who don't usually like yogurt love this soup. And *you'll* love how easy it is to make. (But don't tell!)

Incidentally, if you omit the cream and add a bit more yogurt, it becomes a lovely addition to a low-calorie diet. And still tastes great!

1 cucumber
14 ounces plain low-fat yogurt
15 ounces chilled chicken broth,[2] floating fat skimmed off
5 ounces half & half or light cream
5 ounces canned tomato juice
1 bunch fresh dill weed
1 clove garlic, cut in half

Peel, seed, and dice cucumber. Sprinkle lightly with salt and let drain on a plate for 30 minutes. Meanwhile, mix yogurt, stock, and juice together; refrigerate in a bowl the inside of which you have rubbed with the cut garlic. (Garlic should then be discarded.) Blot drained cucumber with a paper towel, then add to yogurt mixture. Refrigerate for as few as two hours or as long as several days. Just before serving, mix in half & half or light cream. Garnish each portion with several snips of fresh dill.

[2]If you have neither homemade broth nor time to prepare it, you may—just this once—substitute a good canned broth. *College Inn* brand is widely available and tastes fine.

RACK OF LAMB

> 2 *racks of lamb*
> 2 *tablespoons minced dill*
> 2 *tablespoons Dijon mustard*
> 1½ *tablespoons melted butter*
> ⅓ *cup plain bread crumbs*
> 3–4 *bunches curly parsley, trimmed and rinsed*

Have your butcher prepare your racks by removing the backbones, frenching the bones (which exposes the bare ends), and trimming the fat.

Cover bone ends with aluminum foil and place lamb, meat side up, on a rack in a shallow roasting pan. Cover lightly and refrigerate.

Forty minutes before you plan to serve the soup course, preheat oven to 500°F. Bring lamb to room temperature.

Twenty-five minutes before serving, put lamb in upper middle portion of oven. Heat ten minutes. Meanwhile, mix the butter with bread crumbs and dill.

Reduce heat to 400°. Remove lamb, brush with the mustard, and sprinkle well with bread crumbs. Return immediately to oven and roast another fifteen to eighteen minutes or so.

Remove to a wooden serving board when meat temperature reaches 125°–135°F (rare to medium rare). Cover with towel until ready to serve (which should be within ten minutes).

To serve, remove towel, set racks on their ends, slip off the foil, and let the bones interlace to form a tent-like structure. Place bunches of parsley under the "tent" for garnish.

To carve, hold bony end and cut down between ribs. Serve two to three ribs per guest, reserving the rest for seconds.

ASPARAGUS

Note: When asparagus is not in season, use broccoli. Slice off tough ends, trim the leaves, and peel away skin; slit the stalks lengthwise to speed cooking.

> 2 *pounds fresh green asparagus*
>   *Big pinch of salt*
> 2 *tablespoons butter*

Rinse asparagus; break off tough ends at point of least resistance. With a vegetable peeler, carefully scrape off large scales and tough skin on the lower two-thirds of the stalks.

Steam asparagus if you have a steamer (five to seven minutes) or place in boiling salted water in a pan large enough for stalks to lie on their sides (seven to ten minutes). When a knife easily pierces a stalk, cut off a large end and test for doneness. Do not overcook; aim for crisp-tender.

Immediately immerse cooked stalks in ice water. When cool, blot dry. Place in a plastic bag and refrigerate.

When ready to serve, heat 2 tablespoons of butter in a large skillet over a very low flame. Heat asparagus until hot—about five minutes. They will remain very green using this method.

Serve with hollandaise sauce.

HOLLANDAISE SAUCE [3]

Here are two methods. The first is my favorite—if you have a double boiler. If not, you're probably better off with Method II.

Method I

> 3 *egg yolks (not whole eggs)*
> 2 *tablespoons fresh lemon juice*
> 1½ *sticks butter*
>   ⅛ *teaspoon cayenne pepper*

In the top of a double boiler, slowly heat egg yolks. You must keep stirring from start to finish. (If, despite your efforts, the eggs begin

---

[3] Hollandaise sauce is really easy to make, but it doesn't hold well and is thus best made at the last minute. You will, therefore, fare better with a little assistance at this point. If you won't have help, you might consider forgoing the hollandaise in favor of simple melted butter. Just don't forget to supply extra butter on the table.

to scramble, toss them out. Fixing them is more trouble than it's worth.)

As eggs thicken (about two minutes) stir in lemon and pepper, and heat another minute. Add two large pats of butter and stir until they melt. Continue adding two to three pats of butter at a time, stirring continuously until all butter has melted. Sauce should be yellow and very thick.

Method II
(You must use a blender.)

> 3 egg yolks (not whole eggs)
> 1 tablespoon fresh lemon juice
> ⅛ teaspoon cayenne pepper
> 1 stick butter

Place first three ingredients in a blender and mix lightly. With machine running, *slowly* add butter, which has been heated until foamy, but not brown. Sauce should be yellow and thick. Serve immediately.

BUTTERY NEW POTATOES

> 12–16 new potatoes: small, colorful, and as unblemished as possible
> 3–4 tablespoons butter
> Big pinch of salt
> Parsley for garnish

Rinse potatoes well, place in a large pot, and cover with warm tap water. Add salt; cover pan. Boil fifteen to twenty-five minutes depending on size. Eat one to test doneness.

Drain well; return to dried pot. Add butter and shake gently to coat potatoes.

Serve immediately or hold a short while by loosely covering pan.

To present, pile in a pretty warm bowl and top with a big sprig of parsley or snipped chives.

CRÈME CARAMEL (krehm kahr ah MEHL)

I am absolutely crazy about this dessert! It's easy to make if you are careful and follow directions precisely. Best of all, it can be prepared a day or two in advance.

Creme (makes six custards)

    1 quart cold whole or low-fat milk
    ½ cup sugar
    2 teaspoons vanilla
      Pinch of salt
    4 whole eggs
    3 egg yolks

Heat milk over medium flame. Just before it reaches a boil, reduce heat to low and stir in sugar, vanilla, and salt. Simmer fifteen minutes. Cool. Prepare caramel portion.

Next, fill a large shallow pan with water (about an inch deep). Place in an oven preheated to 300°F and bring water to a simmer.

In the meantime, beat eggs and yolks until well blended. Add to cool milk mixture, stir well, and pour through a strainer into the caramel-coated dishes. Cover each dish securely with a circle of foil.

Place the dishes in the pan of simmering water—called a *bain marie* (ban mah REE)—and cook twenty to thirty minutes, or until a knife inserted one-half inch from the edge of the dish comes out clean. (Make certain water remains at a simmer, not a boil. If little bubbles begin to form in the bottoms of the custards, the oven is too hot; reduce the temperature 50°F or so.)

Let custards cool on a rack on the counter for one minute—no more. Cut wax paper circles to place on custard surface to prevent thick film from forming. Cover and refrigerate two hours to two days.

To serve, uncover dishes and set in a shallow pan of hot water (one-half to one-inch deep) for one minute. Then run a knife carefully around each dish's edge to loosen custard. Discard wax paper;

cover with a small dessert plate and invert. Custard will land caramel side up.

Caramel
>   ½ cup granulated sugar
>   6 custard dishes (buttered or sprayed with no-stick coating)

In a heavy, medium-sized saucepan set over medium-low flame, heat sugar until melted and transparent. Raise flame to medium and stir with a wooden spoon until dark and frothy—but not burnt. Test occasionally by cooling a drop in water, then tasting. (Note: It is very, very hot.)

Pour several spoonfuls caramel into each dish, swirling the dish around to coat the bottom. Cool until hard, then proceed with instructions to finish the custard.

COUNTDOWN TO DINNER AT 8:30

Up to 2 days before party
___ Prepare *crème caramel*.

Up to 1 day before party
___ Prepare lamb for cooking; cover and refrigerate.
___ Clean and cook asparagus; bag and refrigerate.
___ Prepare soup; cover and refrigerate.
___ Wash and bag parsley and dill.
___ Refrigerate white wine.

Evening of party

7:50 P.M.
___ Set timer for 15 minutes.
___ Preheat oven to 500°F.
___ Bring lamb to room temperature.
___ Prepare crumb mixture.
___ Open Chablis. Recork and refrigerate.
___ Open Bordeaux. Leave to aerate.

8:05 P.M.

__ Put lamb in upper middle oven.

__ Cook potatoes.

__ Set oven for 10 minutes.

8:15 P.M.

__ Reset oven to 400°F.

__ Quickly brush lamb with mustard, liberally sprinkle top with bread crumbs, and return to oven.

__ Set timer for 15 minutes.

__ Make hollandaise.

8:30 P.M.

__ Check lamb. Remove to platter if done (125°–135°F). Cover with towel.

__ Set timer for 10 minutes. Turn off oven.

__ Drain potatoes; dry and butter. Cover.

__ Take hollandaise to table.

__ Serve soup.

__ Warm asparagus (hold off until lamb is done).

8:40 P.M.

__ Garnish lamb and serve. Have helper carve.

__ Clear soup bowls.

__ Serve asparagus.

__ Serve potatoes.

After main course

__ Clear dishes.

__ Serve *crème caramel* and coffee.

__ Offer liqueurs and brandy.

Lunch

During my years in California, I often visited a friend's summer home in lovely Palma Valley. A perfect little town, really just a country club surrounded by expensive houses and well-placed mountains, it will always hold a special place in my heart.

After almost any exhausting morning on the Palma Valley courts, you could find a group of us chowing down at The Club, sipping margaritas and enjoying a heavenly salad.

We occasionally got a bit tipsy and made moves on visiting movie stars and magnates, but nobody minded. It was California, after all.

Here's my version of the menu:

Pitchers of Margaritas
Cobb Salad
Buttered English Muffins
Tipsy Fruit

MARKETING LIST

Dairy:
   1½ ounces Roquefort cheese
   2 eggs
   1 pint whipping cream
   butter
Meat:
   1 small chicken breast, boned and skinned
   4 slices bacon
Produce:
   1 head iceberg lettuce
   1 head romaine lettuce
   1 large tomato
   1 ripe avocado
   5–6 shallots
   4 lemons
   10 limes
   4 cups fruit (See Tipsy Fruit recipe, page 262.)
Spices and Staples:
   Salt
   Imported olive oil
   Fine red wine vinegar
   Freshly ground pepper

Dijon mustard
Dried dill
Dried thyme
Confectioners' sugar
Bread:
Six high-quality plain English Muffins
Liquor:
Fifth tequila
Fifth Triple Sec
1 cup Grand Marnier
Miscellaneous:
Several bags of ice
1 can frozen lemonade concentrate

SPECIAL EQUIPMENT

Egg beater or whisk
Large, attractive pitcher
Carafe for salad dressing
Large, clear salad bowl

LUNCH RECIPES

PITCHER OF MARGARITAS

1 cup Triple Sec
4 cups tequila
Juice of 6–8 freshly squeezed limes
1 can frozen lemonade concentrate (optional)
Ice cubes
Salt
2 extra limes

Squeeze one extra lime into a saucer. Dip the rims of eight-ounce old-fashioned glasses into the lime, then into a saucer of salt. Place in freezer for several hours if possible.

Just before serving, mix all liquids together in pitcher. Add ice to fill. Stir quickly.

Slice four thin rounds from remaining lime, making a radial slice in each and perching one on the rim of each glass.

Bring ice-filled glasses and pitcher to table. Serve. Don't drink too much. These little darlings are lethal!

COBB SALAD

(Originated by Robert Cobb in 1936 at the Brown Derby Restaurant at Hollywood and Vine in Los Angeles)

¾ cup vinaigrette (recipe to follow)
1 small, firm head of iceberg lettuce
1 head romaine
1 small chicken breast, boned and skinned
1 large tomato, firm and beautiful
4 slices bacon
1½ ounces Roquefort cheese
1 ripe but firm avocado
2 hard-boiled eggs
½ lemon
4 teaspoons diced shallots

SEVERAL HOURS BEFORE SERVING

Chicken — Bring to a simmer (140°F) just enough water to cover chicken. Add 1 teaspoon thyme, stir, and add breast. Simmer for 20 minutes, remove from saucepan, and cool just to room temperature. Dice in half-inch cubes, bag, and refrigerate.

Shallots — Smash, peel, dice, bag, and refrigerate.

Bacon — Cook crisp and crumble. No substitutes! Bag and refrigerate.

Lettuce — Discard bruised leaves. Rinse and dry remaining leaves. Wrap in a towel and refrigerate.

Cheese — Crumble, bag, and refrigerate.

Egg — Hard-boil; bag and refrigerate. When cool, shell and dice using three-way egg slicer or sharp knife. Mix with minced shallots. Salt lightly. Bag and refrigerate.

Tomato   Cut in half horizontally, squeeze out seeds and juice, then dice. Bag and refrigerate.

45 MINUTES BEFORE SERVING

Carefully dice lettuce (yes, just this once, I mean dice, not tear) using a very sharp knife. Place in bottom of a large chilled salad bowl, preferably a glass one.

Prepare remaining ingredient:

Avocado   Slice in half; discard seed. Peel off and discard skin. Slice and dice pulp. Sprinkle with lemon juice to avoid discoloration.

Layer ingredients in rows over lettuce. Put bacon in middle row, cheese on either side of that, tomatoes on either side of cheese, etc. Be as artistic as possible. Toss with dressing at the table after showing off your handiwork.

VINAIGRETTE

>   6 *tablespoons fine French olive oil*
>   3 *tablespoons first-rate red wine vinegar*
>   2 *teaspoons lemon juice*
>   *Small pinch of salt*
>   2 *teaspoons Dijon mustard*
>   1 *teaspoon dried dill*
>   1 *teaspoon minced shallots*
>   ¼ *teaspoon freshly-ground pepper*

Vigorously shake together all ingredients. Refrigerate. Shake again just before serving and pour into a pretty little carafe. (Note: I cut the oil in this dressing to reduce the caloric content. If you're a string bean, and your guests are too, you may wish to add a few more tablespoons of oil.)

ENGLISH MUFFINS

> 6 high-quality English Muffins
> Butter

Tear muffin halves apart. Do not slice. Butter well. Broil in foil-lined broiler, three to four inches from flame, until just lightly toasted. Serve immediately on napkin-lined plate or in a basket.

TIPSY FRUIT

> 4 cups of cut-up fresh fruit. A colorful mélange of blueberries, bananas, strawberries, and pineapple is my favorite, but any of these plus peeled and cored apples or pears, or skinned and pitted oranges or peaches, are also good. (Never use canned or frozen fruit!)
> Juice of 3 lemons
> ½ cup Grand Marnier

Fruit (devoid of skins, seeds, and pits) should be cut into bite-sized pieces. Place in a bowl, squeeze lemon over fruit, and toss well. (Apples and pears should get lemon immediately after cutting.) Cover and refrigerate overnight, or for at least 3 hours.

Before serving, drain off lemon, add Grand Marnier, and mix well. Put into chilled individual serving dishes or all-purpose wineglasses; top with freshly whipped cream. Pass extra whipped cream in a chilled serving dish.

WHIPPED CREAM

> 1 pint fresh, cold whipping cream
> Confectioners' sugar to taste

Put a large (preferably copper) mixing bowl and your wire whisk or beater blades in the freezer till very cold. Whip cream until mixture has body, then gradually add sugar to taste. Continue beating till cream holds soft, glossy peaks. Cover and refrigerate; it will hold several hours. (Make certain that there's no garlic, fish, or onion in the refrigerator; the cream will absorb the odor.)

COUNTDOWN TO LUNCH AT 1:00 (*DRINKS AT 12:30*)

1 day to 3 hours before lunch
___ Prepare dessert fruit. Marinate.
___ Refrigerate bottles of tequila and Triple Sec.

Up to 3 hours before lunch
___ Prepare margarita glasses. Place in freezer.
___ Squeeze limes. Cover and refrigerate.
___ Whip cream; place in chilled service bowl. Cover and refrigerate.
___ Prepare ingredients for salad (except avocado).
___ Clean lettuce. Wrap in towel and refrigerate.
___ Set table with salad plates and bread-and-butter dishes.
___ Put salad dressing ingredients in shaker.

12:00 P.M.
___ Set timer for 30 minutes.
___ Dice lettuce.
___ Peel and dice avocado. Sprinkle lightly with lemon.
___ Assemble salad. Cover with plastic wrap and refrigerate.

12:30 P.M.
___ Set timer for 25 minutes.
___ Prepare and serve margaritas.
___ Preheat broiler.

12:55 P.M.
___ Tear apart muffins. Butter liberally. Heat three to four inches from flame in foil-lined broilers until lightly toasted.
___ Place on a napkin-covered plate or in a basket.

1:00 P.M.

__ Serve muffins.

__ Serve salad. Dress and toss at table.

__ Replenish margaritas.

After main course

__ Clear margarita glasses.

__ Pour liquid off fruit. Add Grand Marnier and mix. Put into service glass or bowl. Top with whipped cream and serve.

__ Take additional whipped cream to the table.

__ Serve coffee and tea, if desired.

Pre-Theater

Shall we talk *chichi?* I mean really First Cabin? Well, this is it.

Invite a well-chosen handful of the very best people, then serve this little menu and bask in a flood of compliments.

Vodka in Ice
Caviar Stuffed Avocado
Buttered French Bread

MARKETING LIST

Dairy:

    8 ounces sour cream

    1 tub sweet whipped butter

    6 eggs

Produce:

    3 ripe avocados

    1 large Bermuda onion

    3 lemons

Spices and Staples:

    Fresh black peppercorns

Bread:

    1 loaf very fresh French bread

Liquor:

    Imported vodka, like *Stolichnaya* (stah LEECH nah yah)

Miscellaneous:
  1–2 jars of the best caviar that you can afford

SPECIAL EQUIPMENT

Empty gallon ice cream carton or similar container
Attractive pepper mill
4 shot glasses

PRE-THEATER RECIPES

VODKA IN ICE

  1 fifth imported vodka

Place vodka in a clean, empty one-gallon ice cream container. Fill
carton with cool water to cover bottle label, then freeze.
  To serve, remove carton and display bottle in the chunk of ice.
It will slip out to pour.
  Offer vodka in shot glasses and grind the pepper mill over each
glass for garnish.

CAVIAR-STUFFED AVOCADO

  1–2 jars fine-quality caviar
  3 ripe avocados
  1 large Bermuda onion, peeled and diced
  8 ounces sour cream
  3 lemons, cut in wedges
  6 hard-boiled eggs, yolks and whites diced separately

Prepare eggs, onion, and lemons as directed, no more than 2
hours before serving. Bag separately and refrigerate.
  Just before serving, halve 2 avocados and carefully remove
seeds. Reserve the other avocados for seconds. Squeeze lemon
over all exposed surfaces to avoid discoloration. Pour off excess.
  Set avocados in a spoke pattern, smaller ends touching, on an

attractive platter. Surround with small spoons and bowls containing caviar and individual condiments (egg white, egg yolk, sour cream, onion, lemon). Provide plates and let each guest "stuff" an avocado as he or she prefers.

BUTTERED FRENCH BREAD

> 1 loaf very fresh French bread
> 1 tub sweet whipped butter

Cut loaf into 1¼-inch-wide pieces. Spread liberally with butter and arrange attractively on a platter. Serve at room temperature.

COUNTDOWN TO PRE-THEATER SNACK AT 6:00

1 to 3 Days Before Snack
___ Freeze vodka.

Up to 2 Hours Before Snack
___ Prepare eggs, onion, and lemons. Bag and refrigerate.

5:50 P.M.
___ Halve avocados. Sprinkle with lemon. Arrange on platter.
___ Place condiments in individual bowls.
___ Prepare bread.

6:00 P.M.
___ Serve avocados and condiments.
___ Serve caviar in tin(s).
___ Serve bread.
___ Serve vodka.

The Fine Art of Hand Kissing

GENTLEMEN:

Kissing a lady's hand is one continental custom most women adore. But you can't just reach out and do it! This is a ritual requiring considerable finesse. And there are very definite rules about how to proceed:

A woman must *voluntarily* extend a bare hand to be shaken before you may presume to kiss it.

If she does, grasp the hand as if to shake it, then rotate the palm downward.

Next, bend gracefully at the waist and barely touch your mouth to the back of her hand. Do *not* raise the hand more than a few inches. Do *not* plant a big kiss.

Complete the gesture by raising your eyes to meet her gaze; release her hand immediately (unless you have reason to believe that the lady has a more serious finale in mind).

LADIES:

Though you may love to have your hand kissed, you must never suggest it by your actions. (Socialites never beg; they are ever so gently *persuaded!*)

Feel free to refuse to have your hand kissed, if you like, but know that it is a great insult, akin to throwing caviar in someone's face (though infinitely less expensive). So don't do it without cause.

Farewell

I simply adore grand entrances. Lots of fanfare. Plenty of fuss. Photographers. Reporters. The whole ball of wax. Don't you?

As for goodbyes, well, I generally feel more comfortable with a few carefully chosen words, a fond farewell, and a quick exit. *Very* low profile.

So let me just say that I hope you enjoyed reading this book as much as I enjoyed writing it. Sophistication is an endlessly fascinating subject, though you must remember that it's not a *static* one. If you are seriously determined to keep outclassing the competition (and people like us practically consider it our birthright!), then you must not be tempted to rest on your laurels. Learn. Search. Investigate. Take risks. And don't ever settle for the mere *approval* of your peers. Nothing short of *adoration* and *envy* is suitable for you!

Au revoir.[1] *Et bonne chance!*[2]

---

[1] Au revoir (oh ruh VWAHR), of course, means "goodbye."
[2] Et bonne chance! (ā bohn SHAHNss) means "and good luck!"

THE V.I.P.'S
VOCABULARY GUIDE

· Foreign Words and Phrases ·
· Wines and Related Terms ·
· French Foods ·

---

*They spell it Vinci and pronounce it
Vinchy; foreigners always spell better
than they pronounce.*

— MARK TWAIN

—

Foreign Words and Phrases[1]

When it comes to foreign languages, you're damned if you do and damned if you don't.

Season your speech too liberally, or unwisely, and you're considered pretentious. Or *gauche*. Or both. Stick to English exclusively and you're unsophisticated and narrow.

Perhaps the only way to sound polished and well-educated is to limit yourself to the prudent use of only the most common words and phrases. Priority coding in the upcoming mini-dictionary facilitates this process.

An asterisk (*) marks the words you'll want to learn—those most often used, too often abused, and even more often mispronounced. The unmarked words and phrases are primarily for reference. Learn them as necessary; use them at your own risk.

À bientôt!   (ah BYEHn toh) so long!
Accoutrement   (ah koo truh MAHn) equipment

[1] All words, terms, and phrases are French unless otherwise indicated. Parts of speech are noted only where necessary for clarification.

Addition,l' (lah dee SYAHn) the bill for a meal

À demain (ah duh MEHn) until tomorrow; goodbye

Ad hoc (ad HAHK) *Latin* for this purpose only; "We formed an ad hoc committee to study discrimination."

Adieu (ah DYUH) go with God; goodbye

Ad infinitum (ad in fuh NĪ tuhm) *L.* endlessly; indefinitely

Ad nauseum (ad NAH zee uhm) *L.* to a sickening degree; "The speaker went on ad nauseum."

Ad valorem (ad vuh LOHR uhm) *L.* according to the value, as in an "ad valorem" tax

À la mode (ah lah MOHD) in style; in fashion; also, with ice cream

Ambiance (ahm BYAHnSS) atmosphere; "The restaurant had a charming ambiance."

Ami(e) (ah MEE) friend

Amour (ah MOOR) love

Andiamo! (ahn DYAH moh) *Italian* Let's go!

Apartheid (uh PAHRT hāt *or* uh PAHRT hīt) *Africaans* segregation of and discrimination against black people

Apéritif (ah peh ree TEEF) a drink that stimulates the appetite

À point (ah PWAn) in the nick of time; or meat cooked to medium doneness

Après (ah PREH) after

Argent (ahr ZHAHn) silver; money

Armoire (ar MWAHR) a large, free-standing, wooden wardrobe closet

Arrivaderla (ah ree veh DEHR lah) *It.* goodbye; until I see you again (formal)

Arrivederci (ah ree veh DEHR chee) *It.* goodbye; until I see you again (informal)

Atelier (ah teh LYĀ) artist's workshop or studio

À tout à l'heure (ah too tah LUHR) see you later

Attaché (ah tah SHĀ) a briefcase; or, an official attached to an embassy

Auberge (oh BEHRZH) a tavern or inn

Aubergine (oh behr ZHEEN) eggplant or the purplish color of the eggplant's skin

Au (OH, *not* OW) with; or, to the; see examples below

Au contraire (oh kahn TREHR) to the contrary; "Is he coming? *Au contraire,* my dear. He has already come and gone."

Au courant (oh koo RAHn) up to date

Auf wiedersehen (owf VEE duhr ZĀ uhn) *German* goodbye; until we meet again

*_Au gratin_   (oh grah TA*n*) topped with crumbs or cheese, or both

*_Au jus_   (oh ZHOO) with natural meat juices; note: meat is served "au jus," not "with au jus."

*_Au lait_   (oh LĀ) with milk

*_Au naturel_   (oh nah too REHL) in the natural way; nude

Au pair   (oh PEHR) member of the household staff who works in return for room and board

*_Au revoir_   (oh ruh VWAHR) goodbye; until I see you again

Autre chose   (oh truh SHOHZ) other things

*_Avant garde_   (ah vah*n* GAHRD) the unorthodox advance group in any field, especially the arts

*_À votre santé_   (ah VOH truh sah*n* TĀ) a French toast "to your health!"

Baccarat   (bah kah rah) a famous game of chance; also the name of one of the world's finest glassmakers

Baroque   (bah ROHK) so extravagant as to be in bad taste

Barrio   (BAH ryoh) _Spanish_ slang term meaning a slum inhabited by Latinos

Basta!   (BAHS tah) _It_. Enough! Stop!

*_Beau_   (BOH) beautiful or handsome (modifies a masculine noun); boyfriend

*_Beaucoup_   (boh KOO) very much

Beau geste   (boh ZHEHST) beautiful gesture

*_Beaux arts_   (boh ZAHR) fine arts

Bel ésprit   (beh leh SPREE) life of the party; beautiful spirit

*_Belle_   (BEHL) beautiful; see _Beau_

Belles lettres   (bel LEH truh) fine literature

Bene   (BEH neh) _It_. good

Benvenuto!   (behn veh NOO toh) _It_. Welcome!

Beret   (beh RĀ) a soft, flat French cap

*_Bête noire_   (beht NWAHR) a thing or person loathed, feared, and avoided; literally: black beast

*_Bienvenu(e)!_   (byeh*n* veh NOO) Welcome!

Bijoux   (bee ZHOO) jewels

*_Bistro_   (bee stroh) a nightclub

Bitte   (BIT eh) _Ger_. please; you're welcome

Boîte de nuit   (bwaht duh NWEE) a nighclub

*_Bon appétit!_   (boh nah peh TEE) Eat well! Enjoy!

Bonbon   (bohn bohn) small chocolate-covered ice cream treat

Bonhomie   (boh nuh MEE) friendliness

*_Bonjour_   (bohn ZHOOR) good day; hello

Bon marché (bohn mahr SHĀ) inexpensive

* *Bon mots* (bohn MOH) witticisms

* *Bonne* (BOHn) good

* *Bonne chance!* (bohn SHAHnSS) Good luck!

Bonne nuit (bohn NWEE) Good night

* *Bonsoir* (bohn SWAHR) Good evening

* *Bon vivant* (bohn vee VAHn) a playboy; or, anyone who lives "the good life"

* *Bon voyage!* (bohn vwah YAHZH) Have a good trip!

* *Boudoir* (boo DWAHR) a woman's bedroom

* *Bouquet* (boo KĀ) a bunch of flowers

* *Bourgeois* (boor ZHWAH) *n.* a member of the middle class; a group with middle-class ideas. *adj.* characteristic of the middle class; vulgar

* *Bourgeoisie* (boor zhwah ZEE) *n.* the middle class

* *Boutique* (boo TEEK, *not* boh teek) a small shop

* *Brava!* (BRAH vah) *It.* used to commend female performers; "When the prima ballerina finished, shouts of 'brava' could be heard everywhere."

Buenas noches (BWEH nahs NOH chehs) *Spanish* Good night

Buenos dias (BWEH nohs DEE ahs) *Sp.* Good day

Buona notte (BWOH nah NOH tā) *It.* Good night

Buona sera (BWOH nah SEH rah) *It.* Good evening

Buon giorno (bwohn JOHR noh) *It.* Good day

Bustier (boo STYĀ) a strapless tube top

* *Cachet* (kah SHĀ) distinguishing feature; prestigious stamp of approval

* *Carafe* (kah RAHF) vessel for serving water or wine

* *Carte blanche* (kahrt BLAHnSH) full power or authority; "I gave the decorator *carte blanche*."

Cause célèbre (kohz seh LEH bruh) a celebrated event, trial, or controversy

* *Caveat emptor* (KĀ vee AHT EMP tohr) *L.* Let the buyer beware

* *C'est la guerre!* (sā lah GEHR) That's war for you! Too bad!

* *C'est la vie!* (sā lah VEE) That's life!

* *C'est magnifique!* (sā mah nyee FEEK) That's wonderful! That's magnificent!

* *Chacqu'un à son goût* (shah KUH nah sohn GOO) Each to his own taste

* *Chaise longue* (shehz LAHn guh) reclining chair

Challis (SHAHL ee) soft, expensive wool or cotton fabric of plain weave, often with a small printed pattern

Chanson (shahn SAHn) a song

Chanteuse (shahn TUHZ) a female singer

Charcuterie (shahr KOO tehr EE) a butcher shop or delicatessen

***Chargé d'affaires* (shahr zhā dah FEHR) a diplomatic official

Châtelaine (shah TLEHN) mistress of an elegant residence

Chef d'oeuvres (sheh DUHV ruh) a masterpiece

Chemin de fer (sheh mehn duh FĀR) a variation of the game baccarat

**Cherchez la femme* (shehr SHĀ lah FAHM) look for the woman; "When a crime of passion has been committed, *cherchez la femme.*"

Cheval (sheh VAHL) horse

*Chichi (shee shee) elegant; sophisticated

*Chignon (shee NYOHn) a knot of hair worn at the nape of a woman's neck

Chinoiserie (shee nwahz ehr EE) *n.* 18th-century style of decoration that was supposedly Chinese; an object decorated in this style

*Chutzpah (KHOOT spuh) *Yiddish* audacity; insolence; gall

**Ciao!* (CHAH oh) *It.* Hello! Goodbye! (informal)

Cinéma verité (see nā mah veh ree TĀ) a filmmaking technique that records life as it really is

Cocotte (koh KAHT) a prostitute

*Coeur (KUHR) a heart

*Cognac (koh NYAHK) a fine brandy from Cognac, France

Coiffeur (kwah FUHR) a male hairdresser

Coiffeuse (kwah FUHZ) a female hairdresser

*Coiffure (kwah FOOR) a hairdo

Comme çi comme ça (kuhm SEE kuhm SAH) so so

Comme d'habitude (kuhm dah bee TOOD) as usual

Comme il faut (kuh meel FOH) stylish; proper

Comment allez-vous? (koh mahn tah lā VOO) How are you? (formal)

**Comment ça va?* (koh mahn sah VAH) How goes it?

Concierge (kahn SYEHRZH) in America, a specially trained social director for a hotel

*Connoisseur (kah nah SUHR) a person considered competent to pass judgment in matters of art and taste; connoisseur

Contretemps (kahn truh TAHn) a mishap or inconvenience

Coquette (koh KEHT) a woman who flirts excessively

*Cordon bleu (kohr dahn BLUH) a method of preparing veal with layers of ham and cheese; also, the name of a famous London cooking school; literally: blue ribbon

*Corps (KOHR) a unit of persons acting together

Corps diplomatique　(kohr dee ploh mah TEEK) diplomatic corps (surprise!)

Corpus delecti　(KOHR puhs deh LIK tī) *L.* the fundamental element of a crime

* *Coup d'état*　(koo dā TAH) sudden political action, often a violent overthrow of a government; "A *coup d'état* was inevitable after the dictator's last proclamation."

* *Coup de grâce*　(koo duh GRAHSS, *not* GRAH) a merciful end; a death stroke; "Considering his long suffering, the accident was a *coup de grâce.*"

Coup d'oeil　(KOO DUH yuh) a quick glance

* *Couture*　(koo TOOR) fashion designing; see also Haute couture

* *Couturier*　(koo toor RYEH) male fashion designer

* *Couturière*　(koo toor RYEHR) female fashion designer

* *Crème de la crème*　(KREHM duh lah KREHM) the best of the best

* *Crêpe*　(KREHP) a thin sweet or savory pancake enclosing a variety of fillings

* *Croissant*　(krwah SAHn) a crescent-shaped breakfast roll

* *Cuisine*　(kwee ZEEN) cooking; see also *Haute cuisine*

* *Cum laude*　(kuhm LOW dā) *L.* in academic work, praise just short of *magna cum laude*

Danke　(DAHNG kuh) *Ger.* Thank you

Danke schön　(DAHNG kuh shuhn) *Ger.* Thank you very much

* *Déclassé*　(dā klah SĀ) low in status; "Wearing polyester is so *déclassé.*"

Décolletage　(dā kohl TAHZH) *n.* a low neckline on a dress; "The best feature of that garment is its *décolletage.*"

Décolleté　(dā kohl TĀ) *adj.* low-necked; wearing a low-necked garment

Découpage　(dā koo PAHZH) an art form created by a conglomeration of cut-out materials

* *Déjà vu*　(dā zhah VOO) an eerie sense of having seen something before

Dénouement　(dā noo MAHn) in drama, the resolution of a plot; also, the outcome of a doubtful series of events

De novo　(dā NOH voh) *L.* again; from the beginning

* *De rien!*　(duh RYEHn) It's nothing! Forget it!

* *De rigueur*　(duh ree GUHR) required; fashionable; "Horseradish is *de rigueur* with roast beef."

* *Dernier cri*　(dehr nyā KREE) the latest fashion; the ultimate

* *Derrière*　(deh RYEHR) rear end; buttocks

* *Détente*　(dā TAHNT) an easing of tension between nations

De temps en temps (duh TAHN zahn TAHN) from time to time

* *Dévote* (dā VOH tuh) or devotee (dā voh TEE) is a person devoted to something

Do svidaniya (doh svee DAH nyah) *Russian* Until we meet again

* *Éclat* (ā KLAH) clout; success; fame

* *Élan* (ā LAn) enthusiasm; dash; ardor

Élégant(e) (eh leh GAHn[T]) elegant

Éminence grise (ā mee nahns GREEZ) the power behind the power

* *Enchanté!* (ahn shahn TĀ) Enchanted! (used as a greeting)

* *Enfant terrible* (ahn fahn teh REE bluh) literally: terrible child; also, someone who is divinely wicked or avant garde; "Truman Capote was the *enfant terrible* of the literary set."

Engagé (ahn gah ZHĀ) engaged in, or committed to, something

En français (ahn frahn SĀ) in French

* *Ennui* (ahn NWEE) boredom; annoyance

* *En masse* (ahn MAHSS) all together; in a group

En passant (ahn pah SAHn) in passing; "*En passant,* I would like to add the following."

* *En rapport* (ahn rah POHR) in agreement; in accord

* *Entre nous* (ahn truh NOO) between us; "*Entre nous,* her dress is hideous."

Ergo (uhr GOH) *L.* therefore

* *Ésprit de corps* (eh SPREE duh KOHR) team spirit

Et (EH) and

* *Étagère* (eh tah ZHEHR) open shelving unit

* *Et al.* (eht ahl) *L.* and others; "I am inviting Jim Smith, et al.," means "Jim Smith and the other members of his household."

* *Eau de toilette* (oh duh twah LEHT) toilette water

* *Façade* (fah SAHD) front; "His ulcer belies his smooth *façade.*"

Faille (FAH yuh *or* FĪL) soft, transversely ribbed fabric, often of silk

* *Fait accompli* (feh tah kahn PLEE) something already done, therefore requiring no discussion; "I'm sorry, my resignation is a *fait accompli.* That is all I have to say on the matter."

Faites vos jeux (FEHT voh ZHUH) Place your bets (a term used at gaming tables)

Faux (foh) false

* *Faux pas* (foh PAH) a social blunder

* *Femme* (FAHM) woman

* *Femme fatale* (FAHM fah TAHL) a dangerously beautiful woman

Fête (FEHT) holiday

Filet (fee LĀ) a boneless cut of meat or fish; note that the English say "FIL it" and spell it *fillet*.

Fin de siècle (fan duh SYEHK luh) end of the century, especially the nineteenth century, a time noted for its elegance

*Flambé (flahn BĀ) flamed

Fleur (FLUHR) flower

Formidable (fohr mee DAHB luh) dreadful; formidable

*Forte (FOHRT, *not* fohr TĀ) strong point; "Grammar is not my *forte*."

*Foyer (foh YEH) lobby or entry way

Français(e) (frahn SEH; frahn SEHZ) French

Froufrou (froo froo) excessively ornate

Gaffe (GAHF) a blunder; see *Faux pas*

*Garçon (gahr SAHn) boy

Gauche (GOHSH) tacky, awkward

*Gaucherie (goh SHREE) *n.* that which is *gauche*

Gendarmes (zhahn DAHRM) French policemen

*Genre (ZHAHn ruh) kind; literary or artistic form; "They are of the same *genre*."

Gentilhomme (zhahn tee YUHM) gentleman

Goût (GOO) *n.* taste

Goût raffiné (GOO rah fee NĀ) refined taste

Guerre, la (lah GEHR) the war; see also *C'est la guerre!*

*Habeas corpus (HĀ bee uhs KOHR puhs) *L.* a writ to bring someone before the court

*Hara-kiri (HAH ruh KEE ree) *Japanese* method of committing suicide by stabbing oneself in the abdomen

Hasta la vista (AH stah lah VEE stah) *Sp.* Until I see you again

*Haute couture (OHT koo TOOR) high fashion

*Haute cuisine (OHT kwee ZEEN) fine cooking

Hauteur (oh TUHR) snobbery

Hoi polloi (HOY puh LOY) *Greek* the masses

*i.e. (Ī Ē) that is

*In flagrante delicto (in flah GRAHN tā deh LIK toh) *L.* red-handed; in the act; "I caught him *in flagrante delicto*, his hand in the cookie jar."

Ingénue (an zheh NOO) on the stage, the role of an innocent young girl; also, an actress who plays such parts

In perpetuum (in pehr PEH too uhm) *L.* forever

Ipso facto (IP soh FAHK toh) *L.* by that very fact; "He was condemned *ipso facto*."

Inconnu(e)   (ehn kohn NOO) unknown

Je ne sais pas   (zhuhn sā PAH) I do not know

Je ne sais quoi   (zhuhn sā KWAH) I don't know what; that special something; "This soup has that certain *je ne sais quoi*."

Je pense, donc je suis   (zhuh PAHnSS, dahn zhuh SWEE) existential statement: I think, therefore I am.

Je t'adore   (zhuh tah DOHR) I adore you; I love you

Jeune fille   (zhuhn FEE) young girl

Je vous aime   (zhuh voo ZEHM) I love you

Je vous en prie   (zhuh voo zahn PREE) I pray you; please

*Joie de vivre   (ZHWAH duh VEE vruh) joy of living

La dolce vita   (lah DOHL chā VEE tah) *It.* The sweet life.

*Laissez faire   (leh sā FEHR) government policy of interfering as little as possible in the course of economic affairs

Lamé   (lah MĀ) ornamental, metallic fabric

*Le smoking   (luh SMOH keeng) dinner jacket; "black tie"

*Le   (luh) French for "the"; modifies masculine nouns; the plural is *les* (LĀ)

Lehayim!   (luh KHAH yim) *Hebrew* toast: To life!

*Lingerie   (lan zhehr EE) ladies' undergarments and night clothes

Littérateur   (lee teh rah TUHR) writer of literature

Macabre   (mah KAHB ruh) gruesome

*Machismo   (mah CHÉZ moh) *Sp.* aggressive masculinity

*Macho   (MAH choh) *Sp. n.* a virile man; *adj.* aggressively male

*Madame   (mah DAHM) a married woman's title

*Mademoiselle   (mahd mwah ZEHL) an unmarried woman's title

Mafioso   (mah fee OH soh) *It.* Mafia member

Magna cum laude   (MAHG nah kuhm LOW dā) *L.* in academic work, praise higher than *cum laude* but lower than *summa cum laude*

*Maillot   (mah YOH) one-piece swimsuit

*Maison   (mā ZAHn) house

**Mais oui!*   (mā WEE) Of course!

**Maître d'hôtel*, also *maître d'*   (meh truh doh TEHL, *also* meh truh DEE) headwaiter or owner of a restaurant

*Malaise   (mah LEHZ) a vague feeling of uneasiness or discomfort

Mal à propos   (mah lah proh POH) inappropriate

*Mal de mer   (mahl duh MEHR) seasickness

Malentendu   (mahl ahn tahn DOO) a misunderstanding

Manqué   (mahn KĀ) unfulfilled or failed

*Masseur   (mah SUHR) a man who gives massages

*Masseuse   (mah SUHZ) a woman who gives massages

Mauvais(e)   (moh VEh, moh VEHZ) bad

*Mauve   (MOHV) purplish-blue color

Mea culpa   (MEH ah KUHL pah) L. my fault

*Mélange   (meh LAHZH) hodgepodge; assortment

*Mémoire   (mehm MWAHR) a record of one's life experiences

*Menage à trois   (meh NAHZH ah TWAH) three people living together
      in a love relationship

*Merci   (mehr SEE) Thank you

*Merci beaucoup   (mehr see boh KOO) Thanks very much

*Mesdames et messieurs   (mā DAHM ā mā SYUH) ladies and gentlemen

*Métier   (meh TYĀ) occupation; field of endeavor

*Milieu   (mee LYUH) n. medium; environment

Mille fois   (meel FWAH) a thousand times

Misérable   (mee sehr AH bluh) miserable

*Modus operandi   (MOH duhs oh peh RAHN dee) L. mode of operation
      (M.O.); procedure

Moi   (MWAH) me

Mon Dieu!   (mohn DYUH) My God!

*Monsieur   (muh SYUH) mister; Mr.

Mort, la   (lah MOHR) death

Mot juste   (moh ZHOOST) the right word

*Naïveté   (nah EEV tā) inexperience

Né(e)   (NĀ) born (refers to someone's original name)

*Négligé   (neh gleh ZHĀ) woman's elegant night things

N'importe   (nan POHRT) unimportant; it's unimportant

*Ne plus ultra   (nuh ploo ZOOL truh) L. the ultimate

*N'est-ce pas?   (ness PAH) Is it not? Is it not the truth?

*Noblesse oblige   (noh BLESS oh BLEEZH) obligation of the rich to be-
      have charitably and honorably

Nolo contendere   (noh loh kuhn TEHN duh REE) L. a legal plea of no
      contest which subjects the defendant to the same penalty as a guilty
      plea

Nom de guerre   (nohn duh GĀR) pseudonym

*Nom de plume   (nohn duh PLOOM) pen name

Non compos mentis   (nohn KOHM pohs MEHN tis) L. not of sound
      mind; "They pronounced him non compos mentis."

*Non sequitur   (non SEHK wih tuhr) L. an illogical inference

Noir   (NWAHR) black

Nôtre dame (noh truh DAHM) our lady

Nouveaux riches (noo voh REESH) the newly wealthy

Nouvelle (noo VEHL) feminine form of *nouveau* (noo VOH)—both mean "new"

Nouvelle cuisine (noo vehl kwee ZEEN) newer, lighter style of French cooking

Nuance (noo AH*n*SS) a subtlety; "I detected a *nuance* of garlic in the sauce."

Nuit (NWEE) night

Objets d'arts (oh zhā DAHR) art objects

Oenophile (EE nuh FĪL) *Greek.* a wine lover or connoisseur

Outré (oo TRĀ) improper; eccentric; bizarre; *déclassé*

Paisano (pī SAH noh) *It.* countryman

Palais (pah LĀ) palace

Panache (pah NAHSH) flair; flamboyance; style

Papillon (pah pee YOH*n*) butterfly

Paparazzi (pah pah RAHTZ ee) *It.* street photographers who snap celebrities

Par (PAHR) by

Parce que (PAHR skuh) because

Parisien(ne) (pah ree SYEH*n*, pah ree SYEHN) of Paris

Par excellence (pahr ek sā LAH*n*SS) absolutely excellent; the best; "This is a recipe *par excellence.*"

Par exemple (pahr ek ZEHM pluh) for example

Parfum (pahr FUH*n*) perfume

Parvenu(e) (pahr veh NOO) upstart; one of the *nouveau riche*

Pas de deux (pah duh DUH) a dance performed by two people

Pas de quoi (pahd KWAH) Don't mention it; you're welcome

Pas du tout (pah doo TOO) Not at all

Passé (pah SĀ) dated; old; out of style

Pastiche (pah STEESH) a hodgepodge; usually refers to an artistic or literary piece

Pavé (pah VĀ) placement of gems so close together that you cannot see the setting underneath; common way to mount diamond chips

Peignoir (peh NWAHR) woman's dressing gown

Penchant (pah*n* SHAH*n* *or* PEN chant) a fondness or inclination; "I have a *penchant* for emeralds."

Pension (pah*n* SYO*n*) a boarding house; a hostel

Per favore (pehr fah VOH rā) *It.* Please

Persona non grata (pehr SOH nah noh GRAH tah) *L*. an unwelcome person; "After planting a bomb in the men's room, I became *persona non grata* at the club."

Petit(e) (puh TEE, puh TEET) little; diminutive

Peu,un (uhn PUH) a little bit

Peut-être (puh TEH truh) perhaps

Piacere (pee ah CHEH rā) *It. v.* to please

Pièce de résistance (PYEHSS duh rā seess TAHnSS) the main, or most irresistible, course of a meal; the best in a series

Pied-à-terre (pyeh dah TEHR) an apartment for occasional, or part-time, use; a city apartment for suburban dwellers

Pince-nez (pan SNEH) little eyeglasses that sit on the nose, like Ben Franklin's

Piquant (pee KAHnT) tart or biting flavor

Pirouette (pee RWEHT) in ballet, a whirl

Plus ou moins (ploo oo MWAn) more or less

Por favor (pohr fah VOHR) *Sp*. Please

Potpourri (poh poor REE) an assortment of things

Pousse-café (pooss kah FĀ) multi-layered liqueur served with coffee

Pourquoi (poor KWAH) Why?

Prego (PREH goh) *It*. Please; you're welcome

Premier (preh MYĀ) *adj*. the first (modifies a masculine noun)

Première (preh MYEHR) *n*. a theatrical opening; *adj*. the first (with a feminine noun)

Prêt-à-porter (preh tah pohr TĀ) ready-to-wear garments (as opposed to couture)

Prima donna (pree mah DOH nah) *L*. Female opera star; a pompous person

Prima facie (PRĪ mah FĀ shee) *L*. immediately evident; at first sight; "The abundance of *prima facie* evidence is going to bury that turkey."

Pro bono publico (proh BOH noh POO blee KOH) *L*. for the public good

Pro forma (proh FOHR mah) *L*. as a matter of form

Pro rata (proh RAH tah) *L*. proportional

Protégé (proh teh ZHĀ) someone whose career is to be furthered by an older, more experienced person

Pro tem, pro tempore (proh TEHM, proh TEHM poh REH) *L*. temporarily; "She is President *pro tem*."

Puissance (pwee SAHnSS) *n*. great power

Puissant   (pwee SAH*n*) *adj.* powerful

Quartier latin   (kahr TYEH lah TA*n*) Latin quarter; arty area of Paris and New Orleans

Quel dommage!   (kehl doh MAHZH) Too bad!

Quelque choses   (kehl kuh SHOHZ) several things

* *Qu'est-ce que c'est?*   (kess kuh SĀ) What is this?

Qu'est-ce que c'est que cela?   (kess kuh sā que SLAH) What is that?

* *Quid pro quo*   (kwid proh kwoh) *L.* tit for tat; one thing for another

* *Raconteur*   (rah kah*n* TUHR) a skilled storyteller

Raffiné   (rah fee NĀ) refined

* *Raison d'être*   (reh zah*n* DEH truh) reason for living

* *Recherché*   (reh shehr SHĀ) sought after; precious; rare

Renaissance   (reh nā SAH*n*SS) rebirth

* *Rendez-vous*   (rah*n* dā VOO) a date; a meeting of two lovers

* *RSVP, short for répondez s'il vous plaît*   (reh poh*n* dā seel voh PLĀ) Please respond

Rive Droite   (reev DRWAHT) Right Bank (of the Seine River in Paris)

Rive Gauche   (reev GOHSH) Left Bank (of the Seine)

Roman à clef   (roh ma*n* ah KLĀ) a novel portraying real people and events as fictional

Rouge   (ROOZH) red

Royale   (rwah YAHL) royal

Sacre-bleu!   (SAHK ruh BLUH) Damn it!

Saint   (SA*n*) saint

Salle de bain   (sahl duh BEH*n*) bathroom

Salud   (sah LOOD) *Sp.* To your health! (a toast)

Salon   (sah LAH*n*) a drawing room; also, a beauty shop

Sang-froid   (sa*n* FRWAH) poise; composure; literally, cold blood

* *Sans*   (SAH*n*) without (Note: Pronounced SAH*n*Z only if the word it precedes begins with a vowel; thus, *sans argent* [without silver] is SAH*n*Z ahr ZHAH*n*.)

* *Sans doute*   (sah*n* DOOT) without doubt

* *Sans-souci*   (sah*n* soo SEE) carefree; carefree person

* *Santé!*   (sah*n* TĀ) Health! (a toast)

Savant   (sah VAH*n*) a knowledgeable person

* *Savoir-faire*   (sah vwahr FEHR) know-how; knowledge of the ways of the world; sophistication

* *Savoir-vivre*   (sah vwahr VEEV ruh) literally, know how to live; knowledge of how to live well

* *Shalom!*   (shah LOHM) *Hebrew.* Hello! Goodbye! Peace!

* *S'il vous plaît*   (seel voo PLÃ) If you please

* *Simpatico*   (seem PAH tee koh) *It*. congenial; understanding

* *Sine qua non*   (SIH neh kwah NOHN) *L*. A necessity; "A passport is sine qua non for travel abroad."

* *Soigné*   (swah NYEH) well-groomed; stylish

* *Soirée*   (swah RÃ) an evening engagement; a party

* *Sommelier*   (suh muh LYÃ) wine steward

Sobriquet   (soh bree KÃ) an assumed name; a nickname

* *Soupçon*   (soop SAHn) a dash; a pinch; a touch; "I think I'll add a soupçon of garlic."

* *Specialité*   (speh syah lee TÃ) specialty

Subito!   (SOO bee toh) *It*. Immediately!

Tableau   (tah BLOH) a picture or scene

Tant mieux   (tahn MYUH) So much the better!

Tant pis   (tahn PEE) Too bad!

* *Tempus fugit*   (TEHM puhs FYOO jit) *L*. time flies

* *Tête-à-tête*   (teht tah TEHT) *adj*. between two people *n*. a private conversation between two people

Toilette   (twah LEHT) toilette; see *Eau de toilette*

* *Tour de force*   (toor duh FOHRSS) an extraordinary achievement or performance

Tout à fait   (too tah FÃ) entirely

Tout de suite   (tood SWEET) right away; immediately

Tout le monde   (too luh MOHnD) everyone

Travail   (trah VĪ yuh) work

* *Très*   (TRÃ) very

* *Très chic*   (trã SHEEK) very chic or stylish

Tristesse   (tree STESS) sadness

Trompe d'oeil   (truhnp DUH yuh) usually, a painting or fabric which creates an optical illusion

Tu   (TOO) you (informal)

Valet   (vah LÃ *or* VAL it) a gentleman's gentleman

Vert(e)   (VEHR, VEHRT) green

* *Vignette*   (vee NYEHT) a short literary sketch

* *Vin*   (VEHn) wine; see Chapter 1 for details

* *Vin ordinaire*   (vehn ohr dee NÃR) inexpensive table wine

* *Vis-à-vis*   (vee zah VEE) in relation to; opposite or facing; compared with

* *Vive!*   (VEE vuh) imperative form of the verb *vivre* (VEE vruh)—to live; also means "Long live," as in "Vive la France!"—"Long live France!"

Voulez-vous se couchez avec moi? (voo lā VOO suh koo SHĀ ah vehk MWAH) Will you go to bed with me?

Vous (VOO) You (formal); see *Tu*

Voyeur (vwah YUHR) a peeping Tom

Wunderkind (VOON dehr KINT) *Ger.* a child prodigy

Zeitgeist (tsīt gīst) *Ger.* spirit of the time

Wines and Related Terms

Descriptions and pronunciations of many of the world's finest wines appear in this glossary, along with important terms relating to their production. Also included are words and phrases which describe the various characteristics of, and handling methods for, these great beverages.

As in the preceding mini-dictionaries, what you must know is marked with an asterisk. The remaining terms are for reference or rainy-day reading.

Abbocato (AHB boh KAH toh) *It.* semi-dry or semi-sweet
Abocado (AH boh KAH thoh) *Sp.* delicate; medium-sweet
Acid compounds in wine that provide a tart freshness and assist in aging
*Aftertaste lingering taste which indicates a complex wine
Alameda, California important coastal wine-growing county
*Alsace (ahl ZAHS) region in France producing wines more German than French in character; the finest are Rieslings and Gewürztraminers, and are labeled, in order of descending quality, Grand Vin, Grand Reserve, and Reserve Exceptionnelle
Amontillado (ah MOHN tee LYAH doh) *Sp.* variety of dry sherry which is sweeter and nuttier than Fino
*Anjou (ahn ZHOO) area producing fine rosé wines

Appellation d'Origine Contrôlée (ah peh lah SYO*n* doh ree ZHEEN kah*n* troh LÃ) guarantee of origin, and therefore, of quality; found on French wine labels

Aroma the lingering perfume of a young wine

Asti Spumante (AHS tee spoo MAHN teh) *It.* sparkling white, somewhat sweet wine of only fair quality

*Auslese (OWS lā zuh) *Ger.* one of the quality designations of German wines; means "made of selected grapes" and indicates a sweet white dessert wine

Ayler Kupp (Ī luhr koop) *Ger.* fine fruity white wine

Balance harmony of ingredients

Barbaresco (BAH bah REHZ koh) *It.* an excellent dry red wine

Barbera (bahr BEH rah) *It.* and *Cal.* a good red wine

Bardolino (BAHR doh LEE noh) *It.* good dry red wine

*Barolo (bah ROH loh) *It.* King of Italian red wines

Barsac (bahr SAHK) sweet white dessert wine from Sauternes; excellent with sweet fruit

Bâtard-Montrachet (bah TAHR mah*n* rah SHÃ) Grand Cru dry white Burgundy wine

*Beaujolais (boh zhoh LÃ) fruity red wine; best are Moulin-à-Vent and Fleurie

Beaulieu (boh LYUH) *Cal.* name of a famous winery

Beaune-Grèves (bohn GREHV) Premier Cru dry red Burgundy

Beaune-Les-Fèves (bohn lā FEHV) Premier Cru dry red Burgundy

Beerenauslese (BÃ ruhn OWS lā zuh) *Ger.* one of the finest designations of high-quality German wine; signifies a "wine made from grapes picked one at a time from selected bunches"; denotes rare, sweet, and expensive white dessert wines

*Bernkasteler Doktor (BEHRN kahs tuh luhr DOHK tohr) *Ger.* the most renowned and expensive fruity white Riesling

Bernkasteler Graben (BEHRN kahs tuh luhr GRAH buhn) *Ger.* fine fruity white wine; almost as good as Doktor, but much less expensive

Bianco (BYAHNG koh) *It.* white

Bienvenue-Bâtard-Montrachet (byeh*n* veh NOO bah TAHR mah*n* rah SHÃ) Grand Cru dry white Burgundy

*Blanc (BLAH*n*) white

*Blanc de Blancs (blahn duh BLAH*N*) *Fr.* and *Cal.* type of Champagne made only from white grapes; elegant and expensive

Blanc de Noirs (blah*n* duh NWAHR) *Fr.* and *Cal.* type of Champagne made only from Pinot Noir grapes

Body   refers to the substance and weight of wine

Bonnes Mares, Les   (lā buhn MAHR) Grand Cru dry red Burgundy

*Bordeaux   (bohr DOH) district which produces most of the finest dry red, and sweet white, wines in France—and the world; the red wines (from Médoc, St. Émilion, and Pomerol) are light and elegant; the sweet whites (from Sauternes and Barsac) are wonderful for dessert; the dry whites (from Graves) are also good

Bordelais   (bohrd LEHZ) from Bordeaux

Bottled by   *Cal.* term on California wine bottles meaning that the wine was bottled (but not necessarily grown) at this location

*Bouquet   (boo KĀ) the fragrance first encountered when opening or tasting a mature wine

Bourgogne   (boor GOH nyuh) means Burgundy; wine named Bourgogne Rouge or Blanc is of only fair quality

Breeding   character and excellence a wine obtains

Brauneberger Juffer   (BROW nuh BEHRK ehr YOOF uhr) *Ger.* fine, famous, fruity white wine

Brauneberger Klostergarten   (BROW nuh BEHK ehr KLOHS tehr GAHR ten) *Ger.* very good fruity white wine

Brolio   (BROH lyoh) *It.* one of the finest Chiantis; do *not* buy it in a straw-wrapped bottle

Brouilly, Côte de   (KOHT duh broo YEE) one of the best Beaujolais red wines

*Brut   (BROOT) driest designation for Champagne; it denotes a fine wine with no added sugar

*Burgundy   one of the finest red- and white-wine-producing areas of France; best wines are labeled Grand Cru; next best are Premier Cru; wines are fuller, and more assertive, than those from Bordeaux

Cabernet Rosé   (kah behr NĀ roh ZĀ) *Cal.* one of the better rosés

*Cabernet Sauvignon   (kah behr NĀ soh vee NYOn) name of a grape making fine red wines; varietal name of some of the best California wines

Caillerets, Les   (lā kah yeh RĀ) Premier Cru white Burgundy

*California Champagne   wine made in California by the French method; technically not a Champagne, but a Champagne-like beverage

California Wine   term on a label meaning that the wine is produced from California grapes only

*Capsule   protective seal covering the neck and mouth of a bottle

*Chablis   (shah BLEE) *Fr.* and *Cal.* dry white wine; finest are from

Chablis, France: Best among these are labeled Grand Cru, next best are Premier Cru, then Chablis, then Petit Chablis; the Chablis of California is so named because it resembles the French wine

Chablis Beauroy (boh RWAH) Premier Cru Chablis

—**Beugnons** (buh NYOH*n*) Premier Cru

—**Butteaux** (boo TOH) Premier Cru

—**Blanchots** (blah*n* SHOH) Grand Cru

—**Bougros** (boo GROH) Grand Cru

—**Chapelot** (shah PLOH) Premier Cru

—**Châtains** (shah TEH*n*) Premier Cru

—**Côte de Fontenay** (koht duh FAH*n* tuh NĀ) Premier Cru

—**Côte de Léchet** (koht duh lā SHĀ) Premier Cru

—**Fourchaume** (foor SHOHM) Premier Cru

—**Grenouilles** (gruh NOO yuh) Grand Cru

—**Les Clos** (lā KLOH) Grand Cru

—**Les Fôrets** (lā foh RĀ) Premier Cru

—**Les Lys** (lā LEE) Premier Cru

—**Les Preuses** (lā PRUHZ) Grand Cru

—**Mélinots** (mā lah*n* NOH) Premier Cru

—**Monts-de-Milieu** (mah*n* duh mee LYUH) Premier Cru

—**Montée de Tonnerre** (mah*n* TĀ duh tuhn NEHR) Premier Cru

—**Montmains** (mah*n* MEH*n*) Premier Cru

—**Pied d'Aloup** (pyeh dah LOO) Premier Cru

—**Séchét** (sā SHĀ) Premier Cru

—**Troesmes** (TRUHZ muh) Premier Cru

—**Vaillons** (vā YAH*n*) Premier Cru

—**Valmur** (vahl MOOR) Grand Cru

—**Vaucoupin** (voh koo PEH*n*) Premier Cru

—**Vaudésir** (voh dā ZEER) Grand Cru

—**Vaulorent** (voh loh RAH*n*) Premier Cru

—**Vosgros** (voh GROH) Premier Cru

Chambertin, Le (luh shah*n* behr TA*n*) magnificent Grand Cru dry red Burgundy from Côte de Nuits

Chambolle-Musigny (shah*n* buhl moo seen NYEE) good dry red Burgundy

Chambolle-Musigny-Les Amoureuses (shah*n* buhl moo seen NYEE lā zah moor RUHZ) Premier Cru dry red Burgundy

Champagne (sham PĀN *or* sham PAH nyuh), France, is the only area of the world that may call its pale sparkling wines by the name

"Champagne"; used on wines from other areas, the name simply refers to a beverage resembling Champagne

Chapelle-Chambertin   (shah pehl shahn behr TEHn) Grand Cru dry red Burgundy

*Chardonnay   (shar DNĀ) *Cal.* varietal name given to California's finest dry white wine; also the name of the grape used to make Chablis and Champagne

Charlemagne   (shar LMAH nyuh) Grand Cru dry white Burgundy

Charmes-Chambertin   (shahrm shahn behr TEHn) Grand Cru dry red Burgundy

Chassagne-Montrachet   (shah SAH nyuh mahn rah SHĀ) good dry red or white Burgundy

Château Ausone   (shah toh oh ZUHN) finest dry red Bordeaux from St. Émilion

Château Batailley   (shah toh bah teh YĀ) Fifth Growth dry red Bordeaux from Médoc

Château Belair   (shah toh beh LEHR) fine dry red Bordeaux from St. Émilion

Château Belgrave   (shah toh behl GRAHV) Fifth Growth dry red Bordeaux from Médoc

Château Beychevelle   (shah toh behsh VEHL) very good Fourth Growth dry red Bordeaux from Médoc

Château Bouscaut   (shah toh boo SKOH) good dry red or white Bordeaux from Graves

Château Boyd-Cantenac   (shah toh bwahd kahn tuh NAHK) Third Growth dry red Bordeaux from Médoc

Château Branaire-Ducru   (shah toh brah NEHR doo KROO) Fourth Growth dry red Bordeaux from Médoc

Château Brane-Cantenac   (shah toh brahn kahn teh NAHK) Second Growth dry red Bordeaux from Médoc

Château Broustet   (shah toh broos TĀ) Second Growth sweet white Bordeaux from Barsac

Château Caillou   (shah toh kah YOO) Second Growth sweet white Bordeaux from Barsac

Château Calon-Ségur   (shah toh kah LOHn sā GOOR) fine Third Growth dry red Bordeaux from Médoc

Château Camensac   (shah toh kah mehn SAHK) Fifth Growth dry red Bordeaux from Médoc

Château Canon   (shah toh kah NOHn) fine dry red Bordeaux from St. Émilion

Château Cantemerle (shah toh kahn teh MEHRL) Fifth Growth dry red Bordeaux from Médoc

Château Cantenac-Brown (shah toh kahn teh NAHK BROWN) Third Growth dry red Bordeaux from Médoc

Château Carbonnieux (shah toh kahr boh NYUH) dry red or white Bordeaux from Graves

Château Certan-Giraud (shah toh sehr TAn zhee roh) dry red Bordeaux from Pomerol

Château Chalon (shah toh shah LOn) Bordeaux white

Château Cheval-Blanc (shah toh sheh vahl BLAHn) exceptional dry red Bordeaux from St. Émilion

Château Clerc-Milon-Mondon (shah toh klehr mee LOHn mohn DOHn) Fifth Growth dry red Médoc

Château Climens (shah toh klee MAHn) First Growth sweet white Bordeaux from Barsac

(Château) Clos Fourtet (shah toh kloh foor TÃ) dry red Bordeaux from St. Émilion

(Château) Clos Haut-Peyraguey (shah toh kloh oh pã rah GÃ) First Growth sweet white Sauternes

Château Cos d'Éstournel (shah toh koh deh toor NEHL) Second Growth dry red Bordeaux from Médoc

Château Cos-Labory (shah toh koh lah boh REE) Fifth Growth dry red Bordeaux from Médoc

Château Couhins (shah toh KWAn) dry white Bordeaux from Graves

Château Coutet (shah toh koo TÃ) First Growth sweet white Bordeaux from Barsac

Château Croizet-Bages (shah toh krwah zeh BAHZH) Fifth Growth dry red Bordeaux from Médoc

Château d'Arche (shah toh DAHRSH) Second Growth sweet white Sauternes

Château Dauzac (shah toh doh ZAHK) Fifth Growth dry red Bordeaux from Médoc

Château de Malle (shah toh duh MAHL) Second Growth sweet white Sauternes

Château de Myrat (shah toh duh mee RAH) First Growth sweet white Sauternes

Château d'Issan (shah toh dee SAn) Third Growth dry red Bordeaux from Médoc

Château de Rayne-Vigneau (shah toh duh RÃ nyuh vee NYOH) First Growth sweet white Sauternes

Château Doisy-Daëne (shah toh dwah ZEE dah EN) Second Growth sweet white from Barsac

Château Doisy-Védrines (shah toh dwah ZEE veh DREEN) Second Growth sweet white from Barsac

Château Ducru-Beaucaillou (shah toh doo KROO boh kah YOO) Second Growth dry red from Médoc

Château Duhart-Milon-Rothschild (shah toh doo AHR mee LOHn roh SHEELD) Fourth Growth dry red Bordeaux from Médoc

Château Durfort-Vivens (shah toh duhr FOHR vee VAHn) Second Growth dry red Bordeaux from Médoc

Château du Tertre (shah toh doo TEHRT ruh) Fifth Growth dry red Bordeaux from Médoc

*Château d'Yquem (shah toh dee KEHM) First Growth, extremely fine, sweet white Sauternes

Château Ferrière (shah toh feh RYEHR) Third Growth dry red Bordeaux from Médoc

Château Fieuzal (shah toh fyuh ZAHL) dry red from Graves

Château Figeac (shah toh fee ZHAHK) fine dry red Bordeaux from St. Émilion

Château Filhot (shah toh fee LOH) Second Growth sweet white from Sauternes

Château Gazin (shah toh gah ZAn) fine dry red Bordeaux from Pomerol

Château Giscours (shah toh zhees KOOR) fine Third Growth dry red Bordeaux from Médoc

Château Grand-Puy-Ducasse (shah toh grahn PWEE doo KAHSS) Fifth Growth dry red Bordeaux from Médoc

Château Grand-Puy-Lacoste (shah toh grahn PWEE lah KOHST) Fifth Growth dry red Bordeaux from Médoc

Château Grillet (shah toh gree YÃ) very good dry white wine from Côtes du Rhône

Château Gruaud-Larose (shah toh groo OH lah ROHZ) Second Growth dry red Bordeaux from Médoc

Château Guiraud (shah toh ghee ROH) First Growth sweet white Sauternes

Château Haut-Bages-Libéral (shah toh oh BAHZH lee beh RAHL) Fifth Growth dry red from Médoc

Château Haut-Bailly (shah toh oh beh YEE) fine dry red Bordeaux from Graves

Château Haut-Batailley (shah toh oh bah teh YÃ) Fifth Growth dry red Bordeaux from Médoc

Château Haut-Brion (shah toh oh bree AHn) First Growth dry red Bordeaux from Graves

Château Haut-Brion Blanc (shah toh oh bree ahn BLAHn) dry white Bordeaux from Graves

Château Kirwan (shah toh keer WAHn) Third Growth dry red Bordeaux from Médoc

Château La Conseillante (shah toh lah kohn sā YAHnT) excellent dry red wine from Pomerol

Château Lafaurie-Peyraguey (shah toh lah foh REE peh rah GĀ) First Growth sweet white Sauternes

Château Lafite-Rothschild (shah toh lah FEET roh SHEELD) First Growth dry red from Médoc

Château Lafleur (shah toh lah FLUHR) fine dry red from Pomerol

Château La Fleur-Pétrus (shah toh lah FLUHR peh TROOSS) fine dry red from Pomerol

Château Lafon-Rochet (shah toh lah FOHn roh SHĀ) Fourth Growth dry red Bordeaux from St. Émilion

Château La Gaffelière (shah toh lah gah fuh LYEHR) excellent dry red Bordeaux from St. Émilion

Château La Garde (shah toh lah GAHRD) dry red from Graves

Château Lagrange (shah toh lah GRAHNZH) Third Growth dry red Bordeaux from Médoc

Château La Lagune (shah toh lah lah GOON) Third Growth dry red Bordeaux from Médoc

Château La Mission Haut-Brion (shah toh lah mee SYOn oh bree OHn) fine dry red Graves

Château Lamothe (shah toh lah MOHT) Second Growth sweet white Sauternes

Château Langoa-Barton (shah toh lahn GWAH bahr TOn) Third Growth dry red Bordeaux from Médoc

Château Lapointe (shah toh lah PWAnT) fine dry red Bordeaux from Pomerol

Château Larrivet Haut Brion (shah toh lah ree VEH oh bree AHn) dry white Bordeaux from Graves

Château Lascombes (shah toh lahs KOHnB) very fine dry red Second Growth from Médoc

Château Latour (shah toh lah TOOR) famous First Growth dry red Bordeaux from Médoc

Château La Tour-Blanche (shah toh lah toor BLAHnSH) First Growth sweet white Sauternes

Château La Tour-Carnet   (shah toh lah toor kahr NÃ) Fourth Growth dry red Bordeaux from Médoc

Château La Tour Haut-Brion   (shah toh lah TOOR oh bree On) dry red Bordeaux from Graves

Château La Tour-Martillac   (shah toh lah TOOR mahr tee YAHK) dry red or white Bordeaux from Graves

Château Laville Haut-Brion   (shah toh lah VEE yoh bree On) dry white Bordeaux from Graves

Château Léoville-Barton   (shah toh lã oh VEEL bahr TOn) Second Growth dry red from Médoc

Château Léoville-Las-Cases   (shah toh lã oh VEEL lahs KAHZ) Second Growth dry red from Médoc

Château Léoville-Poyferré   (shah toh lã oh VEEL pwah feh RÃ) Second Growth dry red from Médoc

Château L'Évangile   (shah toh lã vahn ZHEEL) fine dry red Bordeaux from Pomerol

Château Lynch-Bages   (shah toh leensh BAHZH) Fifth Growth dry red Bordeaux from Médoc

Château Magdelaine   (shah toh mahg duh LEHN) very fine dry red Bordeaux from St. Émilion

Château Malartic-Lagravière   (shah toh mah lahr TEEK lah grah VYEHR) dry red or white Bordeaux from Graves

Château Malescot—Saint-Exupéry   (shah toh mah lehs KOH san teh ZOO peh REE) Third Growth dry red Bordeaux from Médoc

*Château Margaux   (shah toh mahr GOH) First Growth dry red Bordeaux from Médoc

Château Marquis d'Alesme-Becker   (shah toh mahr KEE dah LEHM beh KEHR) Third Growth dry red Médoc

Château Marquis de Terme   (shah toh mahr KEE duh TEHRM) Fourth Growth dry red Médoc

Château Montrose   (shah toh mohn ROHZ) Second Growth dry red Bordeaux from Médoc

Château Mouton-Baron-Philippe   (shah toh moo TAHn bah ROn fee LEEP) underrated Fifth Growth dry red Bordeaux from Médoc

*Château Mouton-Rothschild   (shah toh moo TAHn roh SHEELD) First Growth Bordeaux from Médoc; one of the world's best dry red wines

Château Myrat   (shah toh mee RAH) Second Growth sweet white from Barsac

Château Nairac   (shah toh nã RAHK) Second Growth sweet white from Barsac

* *Châteauneuf-du-Pape*   (shah toh nuhf doo PAHP) popular dry red Rhône wine

Château Olivier   (shah toh oh lee VYĀ) dry red or white Graves

Château Palmer   (shah toh pahl MEHR) Third Growth dry red wine from Médoc

Château Pape-Clément   (shah toh pahp klā MAHn) fine dry red Bordeaux from Graves

Château Pavie   (shah toh pah VEE) dry red Bordeaux from St. Émilion

Château Pédesclaux   (shah toh pā desh KLOH) Fifth Growth dry red Bordeaux from Médoc

Château Petit-Village   (shah toh puh TEE vee LAHZH) fine dry red Bordeaux from Pomerol

* *Château Pétrus*   (shah toh peh TROOSS) exceptional dry red Bordeaux from Pomerol; considered one of the world's finest wines

Château Pichon-Longueville (Baron)   (shah toh pee SHOn lohng VEEL [bah ROn]) Second Growth dry red Bordeaux from Médoc

Château Pichon-Longueville-Comtesse   (shah toh pee SHOn lohng VEEL kohn TEHSS) Second Growth dry red Bordeaux from Médoc

Château Pontet-Canet   (shah toh pohn TEH kah NEH) Fifth Growth dry red wine from Médoc

Château Pouget   (shah toh poo ZHĀ) Fourth Growth dry red Bordeaux from Médoc

Château Prieuré-Lichine   (shah toh pree uh RĀ lee SHEEN) Fourth Growth dry red Médoc

Château Rabaud-Promis   (shah toh rah BOH proh MEE) First Growth sweet white Sauternes

Château Rausan-Ségla   (shah toh roh ZAn seh GLAH) Second Growth dry red Bordeaux from Médoc

Château Rauzan-Gassies   (shah toh roh ZAHn gah SEE) Second Growth dry red Bordeaux from Médoc

Château Rieussec   (shah toh ree uh SEHK) First Growth sweet white Sauternes

Château Ripeau   (shah toh ree POH) dry red Bordeaux from St. Émilion

Château Romer   (shah toh roh MEH) Second Growth sweet white Sauternes

Château Saint-Pierre   (shah toh san PYEHR) Fourth Growth dry red Bordeaux from Médoc

Château Sigalas-Rabaud   (shah toh see gah LAH rah BOH) First Growth sweet white Sauternes

Château Smith-Haut-Lafitte   (shah atoh SMEET oh lah FEET) dry red Bordeaux from Graves

Château Suau (shah toh soo OH) sweet white wine from Barsac

Château Suduiraut (shah toh soo dwee ROH) First Growth sweet white Sauternes

Château Talbot (shah toh tahl BOH) Fourth Growth dry red Bordeaux from Médoc

Château Trimoulet (shah toh tree moo LĀ) dry red Bordeaux from St. Émilion

Château Troplong-Mondot (shah toh troh lohng moh DOH) dry red Bordeaux from St. Émilion

Château Trotanoy (shah toh troh tah NWAH) excellent dry red Bordeaux from Pomerol

Château Trottevieille (shah toh troht VYĀ yuh) fine dry red Bordeaux from St. Émilion

(Château) Vieux Château Certan (shah toh vyuh shah toh sehr TAn) fine dry red from Pomerol

Chénas (shā NAH) one of the better Beaujolais reds

*Chenin Blanc (sheh nan BLAHn) white wine from California

Chevalier-Montrachet (sheh vah LYĀ mohn rah SHĀ) Grand Cru dry white from Burgundy

Chianti (ky AHN tee) dry red wine from Tuscany, Italy; the best is marked "Reserva" and comes in a plain bottle

Chiaretto (kyah RĀ toh) *It.* pale red; also the name of a rosé wine

Chiroubles (shee ROO bluh) one of the better Beaujolais red wines

*Claret (KLĀR reht) British name for red Bordeaux wines

Clos (KLOH) vineyard

Clos Blanc de Vougeot (kloh blahn duh voo ZHOH) Grand Cru white Burgundy

Clos de la Roche (kloh dlah ROHSH) Grand Cru red Burgundy

Clos des Lambrays (kloh dā lahn BRĀ) Grand Cru red Burgundy

Clos des Mouches (kloh dā MOOSH) Premier Cru red Burgundy

Clos des Ruchottes-Chambertin (kloh dā roo SHOHT shan behr TAn) Grand Cru red Burgundy

Clos de Vougeot (kloh duh voo ZHOH) Grand Cru red Burgundy

Clos Saint-Denis (kloh san duh NEE) Grand Cru red Burgundy

Combettes, Les (lā kohn BEHT) Premier Cru dry white Burgundy

Corky description of wine spoiled by a bad cork

Corton, Le (luh kohr TOHn) Grand Cru dry white Burgundy

Corton-Charlemagne (kohr TOHn shahr luh MAH nyuh) Grand Cru dry white Burgundy

Corton-Clos du Roi (kohr TOHn kloh doo RWAH) Grand Cru dry red Burgundy

Corton-Pougets (kohr TOHn poo ZHĀ) Grand Cru dry red Burgundy

Corvo (KOHR voh) good dry red or white from Sicily

Coteaux Champenois (koh TOH shan peh NWAH) still (nonbubbly) white wine from Champagne, France

Coteaux de la Loire (koh TOH duh lah LWAHR) semi-sweet white wine from Loire, France

Côte de Beaune (koht duh BOHN) a fine French growing region in Burgundy

Côte de Brouilly (koht duh broo YEE) a better Beaujolais red wine

Côte de Nuits (koht duh NWEE) one of the best growing regions in Burgundy

Côte de Nuits-Villages (koht duh nwee vee LAHZH) dry red Burgundy

Côte de Provence (koht duh proh VAHnSS) area in France producing much of the country's rosés

Côte D'Or (koht DOHR) Burgundy's finest growing area, composed of the Côte de Beaune and the Côte de Nuits

Côte Rôtie (koht roh TEE) one of the best Rhône reds (second to Châteauneuf-du-Pape)

*Crackling term meaning slightly sparkling

Crémant (krā MAHn) crackling or sparkling wine

Criots-Bâtard-Montrachet (kree oh bah TAHR mohn rah SHĀ) Grand Cru dry white Burgundy

Cru (kroo) growth or vineyard; see Grand Cru and Premier Cru

Cru classé (kroo klah SĀ) officially classified growth

*Crus artisans, bourgeois, exceptionnelle (kroo ZAHR tee ZAn, kroo boor ZHWAH, kroo zek SEHP syohn NEHL) after the 1855 classification of the 62 great growths of France, wines were rated, in order of descending excellence, as Crus Exceptionnelles, Crus Bourgeois, and Crus Artisans; see also First Growth, Second Growth, etc.

Cuvée (koo VĀ) a blend or vatting of wine

Dão (DOW) *Portuguese* dry red or white table wine

*Decant (dee CANT) *v.* to pour wine from its bottle into a container to aerate it quickly, or to separate it from its sediment; not done with Champagne, other sparkling wines, or white wines

Demi-sec (deh mee SEHK) semi-sweet; a designation found on Champagne bottles meaning that sugar was added; not the mark of a fine Champagne

Denominacion de Origen   (dā noh mee naht THYOHN dā oh REE hen) *It*. a guarantee of wine origin

Denominazione di Origine **Controllata**   (dā NOH mee naht SYOH nā dee oh REE zhee nā KOHN trohl LAH tah) *It*. guarantee of the origin and authenticity of a wine, usually abbreviated D.O.C.

—**Controllata e Garantita** (KOHN trohl LAH tah ā GAH rahn TEE tah) adds more controls to the production of wine; a statement found on the finest wines

—**Semplice** (sehm PLEE chā) a simple guarantee of the origin of wine

*Dessert wines   those wines with, or in place of, dessert: Sauternes, Port, sweet Sherries, sweet (demi-sec) Champagne, etc.

Dhroner Hofberg   (DROHN uhr HOHF berk) *Ger*. an excellent Mosel white wine

Dom Avelsbacher **Altenberg**   (dohm AH vuls bahkh er AHL tuhn behrk) *Ger*. good white wine from Mosel

—**Herrenberg** (HĀR uhn BEHRK) good Mosel white

*Dom Pérignon   (DOHn pā ree NYOn) name of a blind Bénédictine monk who is sometimes called the Father of Champagne; his name appears on an exquisite (and very expensive) Champagne from the vineyards of Moët et Chandon (moh EHT teh shan DAHn)

Doux   (DOO) sweet

*Dry   not sweet; without added sugar

Edel   (Ā dl) *Ger*. extra fine; noble

Eiswein   (ĪSS vīn) *Ger*. elegant, rare, rich wine produced when ripe grapes are frozen on the vine

Eitelsbacher Karthäuserhofberg   (ĪT ls BAHKH uhr KAHRT hoi zuhr HOHF behrk) outstanding Mosel white wine

Enkircher Steffensberg   (eng KEERK hehr SHTEHF ehns behrk) *Ger*. good white Mosel wine

Erbacher **Hohenrain**   (EHR BAHKH uhr HOH uhn RĪN) *Ger*. fine white wine from Rheingau

—**Marcobrunn** (MAHR koh bruhn) one of the finest Rheingau whites

—**Siegelsberg** (ZEE guhls BEHRK) fine Rheingau white

—**Steinmorgen** (SHTĪN mohr guhn) fine Rheingau white

Erdener **Prälat**   (EHR duhn uhr PRĀ laht) *Ger*. Outstanding Mosel white

—**Treppchen** (TREHP khen) excellent white Mosel wine

Espumoso   (ess poo MOH soh) *It*. sparkling

Estate bottled   wine bottled at the vineyard

*Extra sec   (EK strah SEHK) extra dry, though not as dry as Brut; both are terms found on Champagne labels

Falkensteiner Hofberg   (FAHLK uhn SHTĪN uhr HOHF behrk) *Ger*. Mosel white wine

Fiasco   (fee AHS koh) straw-wrapped flask usually associated with medium quality Chianti wine

Fifth Growth   See Great Growth

*Fino   (FEE noh) pale, dry Sherry

First Growth   See Great Growths

Fleurie   (fluh REE) one of the best Beaujolais reds

Flinty   term describing the metallic tang found in very dry white wines like Chablis

Fourth Growth   See Great Growths

Foxy   descriptive term for a wine with a very grapey flavor; often used to describe New York State wines

Frascati   (frah SKAH tee) *It*. good dry white wine

Frizzante   (freet TSAHN tā) *It*. crackling or semi-sparkling wine

Gamay   (gahh MĀ) *Fr*. and *Cal*. varietal name given to a dry California red wine resembling French wine made from Gamay grapes

Gamay Beaujolais   (gah MĀ boh zhoh LĀ) name of a California dry red wine

Gattinara   (gah tee NAH rah) *It*. excellent dry red wine from Piedmont

Geisenheimer **Mauerchen**   (GĪ zen HĪ muhr MOW ehr KHUHN) *Ger*. fine white wine from Rheingau

  —**Morschberg**   (MOHRSH behrk) fine Rheingau white

  —**Rothenberg**   (ROHT uhn behrk) fine Rheingau white

Generic labeling   practice of naming a California wine after a famous wine type from another area; for example, California Chablis resembles French Chablis

Gevrey-Chambertin   (zheh VRĀ shahn behr TAn) fine dry red Burgundy

Gewächs   (guh VEHKS) *Ger*. vineyard

Gewürztraminer   (guh VOORTS TRAH mee nuhr) spicy white wine from California, Alsace, or Germany

Graacher Himmelreich   (GRAH kuhr HIM uhl RĪKH) *Ger*. fine Mosel white wine

*Grand Cru   (grahn KROO) literally, Great Growth or Vineyard; used to designate the finest wines of Burgundy, Alsace, and Chablis, France;

see also Premier Cru and Great Growths

Grands Echézeaux, Les   (lā grahn zā shuh ZOH) Grand Cru dry red Burgundy

Grande Réserve   (grahnd reh ZEHRV) designation of one of the better wines of Alsace

Grand Vin   (grahn VAn) designation of the best wines of Alsace; the next best are Grand Reserve, then Reserve Exceptionnelle

Graves   (GRAHV) district producing red and white Bordeaux wines, with the whites being of greatest importance

*Great Growths   The great wines of France were classified for the 1855 Paris Exhibition. In order of descending greatness, they were rated First Growth, Second Growth, Third Growth, Fourth Growth, Fifth Growth, Crus Exceptionnelle, Crus Bourgeois, and Crus Artisan. Though a few class changes have been made in over a century, most of the designations hold true today and thus offer a convenient way to rate French wines. One final note: All the classified wines are of good quality; the various ratings merely point to degree of greatness, not a lack thereof.

Grenache   (gruh NAHSH) name of a better California rosé

Grey Riesling   (grā REESS ling) California white wine of only fair quality

Griotte-Chambertin   (gree UHT shahn behr TAn) Grand Cru dry red wine from Burgundy

Grumello   (groo MEHL loh) *It.* very good dry red from Lombardy; those marked "Riserva" are best

Gunflint   See *Flinty*

Hallgartener **Hendelberg**   (HAHL GAHRT nuhr HEHN dul BEHRK) *Ger.* fine white Rheingau white wine

   —**Schönhell**   (SHUHN hel) very fine white wine from Rheingau

Hattenheimer **Mannberg**   (HAHT uhn HĪ muhr MAHN behrk) *Ger.* very fine white wine from Rheingau

   —**Nussbrunnen**   NOOS BROON en) excellent white Rheingau wine

   —**Wisselbrunnen**   (VĪS uhl BROON uhn) fine Rheingau white wine

Hermitage, L'   (lehr mee TAHZH) distinguished Rhône River red wine

Hochgewächs   (HOHKH guh VEHKS) superior growth or vineyard in Germany

Hochheimer **Domdechaney**   (HOCK HĪ muhr DOM duh KAH nee) fine white wine from Rheingau

   —**Kirchenstück**   (KEER kuhn SHTOOK) fine white Rheingau wine

Inferno   (een FEHR noh) dry red wine from Lombardy, Italy; "Riserva" designates the best

Jerez de la Frontera   (hā REHTH dā lah frohn TĀ rah) *Sp*. famous home of Sherry wine

Johannisberger **Goldatzel**   (yoh HAHN is BEHRK uhr GOHLT AHTS uhl) very fine Riesling from Rheingau, Germany
  —**Hölle**   (HUHL) fine Rheingau white
  —**Vogelsang**   (FOHL guhl ZAHNG) fine Rheingau white

Johannisberg Riesling   (yoh HAHN is behrk REESS ling) *Cal*. good white wine

Josephshöfer   (YOH zefs HOHF uhr) *Ger*. famous, fine Mosel white

*Kabinett; Cabinet   (KAH bee NEHT) the driest of the *Qualitätswein mit Prädikat* wines; term means that the grapes were picked before *noble rot* set in; designates a high-quality table wine

Kellerabfüllung   (KAYL uhr AHP foo loong) German phrase for estate bottled

Kellerabzug   (KAYL uhr AHP tsook) same as *Kellerabfüllung*

Lacrima Christi   (lah KREEM ah KREES tee) good white Italian dessert wine

Lambrusco   (lahm BROOS koh) fair crackling dry red wine from Campania, Italy

La Tache   See *Tache, la*

Latricières-Chambertin   (lah tree SYEHR shahn behr TAn) Grand Cru dry red Burgundy

*Lay down, put down   the practice of storing wine until it reaches maturity

*Lees   (LEEZ) sediment

*Legs   bands of wine running down a glass after swirling the liquid around

*Liebfraumilch   (LEEB frow milkh) any wine from Rheinhessen; may describe one ranging in quality from poor to fair

Loire Valley   (LWAHR) area of France producing such wines as Anjou, Chinon, Muscadet, Pouilly-Fumé, Sancerre, and Vouvray

Made and bottled by   Term on a California wine label meaning that 10–74% of the grapes were crushed and fermented at the stated location

Madeira   (mah DEE rah) fortified wine from the island of Madeira; Sercial is the best dry Madeira; other good, fuller ones include Verdelho, Bual, Malmsey, Rainwater, and especially, a dated Soleras

*Magnum   double-sized bottle, excellent choice for Champagnes and red wines, which tend to age better in large bottles

Málaga   (MAH lah gah) *Sp*. strong dessert wine

Marc   grape skins, peel, and seeds left behind in a wine press; also, the brandy made from marc

Marcobrunn   (MAHR koh BRUHN) one of the most famous vineyards in Rheingau, Germany

Marsala   (mahr SAH lah) Sicilian dessert wine

Mateus   (mah TOOSS) good brand of Portuguese rosé

Mavrodaphne   (mah vroh THAHF nee) Greek dessert wine

Maximim Grünhaüser Herrenberg   (MAHKS see meen GROON hoi zuhr HĀR uhn BEHRK) *Ger.* one of the best Ruwer white wines

May wine   *Ger.* light spring wine flavored with woodruff

Mazis-Chambertin   (mah ZEE shahn behr TAn) Grand Cru dry red Burgundy

Mazoyères-Chambertin   (mah zoh YĀR shahn behr TAn) Grand Cru dry red Burgundy

Médoc   (mā DOK) finest red-wine-producing region in Bordeaux, France; consists of two areas: Médoc and Haut-Médoc

*Meursault-***Charmes**   (muhr soh SHAHRM) fine white Burgundy

   —**Genevrières**   (zhah nuh VRYEHR) as above

   —**Perrières**   (peh RYEHR) as above

Millésime   (mee lā ZEEM) French for "vintage year"

Mis en bouteilles à la propriété   (mee zon boo TĀ yuh ah lah proh pree eh TĀ) estate bottled

Mis en bouteilles au château   (mee zon boo TĀ yuh oh shah TOH) Bordeaux phrase meaning estate bottled

Mis en bouteilles au domaines   (mee zon boo TĀ yuh zoh doh MEHN) Burgundian phrase meaning estate bottled

Montrachet, Le   (luh mohn rah SHĀ) famous Grand Cru dry white Burgundy, felt by many to be the finest white wine in the world

Morgon   (mohr GOn) good Beaujolais red

Mosel, Moselle   (moh ZEHL) German area producing fine white wines, the best being from Mittel Mosel

Moulin-à-Vent   (moo lan nah VEHn) fine Beaujolais red wine

Muscadet   (mooss kah DĀ) very dry white wine from Loire Valley, France

Muscadet de Sèvre-et-Maine   (mooss kah dā duh SEH vruh eh MEHN) the finest Muscadet

Musigny, Les   (lā moo zee NYEE) Grand Cru dry red Burgundy

Musigny-Blanc   (moo zee nyee BLAHn) dry white wine from Burgundy

Must   pressed grape juice before and during fermentation

Nackenheimer Rothenberg   (NAHK uhn HĪM ehr ROHT un BEHRK)

fine white German wine from Rheinhessen

Napa   the most important wine-producing county in California

Natur   (nah TOOR) German for "natural," meaning no sugar was added to the wine

Nature   (nah TOOR) French for "natural," or very dry; for wines from Champagne, France; however, it means still, or nonbubbly

New York   wine made of at least 51% New York grapes, with perhaps some California grapes added to cut down on the local grapes' *foxiness*; sugar may, or may not, also be added; many consider the best product from this state to be the Champagne-like wine from the Finger Lakes region

Niersteiner **Bildstock**   (neer SHTĪN uhr BILT shtohk) *Ger.* one of the best wines of Rheinhessen

　　—**Glöck**   (GLAHK) as above

　　—**Heiligenbaum**   (HI lee guhn BOWN) as above

　　—**Hipping**   (HEEP ing) as above

　　—**Hölle**   (HUHL uh) as above

　　—**Kransberg**   (KRAHNS behrk) as above

　　—**Öelberg**   (OHL behrk) as above

　　—**Orbel**   (OHR behl) as above

*Nose   term meaning bouquet or aroma; a good nose means a good bouquet

Ockfener Bockstein   (OK fān uhr BOHK shtīn) *Ger.* one of the finest wines of Saar

Oeil de perdrix   (UH yuh duh pehr DREE) literally, eye of the partridge; this term refers to the color of pale pink sparkling, or still, wine

Oloroso   (OH loh ROH soh) sweet Sherry from Spain

Oppenheimer **Daubhaus**   (OHP uhn HĪM uhr DOWB HOWS) *Ger.* fine Rheinhessen white wine

　　—**Herrenberg**   (HEHR uhn BEHRK) as above

　　—**Kreuz**   (KROITS) as above

　　—**Sackträger**   (ZAHK TRÄ guhr) as above

Orvieto   (ohr vee Ä toh) *It.* good dry, or semi-dry, white wine

Paulliac   (poh YAHK) one of the most important communes in Haut-Médoc, Bordeaux

Perrier-Jouët Fleur de Champagne   (pehr YÄ zhoo EHT fluhr duh shahn PAH nyuh) is a wonderful Champagne

Pétillant   (peh tee YAHn) French word meaning semi-sparkling or crackling

Petite Sirah   (puh TEET suh RAH) fairly good red California wine

Piesporter Goldtröpfchen (PEES pohrt ehr GOHLD truhpf shen) fine white wine from Mosel, Germany

*Pink champagne an inferior sparkling wine generally colored by the addition of Pinot Noir grapes and often flavored with sugar

Pinot Blanc (pee noh BLAHn) varietal name of a better California dry white wine

*Pinot Chardonnay (pee NOH shahr doh NĀ) varietal name for the best of the California white wines

*Pinot Noir (pee noh NWAHR) varietal name for one of the best dry, red California wines

Pomerol (poh mehr OHL) name of one of the fine red-wine producing areas of Bordeaux

Pommard-**Clos-de-la-Commareine** (poh mahr KLOH duh lah koh mah REHN) a fine dry red Burgundy

—**Garollières** (gah roh LYEHR) as above

—**Les-Épenots** (lā zā puh NOH) as above

—**Les-Rugiens Bas** (lā roo ZHYAN BAH) as above

—**Les-Rugiens Haut** (lā roo ZHYAN OHT) as above

—**Platière** (plah TYEHR) as above

Porto (POHR toh) the fine dessert wine of Portugal, also known as Port; the very best is Vintage Porto, perhaps from a great year like 1945, 1963, or 1970

*Pouilly-Fuissé (poo yee fwee SĀ) very good, though often overpriced, dry white Burgundy wine

Pouilly-Fumé (poo yee foo MĀ) smoky, good, dry white wine from Loire Valley, France

Prädikat see *Qualitätswein mit Prädikat*

Premier Cru (preh myā KROO) for wines of Burgundy, Chablis, and Alsace, a classification meaning a wine second in quality only to those designated Grand Cru; see also *Great Growths*

Produced and bottled by term on a California wine label signifying that at least 75% of the grapes were crushed and fermented at the stated location

Qualitätswein (KVAH li taht SVĪN) designation of a superior German table wine from one of eleven rated areas

**Qualitätswein mit Prädikat* (KVAH li taht SVĪN mit preh di KAHT) *Ger.* describes superior wines with special attributes; the principal grape of these fine white wines is Riesling, with designations like Kabinett, Spätlese, Auslese, Beerenauslese, and *Trockenbeer-enauslese,* describing how and when the grapes were picked—factors influencing the sweetness of the wine

Raffia (RAHF fyah) *It*. straw covering on medium-priced Chianti bottles

Rauenthaler **Baiken** (ROW uhn TAH luhr bī ken) one of the finest, and most expensive, wines in Germany; from the Rheingau region

—**Gehrn** (GĀRM) as above

—**Langenstück** (LAHNG uhn STOOK) as above

—**Rothenberg** (ROHT uhn BEHRK) as above

Recioto della Valpolicella (reh CHOH toh dā lah VAHL poh lee CHĀ lah) *It*. fine Veneto red wine

* *Red Wines* best in the world are the light reds of Bordeaux (see *Great Growths*); others of note are from the *Cote D'Or* of Burgundy; California and Italian wines are also good; wines are generally best served at room temperature after being allowed to breathe for a while.

Reserve Exceptionnelle (reh SEHRV ek SEHP syon NEHL) quality designation of Alsatian wines

Rheingau (RĪN gow) the finest wine-producing area of Germany; home of wonderful fruity white Rieslings

Rheinhessen (RĪN HĀS uhn) a fine wine-growing area of Germany

Rhine Wine (RĪN) light, dry wine produced from the Riesling grape

Rhône Wine (ROHN) area of France producing both red and white wines, including Châteauneuf-du-Pape, Côte Rotie, and Hermitage

Richebourg, Le (luh reesh BOOR) Grand Cru dry red Burgundy

Riesling (REES ling) dry or sweet white wine produced by the grape of the same name; a principal wine in California, Germany, and Alsace

Rioja (RYOH hah) one of the best types of Spanish red wine

Riserva (ree SEHR vah) *It*. term meaning that the wine has been aged an extra period of time; denotes quality

Riserva Speciale (ree SEHR vah spech YAHL lā) *It*. term meaning that a wine has been aged even longer than one labeled Riserva

Romanée, La (lah roh mah NĀ) Grand Cru dry red Burgundy

* *Romanée-Conti, La* (lah roh mah NĀ kahn TEE) name of the finest Grand Cru dry red Burgundy wine

Romanée-Saint-Vivant (roh mah NĀ san vee VAHn) Grand Cru dry red Burgundy

Rosato (roh ZAH toh) *It*. rosé

Rosé (roh ZĀ) pink-colored wine, the best of which comes from Tavel and Anjou (France); rosés are technically red wines, not a special class

Ruchottes-Chambertin (roo SHOHT shan behr TAn) Grand Cru dry red Burgundy

Ruchottes, Les (lā roo SHOHT) Premier Cru dry red Burgundy

Rüdesheimer **Berg Rottland**   (ROO des HĪM uhr behrk ROHT lahnt)
  medium-dry white Rheingau wine
  —**Berg Schlossberg**   (behrk SHLAHS behrk) as above
  —**Klosterberg**   (KLOHS tehr BEHRK) as above
Saint-Amour   (san tah MOOR) a good Beaujolais red
Saint-Aubin   (san toh BAn) red or white wine from Côte de Beaune, Bur-
  gundy
* *Saint-Émilion*   (san tā mee LYOHN) one of the five major growing re-
  gions of Bordeaux; produces excellent dry red wines, the best of
  which are Château Ausone and Cheval-Blanc
Saint-Estéphe   (san tā STEHF) area producing some good dry red Bor-
  deaux wines
Saint-Julien   (san zhoo LYAn) commune of Médoc producing some excel-
  lent dry red wines, like Châteaux Leoville-Las-Cases and Ducru-
  Beaucaillou
San Joaquin Valley   (san wah KEEN) wine-producing area of California's
  Great Central Valley
Sassella   (sah SĀ lah) *It.* one of the better dry red wines of Lombardy;
  purchase it "Riserva"
* *Sauternes*   (soh TEHRN) world-famous dessert wine of the Sauternes
  region of Bordeaux; the finest is the First Growth Château D'Yquem
  Note: The much inferior Sauterne of California is spelled without the
  final "s" and should never be substituted when quality is important.
Sauvignon Blanc   (soh vee nyon BLAHn) a fine white California wine
  ranging from dry to semisweet
* *Schloss Johannisberg*   (SHLAHS yoh HAN is BEHRK) *Ger.* perhaps
  the most consistently fine Riesling from the Rheingau; also the most
  expensive
Schloss Vollrads   (SHLAHS FOHL rahts) exceptionally fine Riesling
  from Rheingau, Germany
Sec   (SEHK) designation for Champagne meaning sweet; sugar has been
  added
Secco, Seco   (SEHK koh) *It.* and *Sp.* dry
Second Growth   See Great Growths
Sekt   (SEHKT) *Ger.* sparkling
Sémillion   (seh mee YOHN) white California wine, drier than a Sauterne
* *Sherry*   fortified wine, the best of which is made in Jerez de la Fron-
  tera, Spain; Fino, or dry, Sherry is served as a cocktail; dessert Sher-
  ries include Oloroso, Cream, and Amoroso
Soave   (SWAH veh) *It.* dry white wine from Veneto, the best of which is

labeled Classico Superiore

Sonoma (soh NOHM mah) one of the most important coastal growing districts of California

* *Sparkling* term describing bubbly wines like Champagne

* *Spätlese* (SHPĀT lā zuh) *Ger.* a sweet wine of fine quality made from late-picked grapes; one of the designations of Qualitätswein mit Prädikat

Split a quarter bottle

Still term describing a wine to which no alcohol, CO_2, or flavoring has been added; a wine which is not sparkling

Superiore (soo peh ree OH rā) *It.* term designating a wine with additional alcoholic content, and perhaps, longer aging

Süss (ZOOSS) *Ger.* sweet

Sylvaner (zil VAH nuhr) dry, fruity wine from Alsace, France, or California

Tâche, La (lah TAHSH) Grand Cru dry red Burgundy

Tavel (tah VEHL) a fine rosé from the Rhône Valley

Tête de cuveé (teht duh koo VĀ) an outstanding growth; a term usually applied to Burgundies

Third Growth See *Great Growths*

Tokaji Aszú (TOH koh yee AH soo) rare Hungarian dessert wine

— **Szamorodni** (SOH MOH ROHD nee) average Hungarian dessert wine

Tokay (toh KĀ) a California dessert wine; also, the Americanization of the Hungarian word *Tokaji*

Trittenheimer **Altärchen** (TRIT un HĪ muhr AHLT ehr shen) a fine white German wine from Mosel

— **Apotheke** (ah poh TĀ kuh) as above

Trockenbeerenauslese (TROHK uhn BĀ ruhn OWS lā zuh) very rare, and expensive, sweet German wine made from selected raisin-like grapes; one of the designations of Qualitätswein mit Prädikat

Ürziger Würzgarten (OORT see guhr vuhrtz GAHR tuhn) *Ger.* fine, spicy white wine from Mosel

Usé (oo ZĀ) a wine which is diminishing in quality

V.D.S.Z. See Vins Délimités de Qualité Supérieure

Valgella (vahl JĀ lah) *It.* good dry red Lombardy wine, the best of which is marked Riserva

* *Valpolicella* (vahl poh lee CHĀ lah) *It.* delicate dry red wine, the best of which is from Veneto

Varietal name *Cal.* name refering to a wine's variety of grape, rather than its place of origin, like Pinot Noir or Cabernet

Verdicchio   (vehr DEE kyoh) *It*. dry, or semisweet, white wine; Verdicchio dei Castelli is best

*Vin   (VAn) wine

Vin Blanc   (van BLAHn) white wine

Vin de Cuvée   (van duh koo VĀ) term designating the best wine a firm has to offer

Vin de garde   (van duh GAHRD) a wine to keep, or put down, until it matures

Vinhos Verdes   (VEE nyoosh VEHR desh) a well-known Portuguese crackling white wine

Viniculture   the science of wine making

Vin Mousseux   (van moo SUH) sparkling French wine not from Champagne

Vin Nature   (van nah TOOR) unsweetened wine

Vino Frizzante   (VEE noh freet TZAHN tā) *It*. sparkling wine

*Vin Ordinaire   (van ohr dee NĀR) ordinary table wine

*Vin Rouge   (van ROOZH) red wine

Vino Santo   (VEE noh SAHN toh) dessert wine from Tuscany

Vins Delimités de Qualité Superiéure   (van dā lee mee TĀ duh kahl ee TĀ soo peh RYEHR) a term appearing on labels which simply means that the wine was produced according to government regulations.

Vins Doux   (van DOO) sweet wine

Vins du pays   (van doo pā EE) wine grown for local consumption

Vins Gris   (van GREE) pale pink wine from Lorraine, France

*Vintage   year in which a wine's grapes were harvested; a guarantee of quality only for Porto and Champagne, but important wherever climate fluctuates dramatically (as in France and Germany)

Viticulture   science of growing grapes for wine

Vitiviniculture   science of all that encompasses grape growing and wine making

Volnay   (vohl NĀ) elegant red Burgundy

Volnay Santenots   (vohl NĀ sahnt NOH) very good dry red Burgundy

Vouvray   (voo VRĀ) good white still, crackling, or sparkling wine from the Loire Valley, France

Weeper   a bottle with a leaky cork

Wehlener **Nonnenberg**   (VĀ luhn ehr NOHN uhn BEHRK) *Ger*. excellent white wine from Mosel

   —Sonnenhur   (ZOHN uhn OOR) as above

Wein   (WĪN) German for wine

Weingut (vīn GOOT) German for vineyard or estate

Weisswein (vīs vīn) German for white wine

Wiltinger Schlarzhofberg (VIL ting ehr SHLAHRS hohf BEHRK) finest white wine from Saar, Germany

Winkeler **Hasensprung** (VINGK el uhr HAH zen SHPROONG) *Ger.* very good white from Rheingau

—**Jesuitengarten** (yā zoo EET uhn GAHR tuhn) as above

Zeller Schwarze Katz (TSEL ehr SHVART seh KAHTS) *Ger.* white Mosel wine of fair quality

Zeltinger Himmelreich (TSELT ing ehr HĬM mel RĬK) *Ger.* fine white wine from Mosel

—**Schlossberg** (SHLAHSS BEHRK) as above

—**Sonnenuhr** (ZOHN uhn OOR) as above

*Zinfandel (TZIN fahn dehl) dry red wine produced almost exclusively in California

French Food

This glossary contains pronunciations and descriptions of popular French foods, of terms related to the methods of preparations, and of terms applying to taste and appearance.

Though all are worth learning, those marked with an asterisk, and those referring to your favorite foods, deserve special attention. Of even more importance are the names of the basic food groups, as listed below.

The Basics

Canapés   (kah nah PĀ) appetizers served on small pieces of bread
Dessert   (dā SEHR) dessert
Entrées   (ahn TRĀ) main courses
Hors d'oeuvres   (ohr DURV) appetizers which may, or may not, be served on bread pieces
Gibier   (zhee BYEH) game
Légumes   (lā GOOM) vegetables
Pain   (pan) bread
Pâtisserie   (pah tee SREE) pastry
Poisson   (pwah SAHn) fish
Poulet   (poo LĀ) chicken

Salade (sah LAHD) salad
Viande (VYAHND) meat
Volaille (voh LAH yuh) fowl

The Specifics

*Agneau (ah NYOH) lamb

Ail (AH yuh) garlic

*À la maison (ah lah mā ZAH*n*) in the style of the house; as prepared at this restaurant

Amandine (ah mah*n* DEEN) with almonds

Ananas (ah nah nah) pineapple

Artichaut (ahr tee SHOH) artichoke

Asperges (ah SPERZH) asparagus

Aubergines (oh behr ZHEEN) eggplant

*Au gratin (oh grah TA*n*) topped with bread crumbs or cheese, or both

*Au jus (oh ZHOO) with natural juices; Note: meat is served "au jus," not "with au jus."

*Au poivre (oh PWAHV ruh) with pepper

Babas au rhum (bah bah zoh RAHM) little yeast cakes soaked in rum and sugar syrup

Bavaroise (bah vah RWAHZ) delicate custard

*Béarnaise (behr NEHZ) delicious egg yolk and butter sauce flavored with wine vinegar, tarragon, and shallots; usually served over meat or eggs

Béchamel (bā shah MEHL) basic French white sauce

Bercy (behr SEE) white sauce with shallots and wine

*Beurre (BUHR) butter

Beurre blanc (buhr BLAH*n*) butter sauce flavored with shallots, a touch of vinegar, and perhaps, white wine

Beurre noisette (buhr nwah ZHET) browned butter

Bifteck (beef TEHK) beefsteak

Bigarade (bee ghah RAHD) sauce made from sour oranges

Bisque (BISK) thick shellfish-and-cream soup

Blanc (BLAH*n*) white; with white sauce

Blanquette de veau (blah*n* keht duh VOH) veal with mushrooms, onions, and vegetables in a white sauce

*Boeuf (BUHF) beef

Boeuf à la bourguignonne　(buhf ah lah boor ghee NYAHn) beef in a rich red-wine sauce, with onions, mushrooms, and other vegetables

Bombe　(BAHMB) usually, a mold of several different ice cream flavors

Bonne femme　(bohn FAHM) simple fare, as prepared by "a good woman"

* *Bordelaise*　(bohr DLEHZ) red-wine sauce, flavored with shallots, butter, tomatoes, and beef marrow

Bouillabaisse　(boo yuh BEHZ) famous Mediterranean stew

Bouillon　(boo YAHn) clear broth

Bouquetière　(boo keh TYEHR) with a variety of vegetables

Bourguignonne　(boor ghee NYAHN) of Burgundy, France; see *Boeuf,* and *Escargots, à la bourguignonne*

Boursault　(boor SOH) creamy cheese with a nutty taste

* *Boursin*　(boor SAn) creamy cheese which may be flavored with garlic, herbs, fruit, or seeds

* *Brie*　(BREE) popular semi-soft cheese

* *Brioche*　(bree OHSH) light bun or roll, sometimes served for breakfast, often hollowed and filled with creamed meat or poultry

* *Brochette, en*　(ahn broh SHEHT) on a skewer

Brûlé　(broo LĀ) broiled

Caille　(KAH yuh) quail

* *Camembert*　(kah mehn BEHR) popular semi-soft cheese with a pungent flavor

Campagne, de　(duh kahm PAHN yuh) country-style

Canard　(kah NAHR) duck

Caneton　(kah nuh TAHn) duckling

Carré d'agneau　(kah rā dah NYOH) rack of lamb

Cèpes　(SEHP) popular French mushroom

Cerises　(seh REEZ) cherries

Cevenale　(seh veh NAHL) with chestnuts

* *Champignon*　(shan peen YOHn) button mushroom

Chanterelles, aux　(oh shan TREHL) with wild, yellow chanterelle mushrooms

Charlotte Russe　(shar LAHT ROOSS) molded custard ringed with ladyfingers or spongecake

Chasseur　(shah SUHR) hunter's sauce, made with sautéed mushrooms, shallots, tomatoes, and white wine

* *Châteaubriand*　(shah toh bree AHn) beef tenderloin, usually served with a sauce

Chaud-froid　(shoh FWAH) a sauce made with broth, cream, egg yolks, and plain gelatin

Chevreuil (sheh VRUH yuh) sauce with venison bits

*Chez (SHĀ) literally, at the house of; means essentially the same as *à la maison*

*Chocolat (shah koh LAH) chocolate

Choron (shoh ROn) a sauce with egg yolk, butter, shallots, and tomato paste

Chou (SHOO) cabbage

Chou-fleur (shoo FLUHR) cauliflower

Citron (see TRAHn) lemon

Cocotte, en (ahn kuh KAHT) in a casserole

Coeur de la crème (kuhr dlah KREHM) dessert, often heart-shaped, made with cream cheese and strawberries

Confiture (kahn fee TOOR) jam; preserves

*Consommé (kahn soh MĀ) clear, seasoned broth

*Coq au vin (koh koh VAn) chicken carrots, mushrooms, and onions stewed in a red-wine sauce

*Coquilles Saint Jacques (koh KEE yuh san ZHAHK) scallops in a sauce of white wine, shallots, mushrooms, cream, butter, and eggs, topped with cheese and served in a scallop shell

*Cordon Bleu (kohr dahn BLUH) Blue ribbon; or, in the style of the London Cordon Bleu Cooking School; or, as Veal Cordon Bleu is sometimes prepared

Cornichons (kohr nee SHAHn) tiny French gherkins

Côte (KOHT) chop

Coupe de fruits (koop duh froo EE) fruit salad

*Crème (KREHM) cream

Crème anglaise (krehm ahn GLEHZ) English cream custard sauce

Crème caramel (krehm kah rah MEHL) unmolded custard with a caramel topping

Crème Chantilly (krehm shahn tee YEE) unsweetened whipped cream flavored with vanilla

Crème fraîche (krehm FREHSH) coddled French cream with a tart flavor

Crème pâtissière (krehm pah tee SYEHR) vanilla custard cream sauce

*Crêpe (KREHP) thin sweet or savory pancake

Crêpe Suzette (krehp soo ZEHT) crêpes heated with sugar, butter, and orange and lemon juices, then flamed with Cognac and Grand Marnier

Crevette (kreh VEHT) shrimp

*Croissant (krwah SAHn) crescent-shaped breakfast roll

Croquette (kroh KEHT) minced meat, fish, or vegetables formed in a ball, then breaded and deep fried

Croûte, en (ahn KROOT) in a crust

Croûton (kroo TAHn) a round or square of bread sautéed in butter

Crudités (kroo dee TĀ) raw vegetables served as appetizers, often accompanied by a dip

Cuisine minceur (kwee ZEEN man SUHR) low-calorie French cooking

Cuisse de (KWEESS duh) legs of

Daube (DOHB) beef stew simmered slowly in a sealed pot

Dauphinoise, à la See *Pommes de terres dauphinoise*

Dijonnaise (dee zhuh NEHZ) with a mustard sauce

Du Barry (doo bah REE) garnished with cauliflower and topped with a cream sauce and cheese

Duchesse, à la (ah la doo SHEHSS) potatoes mashed with egg, cream, and butter, piped from a pastry tube, and browned in the oven

Duxelles (dooks EHL) minced sautéed shallots and mushrooms, used as a stuffing

Écrevisses (eh kreh VEESS) crayfish

Émincé (eh man SĀ) minced or thinly sliced

En croûte See Croûte

Endive (ahn DEEV) curled-leaf salad green

Entrecôte (ahn truh KOHT) beefsteak cut from the ribs; sometimes, the sirloin

Épinard (eh pee NAHR) spinach

Escalope (ess kah LAHP) a boneless piece of pounded meat

Escargots (es kahr GOH) snails

Escargots à la bourguignonne (ess kahr GOH ah lah boor ghee NYAHn) snails baked in their shells with butter, shallots or garlic, and parsley

Escarole (ess kah ROHL) broad-leafed salad green

Escoffier (ess kah FYEH) in the style of the great chef Escoffier; also, in "gourmet" fashion

Estouffade (eh stoo FAHD) beef stew

Faisan (fā ZAn) pheasant

Farci,e (fahr SEE) stuffed

Filet (fee LĀ) a boneless piece of meat or fowl

Fillet (FIL leht) English pronunciation of Filet

Financière (fee nahn SYEHR) a rich sauce made of Madeira wine, broth, mushrooms, and truffles

Fines herbes, aux (oh feen ZEHRB) flavored with chopped parsley, chervil, tarragon, and chives; or, just parsley

Flambé (flahn BĀ) flamed

Flan   (FLAHn) a savory or sweet open tart; a custard

Florentine   (floh rehn TEEN) with spinach; often with a cream sauce and cheese topping as well

Forestière, à la   (ah lah foh reh STYEHR) with mushrooms, diced bacon, and potatoes

Fraise   (FREHZ) strawberries

Framboises   (frahn BWAHZ) raspberries

Frites   (FREET) fried

*Fromage   (froh MAHZH) cheese

*Fruit   (froo EE) fruit

Fumé   (foo MĀ) smoked

Garnie,e   (gahr NEE) garnished

*Gâteau   (gah TOH) cake

Gelée, en   (ahn zhā LĀ) in aspic

Gigot   (zhee GOH) leg of lamb

Glacé   (glah SĀ) candied, glazed, or iced

Gourmandise   (goor mahn DEEZ) mellow, soft, double-cream cheese

Gratin, au   See *Au gratin*

Gratiné   (grah tee NĀ) same as *Au gratin*

Grenouilles   (greh NOO yuh) frog legs

Haricots verts   (ahr ee koh VEHR) string beans

*Haute cuisine   (OHT kwee ZEEN) fine cooking; the style of French cooking preceding *nouvelle cuisine*

*Herbe   (EHRB) herb

*Hollandaise   (ahl lahn DEHZ) or (HAHL uhn dāz) rich sauce for vegetables and seafood made with egg yolk, lemon, and butter

Homard   (oh MAHR) lobster

Huile, à l'   (ah LWEEL) in oil

Huîtres   (WEE truh) oysters

Jambon   (zhahn BAHn) ham

Jardinière   (zhahr dee NYEHR) surrounded by groups of colorful vegetables

Julienne   (zhoo LYEHN) cut into strips

Jus, au   See *Au jus*

Lait   (LĀ) milk

Laitue   (lā TOO) lettuce

Langouste   (lahn GOOST) spiny lobster

Langoustine   (lahn goo STEEN) saltwater crayfish

Lapin   (lah PAn)

Lièvre   (LYEH vruh) hare

Lyonnaise (lyohn NEHZ) with onions or onion sauce

Macédoine (mah seh DWAHN) fruit salad

Macédoine de legumes (duh lā GOOM) mixed vegetables

Maître d'hôtel (meh truh doh TEHL) *adj.*, served with butter and creamed with lemon juice, parsley, and pepper; *n.*, the Headwaiter or owner

Maltaise (mahl TEHZ) orange-flavored Hollandaise sauce

Marchand de vin (mahr shahn duh VAn) with a sauce of shallots, red wine, meat broth butter, and herbs

Maréchale (mah rā SHAHL) breaded, fried, and garnished with truffle slices and asparagus tips

Marinière (mah ree NYEHR) white-wine sauce for seafood, especially mussels

Mayonnaise (mā yah NEHZ) with mayonnaise; mayonnaise

Médaillons (meh dah YAHn) small round slices

Meunière (moon YEHR) method of cooking lightly-floured fish in butter, then making a lemon-parsley sauce from the butter

Mignon (meen YAHn) little

Moelle (MWAHL) bone marrow

Mont Blanc (mahn BLAHn) a "mountain" of sweetened, cooled, and puréed chestnuts topped with vanilla-flavored whipped cream

Morilles (moh REEL) wild morel mushrooms

Mornay (mohr NĀ) delicate cheese-enriched white sauce

Moules (MOOL) mussels

Mousse (MOOSS) airy mixture of puréed sweet or savory ingredients lightened with beaten egg whites, and sometimes, whipped cream

Mousseline (moo SLEEN) a dish enriched with whipped cream; hollandaise similarly enriched

Nage, à la (ah lah NAHZH) shellfish with a seasoned white-wine broth

Napoléon (nah pah LYOn) pastry square filled with light custard or pastry cream

Navarin (nah vah RAn) stew of lamb or mutton

*Niçoise (nee SWAHZ) with tomatoes and garlic, and perhaps, black olives, onions, and peppers

Noisette (nwah ZEHT) hazelnut; or a médaillon of meat

Normande, à la (ah lah nor MAHND) as prepared in Normandy, France; usually with apples or cider or cream, or a combination of these ingredients

Normande, sauce (sohss nohr MAHND) cream sauce containing butter, egg yolk, fish broth, and mushrooms; served over seafood with a shellfish garnish

Nouvelle cuisine (noo vehl kwee ZEEN) new, lighter style of French cooking relying less on heavy sauces than does *haute cuisine*

Oeuf, oeufs (UHF, UH) egg(s)

Oeufs à la neige (uh zah lah NEHZH) meringue "eggs" nestled in a *crème anglaise* "nest"; similar to "Floating Island"

Oignon (ah NYAHn) onion

Omelette (ahm LEHT) egg dish served plain or filled

Orange, à l' (ah loh RAHNZH) style of preparing duck with a white wine–Port–Curaçao sauce that is flavored with herbs and orange peel, then garnished with orange sections

Pamplemousse (pahm pluh MOOSS) grapefruit

Pané (pah NĀ) fried in crumbs

Papillote, en (ahn pah pee YOHT) wrapped in foil or paper before cooking

Parisienne See names à la Parisienne

Parmentier (pahr mahn TYEH) with potatoes

Pâte (PAHT) pastry

Pâté (pah TĀ) fine, spiced French meatloaf usually served as an appetizer

Pâte feuilletée (paht fuh yuh TĀ) puff pastry

Pâtisserie (pah tee SREE) pastry

Pêches (PEHSH) peaches

Perdreau (pehr DROH) partridge

Périgeux (peh ree GUH) with truffles; or, a sauce with minced truffles and Madeira wine

Périgourdine (peh ree goor DEEN) white sauce with sliced truffles

Petite marmite (peh TEE mahr MEET) vegetable-beef soup served in a little bowl

Petits-fours (peh tee FOOR) elegant little cakes

Pigeonneau (pee zhahn NOH) squab

Piquante (pee KAHNT) brown sauce with gherkins and parsley

Poires (PWAHR) pears

Poivre (PWAH vruh) pepper

Poivre, steak au (stāk oh PWAH vruh) steak studded with coarsely-ground black peppercorns, sometimes flamed, sometimes with a sauce

Pomme (PUHM) apple

Pomme de terre (puhm duh TEHR) potato

Pommes à la Parisienne (puhm zah lah pah ree ZYEHN) tiny potato balls sautéed in butter and topped with meat gravy and chopped parsley

Pommes Anna (puhm ZAH nah) a savory cake of buttery potato slices

Pommes Frites (puhm FREET) deep-fried potatoes

Port Salut (pohr sah LOO) yellow semi-soft cheese

Potage (poh TAHZH) soup; more elegant than Soupe

Pot-au-feu (poh toh FUH) boiled meat and vegetables generally served after, not in, the broth in which it was cooked

Pots de crème (poh duh KREHM) elegant little pots in which dessert is served

Poularde (poo LAHRD) a roasting chicken

Poussin (poo SAn) young chicken

Printanière, à la (ah lah pran tan YEHR) garnished with spring vegetables

Profiterole (proh fee teh ROHL) tiny balls of cream-filled puff pastry, usually topped with chocolate sauce

Provencale, à la (ah lah proh VEHn SAHL) usually, a dish served with a sauce of tomatoes, olive oil, and garlic

Purée (poo RĀ) or (pyoor RĀ) meat, fish, or vegetables processed to the consistency of a paste

Quenelles (kuh NEHL) delicate dumplings of poached seafood, veal, or chicken served with a fine sauce

Quiche (KEESH) a savory custard usually flavored with meats, cheese, and/or vegetables

Quiche Lorraine (keesh loh REHN) savory pie of cream, eggs, bacon, and sometimes, cheese

Ragoût (rah GOO) thick stew

Raifort (reh FOHR) horseradish

Raisins (reh ZAn) grapes

Raisins secs (reh zan SEHK) raisins

Ratatouille (rah tah TOO ee) zucchini, tomato, eggplant, green pepper, and onion stewed in olive oil and garlic

Rémoulade (reh moo LAHD) a mayonnaise flavored with capers, anchovy paste, gherkins, mustard, herbs, and spices

Rillettes (ree YEHT) potted pork mixture used as a spread

Ris de veau (ree duh VOH) sweetbreads (pancreas of calf or lamb)

Rissoles (ree SOHL) meat ground, seasoned, wrapped in pastry, and fried

Riz (REE) rice

Robert, sauce (sohss roh BEHR) rich brown sauce flavored with mustard and tomatoes

Rognons (roh NYOn) kidneys

Romanoff (roh mah NAHF) usually, strawberries soaked in orange juice and orange liqueur, served with whipped cream or ice cream

Roquefort (rohk FOHR) blue cheese made from ewe's milk

Rosbif (rohz BEEF) roast beef

Rosetti (roh ZEH tee) raw Lyon sausage

Rossini (roh SEE nee) tournedos garnished with goose liver and truffles

* *Roti* (roh TEE) roasted

Roulade (roo LAHD) rolled roast with a filling that is braised or poached

* *Royale* (roh YAHL) in a royal manner

Royale, sauce (sohss roh YAHL) white sauce with egg yolk, cream, chicken broth, sherry, and perhaps, truffle pieces

Russe, à la (ah lah ROOSS) with caviar or sour cream

Russe, sauce (sohss ROOSS) a mayonnaise with puréed caviar, mustard, and unfertilized lobster roe

Saint-Honoré (san toh noh RĀ) an elegant cream-filled puff pastry "cake"

* *Sauce* (SOHSS) sauce; see individual listings

Saucisses (soh SEESS) fresh pork sausage

Saucisson (soh see SAHn) cured pork sausage

* *Saumon* (soh MAHn) salmon

* *Sauté,e* (soh TĀ) cook quickly in butter, or butter and oil; or, a mixture which is sautéed

Savarin (sah vah RAn) rich cake soaked in rum

Selle (SEHL) saddle; a roast of both loins (usually lamb)

Smitane (smee TAHN) wine, onion, and sour cream sauce

* *Sorbet* (sohr BĀ) sherbet; may be sweet or savory; often served to clear palates between courses

Soubise (soo BEEZ) sauce of puréed onion or onion and rice

* *Soufflé* (soo FLĀ) puffy sweet or savory dish

Suprême (soo PREHM) most delicate, succulent part of meat or poultry

Suprême, sauce (sohss soo PREHM) white sauce enriched with egg yolk, heavy cream, and chicken broth

Tartare, steak (stāk tahr TAHR) chopped lean raw beef served with chopped onions, capers, a raw egg, and seasoning; all ingredients are mixed prior to eating

Tarte (TAHRT) open-faced sweet pie

* *Terrine* (tehr REEN) pâté-like dish served in a small pot called a terrine

Timbale (tan BAHL) usually, an unmolded savory custard in the shape of a dome

* *Tomates* (toh MAHT) tomatoes

Tortue (tohr TOO) turtle

* *Tournedos* (toor nuh DOH) narrow end of the beef tenderloin

Tranche (TRAHNSH) slice

Truffes   (TROOF) truffles

Truite   (troo EE) trout

Vanille   (vah NEEL) vanilla

*Veal Cordon Bleu   (veel kohr dah*n* BLUH) veal stuffed with ham and Swiss cheese, then breaded and sautéed

*Veau   (VOH) veal

Velouté   (veh loo TĀ) velvety white sauce

Véronique   (veh ruh NEEK) garnished with white grapes

Vert,e   (VEHR, VEHRT) green

Verte, sauce   (sohss VEHRT) a mayonnaise flavored with several puréed greens: spinach, chives, tarragon, watercress, parsley, etc.

*Vichyssoise   (vee shee SWAHZ) cold, elegant soup of cream, chicken stock, and puréed leeks and potatoes

*Vinaigrette   (vee neh GREHT) dressed with oil and vinegar

*Vin, au   (oh VA*n*) with wine

*Vin blanc, au   (oh va*n* BLAH*n*) with white wine or a white-wine sauce

*Vin rouge, au   (oh va*n* ROOZH) with red wine or a red-wine sauce

Vol-au-vent   (voh loh VEH*n*) small filled puff pastry pie

Xérès, au   (oh keh REHS) with sherry

Bibliography

While researching this book, I encountered many books I think you will enjoy. They include:

Anderson, Jean, and Elaine Hanna. *The Doubleday Cookbook*. New York: Doubleday, 1975.

Chalmers, Irena. *Napkin Folding*. Greensboro, NC: Potpourri Press, 1978.

Child, Julia, and Simone Beck. *Mastering the Art of French Cooking*. Vol. 2. New York: Alfred A. Knopf, 1970.

Grossman, Harold J. *Grossman's Guide to Wines, Beers, & Spirits*. 7th ed., rev. by Harriet Lembeck. New York: Charles Scribner's Sons, 1983.

Hettich, Arthur. *Best of the Best*. New York: Quadrangle/New York Times Books, 1976.

Jackson, Carole. *Color Me Beautiful*. New York: Ballantine Books, 1980.

Kadish, Ferne, Kathleen Kirtland, and Gladyce Begelman. *New York on $500 a Day*. New York: Collier Books/Macmillan, 1978.

Lichine, Alexis. *Alexis Lichine's New Encyclopedia of Wine & Spirits*. New York: Alfred A. Knopf, 1981.

Marcus, Stanley. *Quest for the Best*. New York: Viking Press, 1979.

Peter, Laurence J. *Peter's Quotations*. New York: William Morrow, 1978.

Robards, Terry. *The New York Times Book of Wine*. New York: Quadrangle/New York Times Books 1976.

Rombauer, Irma S., and Marion Rombauer Becker. *The Joy of Cooking*. Indianapolis/New York: Bobbs-Merrill, 1975.

Schoonmaker, Frank. *Encyclopedia of Wine*. 7th ed., rev. and exp., ed. by Julius Wile. New York: Hastings House, 1980.

Simon, Andre L. *A Concise Encyclopedia of Gastronomy*. Woodstock, NY: Overlook Press, 1981.

Trader Vic's Bartender's Guide, Revised. Edited by Shirley Sarvis. Garden City, NY: Doubleday, 1972.

Weinberg, Julia. *Gourmet Bouquet*. New York: Butterick, 1978.

The Wholesale-by-Mail Catalog, by The Print Project. New York: St. Martin's Press, 1979.

Vanderbilt, Amy. *The Amy Vanderbilt Complete Book of Etiquette*. Rev. and exp. by Letitia Baldridge. Garden City, NY: Doubleday, 1978.

Williams, Sallie Y. *The Art of Presenting Food*. New York: Hearst Books, 1982.

Index